D0104184

Myths of Leadership

Banish the misconceptions and become a great leader

Jo Owen

First published in Great Britain and the United States in 2018 by Kogan Page Limited

2nd Floor, 45 Gee Street
London
EC1V 3RS
United Kingdom

c/o Martin P Hill Consulting
122 W 27th St, 10th Floor
New York, NY 10001
USA

4737/23 Ansari Road
Daryaganj
New Delhi 110002
India

www.koganpage.com

ISBN   978 0 7494 8074 5
E-ISBN   978 0 7494 8075 2

British Library Cataloguing-in-Publication Data

A CIP record for this book is available from the British Library.

Library of Congress Cataloging-in-Publication Data

Names: Owen, Jo, author.
Title: Myths of leadership : banish the misconceptions and become a great
   leader / Jo Owen.
Description: London ; New York : Kogan Page, 2017. | Includes index.
Identifiers: LCCN 2017037653 (print) | LCCN 2017025740 (ebook) | ISBN
   9780749480752 (ebook) | ISBN 9780749480745 (pbk.)
Subjects: LCSH: Leadership.
Classification: LCC HD57.7 (print) | LCC HD57.7 .O9473 2017 (ebook) | DDC
   658.4/092–dc23
LC record available at https://lccn.loc.gov/2017025740

Typeset by Integra Software Services, Pondicherry
Print production managed by Jellyfish
Printed and bound by CPI Group (UK) Ltd, Croydon, CR0 4YY

Myths of Leadership

CONTENTS

Acknowledgements viii

Introduction 1

PART ONE We know what leadership is 5

Myth 1   We know what leadership is 7
Myth 2   The perfect leader 12
Myth 3   Leadership is about your rank, title or position 16
Myth 4   Managers are leaders 20
Myth 5   Leaders know what leadership is 24
Myth 6   The founder is the leader 28
Myth 7   Leadership is universal 32

PART TWO We know what leaders do 37

Myth 8   We know what leaders do (1): top-level leaders 39
Myth 9   We know what leaders do (2): your leadership journey 43
Myth 10   Leaders motivate their followers 48
Myth 11   Leaders communicate well 53
Myth 12   Leaders are decisive 59
Myth 13   Leaders set goals and give directions 63
Myth 14   Great leaders build great teams 68
Myth 15   The leader knows what is going on 72

PART THREE We know what leaders are like: character and traits 77

Myth 16   Leaders are born, not bred 79
Myth 17   Leaders are visionary 83
Myth 18   Leaders are charismatic and inspirational 87
Myth 19   Leaders are honest 91
Myth 20   Leaders are brave 95

Myth 21   The leader is the smartest person in the room 99
Myth 22   The best leaders are clever 103
Myth 23   Male and female leaders are different 107
Myth 24   Psychopaths succeed as leaders 113
Myth 25   Leaders are reasonable 118
Myth 26   An effective leader is a skilled leader 124

PART FOUR   We know how leaders succeed 129

Myth 27   Leaders succeed on merit 131
Myth 28   Leadership is about survival of the fittest 136
Myth 29   It's not what you know, it's who you know 142
Myth 30   Power comes from your position 146
Myth 31   Leaders need experience 150
Myth 32   The first 90 days 155
Myth 33   You have to manage before you can lead 160
Myth 34   Sporting heroes show us how to lead 164
Myth 35   You can teach leadership 169
Myth 36   Leaders know when to move on 173

PART FIVE   We have a theory about leadership 179

Myth 37   Great Man theory of leadership 181
Myth 38   Servant leadership 186
Myth 39   The humble leader 192
Myth 40   Distributed leadership 196
Myth 41   Transactional and transformational leadership 201
Myth 42   Authentic leadership 206
Myth 43   Leadership is a team sport 210
Myth 44   Leadership and money: the dog that didn't bark 214
Myth 45   Leaders are like tea bags 219

PART SIX   We have beliefs about leadership 223

Myth 46   It's lonely at the top 225
Myth 47   The buck stops here 229

Myth 48   It's tough at the top 233
Myth 49   The leader makes a difference 237
Myth 50   The leader is in control 241
Myth 51   Leaders are role models 245
Myth 52   Leaders are popular 249
Myth 53   Leaders deserve exceptional rewards 253

PART SEVEN Conclusions 259

Myth 54   Myths, fads and theories 261
Myth 55   Leaders take people where they would not have got by themselves 266
Myth 56   I have the answer: myth or reality? 270

Index 273

ACKNOWLEDGEMENTS

No one ever achieves anything alone, and that is most certainly true of writing a book. This book is based on 20 years of research and nearly 40 years of work with teams and leaders from organizations around the world. I have been able to learn from them all, and I hope that they have gained something in return. A few of the firms to which I am indebted are below, and my thanks go to all of them.

Accenture, Aegon, AIG, Airbus, ALICO, Allen & Overy, Ambition School Leadership, Amex, ANZ Bank, Apple, Ares & Co, Armstrong Industries, Arrowgrass, AstraZeneca, Aviva, BAML, Bank Indonesia, Barclays, BASF, BNY Mellon, British Council, Canon, Cap Gemini, Citi, CRU, Dentons, Deutsche Bank, Dow, EBRD, EDS, Education Development Trust, Electrolux, EW Payne, Facebook, Financial Times, Fujitsu, Google, The Groove, HCA, HERE, Hiscox Re, Hitachi, House, HSBC, IBM, Ito Chu, JAL, Laird, Mandarin Capital, MetLife, Mitsubishi Chemical, Mitsui OSK Lines, Mitsui Sumitomo Insurance, Modern Tribe, Monsanto, Nationwide, Nokia, Nomura, Nordea, NRI, NTT, Opportunity Network, Pearson, PepsiCo, Philip Morris, Philips, P&G, Premier Foods, Qualcomm, RBS, RELX, Rentokil, Right to Succeed, Rolls Royce, SABIC, San Miguel, SDP, SECOM, Social Media, Spark Inside, Standard Chartered Bank, Start Up, STIR, SWIFT, Symantec, Teach First, Tetrapak, Tokyo Marine, UBS, Unilever, Vastari, Visa, World Bank, World Faith and Zurich Insurance.

I would in particular like to thank the magnificent team at Kogan Page, led by Helen Kogan. They have always been a joy to work with, and this was no exception. Unusually, the idea for this book came from Kogan Page, not from the author. My thanks to my editor, Anna Moss, for thinking of the idea and thinking that I might be the person to do it justice. I hope I have lived up to expectations.

Throughout this and many other books I have been more than ably supported by my long-time agent, Frances Kelly, who lets me focus on writing by looking after the things that I do not want to look after.

Finally, my eternal thanks to my wife, Hiromi, who regularly becomes a book widow for long periods when I am engrossed in writing obsessively. Her patience and support is remarkable.

One theme of this book is that no leader is perfect. The same is true of authors and books: there is no such thing as perfection. Success is always a team effort, but any mistakes are the author's alone.

INTRODUCTION

Why this book is needed

Why another book on leadership when there are already nearly 60,000 to choose from? The reason for this book is *because* there are so many books on leadership out there. They all have their theories which fight with each other for your attention. The result is not clarity, but chaos and confusion.

The purpose of this book is to help you find clarity amid the chaos. *Myths of Leadership* is your practical guide to all the myths, fads, theories and fantasies of leadership. It will help you sort out myth from reality and fact from fiction. If leadership is a journey, you need a map. This book is the map which will help you structure your journey and accelerate your path to success, if only by avoiding the many bear traps that exist on the way.

Why this book is different

This book is unusual for three reasons:

1 **It explores not one leadership idea, but over 50.** It maps out the entire leadership landscape and highlights some of the traps, dead ends and short cuts you may encounter on your leadership journey.

2 **It is based on three perspectives,** whereas most books are based on just one:

   – Twenty years of original leadership research around the world in most industries and countries, as well as research with tribes around the world: truly original insights.

   – Forty years of leading, working with and working for great firms and leaders around the world who are recognized in the acknowledgements. In addition, I am a founder or co-founder of eight not-for-profit organizations with a collective turnover above £100 million annually. This means I respect the challenge of leadership in the real world.

– Extensive secondary research, which is needed when investigating myths of leadership. I hope I will have spared you a lot of pain by removing the need for you to read so many books and articles on leadership. Where appropriate, this research is recognized in the endnotes.

3 It offers insight through questions, not answers. Many leadership books purport to have the secret of leadership, wrapped up in three easy steps for you to follow. But real insight does not come from being told something, even if it is true. Real insight comes from discovering something for yourself. So you can treat this book as your journey of discovery through the land of leadership myths. I hope you discover much that you can use and value.

How this book will help

Myths of Leadership does not just deal with myths; it deals with realities. It constantly compares the theory of the myth to the day-to-day reality of leadership. In doing so, it attempts to answer basic questions every leader faces on their journey:

- How do I know if I am really leading: what is a leader?
- Can I lead if I am not the boss?
- Do I need to be charismatic and inspirational to be a leader?
- Can I learn to lead, and if so how?
- Do I need to be visionary or have a vision?
- What must I do to lead well?
- How do I gain the power to lead?

How to use this book

This book is ordered into several major sections, mainly for ease of reference. In practice, you can read this book in any order you want. You can dip in and out; start at the end and work backwards or even sdrawkcab; read it all at once or read just one chapter on your way into work.

The intent of this book is to provoke thinking about the nature of leadership in general, and about how you can lead better. If the provocation causes you to laugh or curse the book, that is fine. The book does not pretend to have the definitive answer on leadership, because there is no definitive answer on leadership. Instead, it opens new windows on leadership theory and practice and invites you to take a look. You will agree with some perspectives and disagree with others; what you choose to learn from each perspective is up to you.

Finally, I have attempted to make this book readable. A book on leadership myths is an invitation to get lost in jargon. I have declined that invitation as much as possible. Leadership books can also be pretty dull and pompous (like quite a few people who think they are leaders), so I decided to commit the cardinal sin of attempting to make this book enjoyable to read. In this regard at least, I hope I have sinned successfully on your behalf.

Enjoy the book.

PART ONE

WE KNOW WHAT LEADERSHIP IS

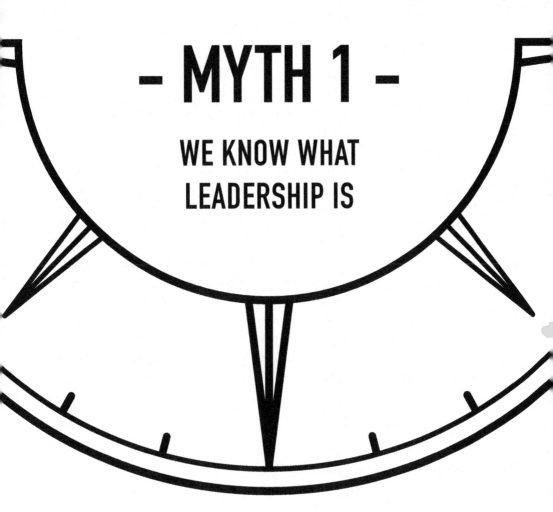

– MYTH 1 –

WE KNOW WHAT LEADERSHIP IS

There is no theory of leadership that can stand up to scientific challenge.

The nature of the myth

Defining leadership is like searching for smoke signals in the fog. It can be an exercise in futility. We all think we know what leadership is like, but when we try to agree on a common definition we find ourselves grappling with the fog. This matters because if we cannot agree what leadership is, then judging, discussing or developing leaders becomes impossible.

To understand this myth, we will look at leadership from four perspectives.

Common sense

We all know a good leader when we see one: Churchill, Martin Luther King, Nelson Mandela and Mother Theresa. But what about Mao Tse-tung or Stalin: should they be revered as national saviours or reviled as mass murderers? Were they good leaders or not?

We need to define what we mean by a 'good' leader. If good means effective, then we can include many dictators and empire builders down the ages. Alexander the Great was named 'the Great' by the Greeks who were on the winning side. The Persians named him 'Alexander the Barbarian' for destroying their civilization. Being a *good* leader and being an *effective* leader are different concepts.

We can try applying common sense, but common sense can be deeply misleading. It was once common sense to think that the sun rotated around a flat earth; all you had to do was to believe the evidence of your eyes which showed the sun moving through the sky and the world was flat to the horizon.

Common sense seems not to help, so let us turn to practising managers who deal day to day with effective and less effective leaders. They should know what leadership is about.

Practising managers

Here is the output of a typical workshop[1] where attendees were asked to define the qualities of a leader:

- ambitious and humble;
- directive and empowering;
- visionary and practical;
- big on ideas and on people;
- coaching and controlling;
- inspiring, charismatic, authentic and regular.

On a good day we might believe that we have all of these talents. On most days we will recognize that no one can embody this cornucopia of contradictions.

Successful leaders

It does not help when we look to successful leaders to define leadership. As a research exercise, 100 successful leaders were asked to define leadership.[2] It soon became clear that they were not describing leadership: they were describing themselves.[3] They all assumed that their personal success formula was a universal success formula. But we know that not many leaders succeed when they move into a different industry; great politicians rarely make great business people. The United States is conducting an experiment to see if the opposite is true: can a rich business person be a successful political leader?

If you have the misfortune to read the autobiographies of successful business leaders you will see they fall into the same trap: they think their success formula is a universal one. These autobiographies are particularly dangerous. Anyone who feels the urge to write an autobiography is likely to be a larger-than-life individual interested in their own self-promotion and immortality. Some of these people can be exceptional leaders, but the problem with these exceptional leaders is exactly that: they are exceptional. Most leaders are not like that, and most of us cannot aspire to be like that, even if we wanted to be.

Academic research

This is deeply dangerous territory. Every academic has their own definition of leadership which they guard jealously. Anyone who argues is likely to suffer the academic equivalent of being burned at the stake for heresy. The challenge for the academic world is that there is no scientific way of establishing what leadership is. There are endless hypotheses, but every hypothesis can be disproven. Even the definitions provided by top thinkers such as Drucker, Kotter and Bennis are inconsistent and do not work.[4]

One paper[5] found 26,000 academic articles on leadership, which it was able to distil down to 90 variables. That is not a recipe for leadership, it is a recipe for confusion.

Why this myth matters

By now we are in danger of slumping into fashionable postmodern scepticism which holds that there is no truth, there is only what we choose to believe. But if no one has any idea what leadership is, we will struggle to develop leaders. You cannot go on a leadership journey, or any journey, if you do not know what the destination is.

So we need some way forward. We need a working definition of leadership which will allow us to make some progress.

So far, we have looked at the qualities of a good or effective leader. And the result is confusion. So it is time to look at leadership from another perspective. Instead of looking at the qualities of a leader, look at what a leader achieves: judge leaders by what they achieve, not what they do or what they are. Looking at what leaders do results in a long and tedious list of activities: leaders motivate people, make decisions, direct resources, breathe and go to the toilet. The list is long because you can always add more activities; it is tedious because it then leads to a debate about which of these activities leaders do and which managers do. It is a debate that leads nowhere.

The ultimate focus, therefore, is not on what leaders do or what they are: the focus is on what leaders achieve.

Of all the attempts at defining leadership, the former US Secretary of State Henry Kissinger has probably come closest. He defined a leader as 'someone who takes people where they would not have got by themselves'. This sounds a slightly boring and underwhelming definition of leadership. But it is revolutionary. It cuts through the debate about the qualities of a leader; it differentiates leaders from managers; it shows that leadership is about your performance, not your position. It sets a high bar for leadership, which even the most exalted people often fail to reach.

'Someone who takes people where they would not have got by themselves' is the definition of leadership this book will follow. It is a definition which consistently works in practice, if not in theory, but there is no theory of leadership which can stand up to scientific challenge. So instead we will have to make do with what works in practice. As we shall see in the following myths, it is a very powerful definition.

Lessons for leaders

If you want to lead, you have to take people where they would not have got by themselves. That means taking risks, challenging the ways things work today, taking on vested interests and making a real difference. Not everyone wants to live and work that way. But for real leaders, it is the only way to live and work.

This book will give each myth a unicorn rating. The more mythical and the more damaging the myth is, the more unicorns the myth earns. This is the biggest and most damaging myth of all. Out of a maximum of five unicorns, it deserves six. We have to settle for five unicorns.

Endnotes

1 The author runs regular leadership workshops with clients around the world; this is a typical group response to the question: 'What makes a good leader?'

2 Jo Owen (2015) *How to Lead*, 4th edn, Pearson.

3 See Myth 5 for details of how leaders define leadership.

4 See Myth 55 for how Drucker and other academics define leadership, and why their definitions fail.

5 Bruce E Winston and Kathleen Patterson (2006) An integrative definition of leadership, *International Journal of Leadership Studies* [online] https://www.regent.edu/acad/global/publications/ijls/new/vol1iss2/winston_patterson.doc/winston_patterson.htm.

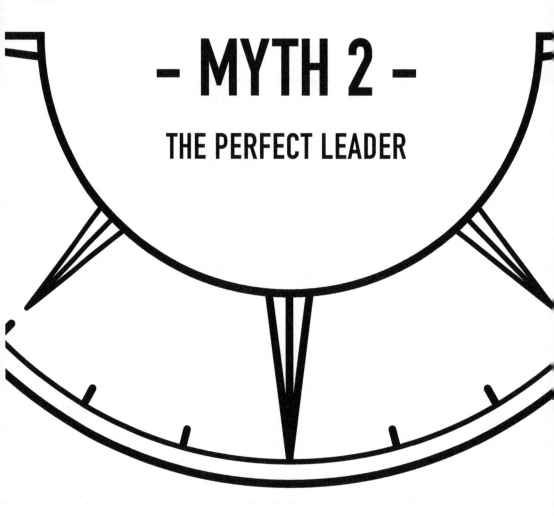

- MYTH 2 -

THE PERFECT LEADER

Perfection is not required to lead. No leader gets ticks in all the boxes.

The nature of the myth

In the last myth we saw how followers expect their leaders to be a perfect cornucopia of contradictions:

- ambitious and humble;
- directive and empowering;
- visionary and practical;
- big on ideas and on people;
- coaching and controlling;
- inspiring, charismatic, authentic and regular.

Leaders who think they are this good are well worth avoiding. For the rest of us, this is a daunting list.

HR systems do not help much either. They also come up with a long list of talents and capabilities which we have to master. How can we achieve perfection in such an imperfect world?

THE PERFECT PREDATOR

It had been a hard research trip with the Pokot and Turkana tribes in northern Kenya. On the way back to Nairobi we went through Samburu National Park. We saw lots of wild animals and started to have an argument about who was the king of the jungle (or, more accurately, the hills and plains). Some favoured the lion, others the crocodile who feared no one, and some the elephant because all animals give way to elephants at a water hole.

We decided to settle the argument by creating the true king of the jungle: the perfect predator. We all took responsibility for one limb. The result was a beast with the jaws of a crocodile, the ears of an elephant, the neck of a giraffe, the hide of a rhino, the tail of a scorpion and the legs of the cheetah. The animal promptly died under the weight of its own improbability.

The same is true of leaders. The perfect leader is not a mix of all the best bits of every leader who has ever breathed air. The perfect leader is the one who fits the context. The lion thrives on the plains and would not last long in the arctic where the reindeer rule; a reindeer on the Serengeti would be called 'lunch'. If you want to lead, find the context where you will succeed.

Why this myth matters

In life there is often a gap between what we want and what we get. This is true of our leaders. We want leaders who are perfect and we end up with [you can name your favourite politicians or bosses here].

As your leadership journey progresses, you will find that you slowly move out of the shadows and into the limelight. In time you might take centre stage, with the spotlight and cameras on you picking up every detail of what you do and every nuance of what you say. Life in the shadows is hard but forgiving. Any minor weaknesses (or 'development opportunities' in HR speak) will only be seen by the people closest to you. When you are centre stage, every minor blemish and every misstep is magnified 100-fold and is seen by everyone. The result is that we see the weaknesses of our leaders very clearly. We know that they are not perfect, and in our hearts we know they never can be.

This is exceptionally good news for all leaders. It means that perfection is not required to lead. No leader gets ticks in all the boxes.

Lessons for leaders

The most important lesson is a lesson of hope: you do not need to be perfect to succeed. Besides this inspirational lesson, there are five practical lessons which will help you on your leadership journey to success, not perfection.

Chase fit, not perfection

Instead of perfection, you have to seek fit. You either have to develop the talents to suit your context or you have to find the context to suit your talents. The latter is more effective than the former; it is easier to change your context than to change your talents.

Build on your strengths

Everyone has a few signature strengths, which can be anything from being deeply analytical or creative, to being highly effective working in teams. These strengths are the fuel for your leadership journey; make sure you find the context where they are vital to success, and you will flourish.

Work around your weaknesses

Corporate development systems often require you to work on your weaknesses. This is catastrophic advice. Weight lifters do not win in the Olympics by working on their weakness in synchronized swimming. If you are highly analytical but less creative, you will not succeed by trying to become the creative heart of your firm. You can work around your weaknesses in three ways:

- Avoid working in contexts where your weaknesses are the key skills required. Find the context where you and your strengths flourish.

- Build a team which is strongest where you are weakest. If you hate book keeping, love book keepers: they can do what you prefer not to.

- Learn enough to ensure that your weakness is not fatal, but do not try to turn it into a strength.

Keep on learning

Leadership is a journey, not a destination. The nature of your leadership challenge keeps on changing, at each level of the firm (see Myth 10) and with each assignment. When the context changes, you have to change. This is what makes the leadership journey so fulfilling and exciting: enjoy the ride.

Avoid the prison of success

Success can be lethal to a career. Many leaders fail because they have huge success in one context. This then becomes their success formula, which they want to apply to every situation. But not every problem is solved with a hammer; you need different tools and different approaches for different situations. The prison of success is the prison of your past. Avoid it.

Conclusion

The perfect leader is like a unicorn: completely mythical. It makes leadership seem unattainable for mere mortals. But this is good news for leaders. You do not need to be perfect, nor do you need a unicorn, to succeed. A full five-unicorn myth.

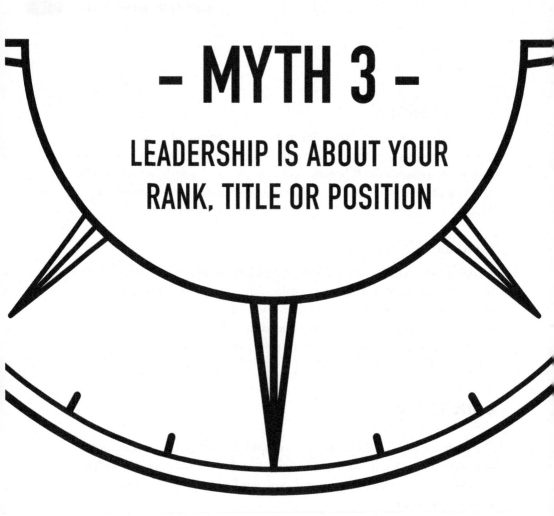

– MYTH 3 –

LEADERSHIP IS ABOUT YOUR RANK, TITLE OR POSITION

Never confuse position with performance.

The nature of the myth

Organizations are hierarchies. This leads to a fatal mistake: everyone assumes that their boss is the leader. Even in the largest and most prestigious firms, you can ask a group of senior executives who is the leader, and they will all point to their boss.

Why this myth matters

The myth is dangerous for two reasons.

Having a grand title does not make you a leader

It simply means you have a grand title. There are plenty of CEOs, presidents and prime ministers who failed to lead: they simply administered a legacy they inherited. There is nothing wrong with managing a legacy. As a good steward of a legacy you should hope to leave the legacy better than when you found it. This was explained well by the CEO of the Grosvenor Group, which is over 300 years old. His job was not to transform the ancient property company into a glorious high-tech firm that would go bust; his job was to manage the legacy for future generations. This is the art of management, and it is much underrated. But it is not leadership.

A leader has to take people where they would not have got by themselves. As an exercise, think of how many presidents or prime ministers you can recall who succeeded in taking the country in a new direction, and a direction they intended to go in. Most of these famous people fail. When I do this exercise with groups in the UK, only two prime ministers out of 13 since 1945 pass the test: Attlee founded the Welfare State, and Thatcher gave us the word Thatcherism. All the others are remembered for trivia or mistakes.

Just because you have the big title, that does not mean you are a leader. Never confuse position with performance. Leadership is about what you do, not what your title is. This gives the clue to the second reason the myth is dangerous.

Having a boss does not stop you from leading

If leadership is about what you do, not about your title, then you can lead wherever you are in the firm. You do not have to lead people to the Promised Land to be a leader. If you change the way your service team works, you are taking people where they would not have got by themselves: you are leading.

You will never reach the corner office unless you learn to lead from an early stage. You have to show that you can make a difference. Fortunately, there are always opportunities to grow your leadership capabilities. In every firm, there are moments of uncertainty, doubt and ambiguity; there are crises and new opportunities where no one is sure what to do. These are the moments of truth when leaders step up and followers step back.

PASSING THE LEADERSHIP TEST

Duncan was the facilities manager. This is the role where everyone ignores you or moans at you. They moan about the catering, the furniture, the lighting, the toilets, the flowers, the car parking, the signage: you name it, it is your fault if you are the facilities manager.

So how can you be a leader if you are the lowly facilities manager?

One day, the partners of the firm went to their global meeting. Duncan was not invited, but he heard the senior partner had made a big speech about working as teams and being more customer focused. It was the sort of standard speech that everyone ignores. But Duncan chose not to ignore it.

Duncan decided to approach the senior partner, which meant going to the office with the deep carpet and reproduction antiques which Duncan had supplied. He was ushered into the presence of the senior partner.

Duncan laid out his idea. 'If you really want teamwork, we will have to get rid of all the private offices and little cubicles, and go open plan… which should save a lot of money.' The partner smiled, so Duncan carried on: 'Of course, that means leadership will have to set an example: the senior partners will need to start by sharing an office.' The partner's smile evaporated: he had been caught. He could not say 'no' but did not want to say 'yes'.

Duncan then carried on: 'In practice we need only about 70 desks for every 100 staff. We should get as many staff out working with clients: more client focus and less cost to us.' The senior partner began to wonder who he had hired as facilities manager.

Duncan may have been a manager by title, but he was a leader by action. He was actively taking the firm where it would not have got by itself. He was even leading the senior partner. Duncan persuaded the senior partner to do something he would never have done by himself.

Lessons for leaders

This myth is bitter sweet. There are different lessons for you, depending where you are in the hierarchy:

- If you are at the top of the firm, do not assume that means you are leading. Being at the top simply means you have a big title and perhaps a big salary. If you want to lead, you will have to show that you are taking the firm where it would not have got by itself.

- If you are at the top of the firm, do not feel the need to be a transformational leader. Being a good steward of a legacy you inherited is worthwhile if you want the firm to survive for 300 years.

- If you are in the middle or junior ranks of management, that should not stop you from thinking and acting as a leader. Inevitably, most of your time will be spent on management tasks, because that will be your job. But within your job, you should find opportunities to reshape how your section operates; you may even find a chance to change the wider firm.

- Thinking and acting like a leader does not start when you reach the 'corner office'. By then it is too late: you will already have the habits of a lifetime which will condition how you act. That means that if you want to lead, you have to start thinking and acting as a leader from the earliest stage.

Leadership is about performance, not position. You can lead whatever your title is. You can be at the top of the firm and not leading; you can be at the bottom of the firm and be a leader. Your choice. Choose well.

Conclusion

This earns a full five unicorns. It cuts to the heart of the leadership debate and overturns the lazy assumption that the boss is a leader. It challenges those at the top and liberates those at the bottom to be real leaders.

- MYTH 4 -

MANAGERS ARE LEADERS

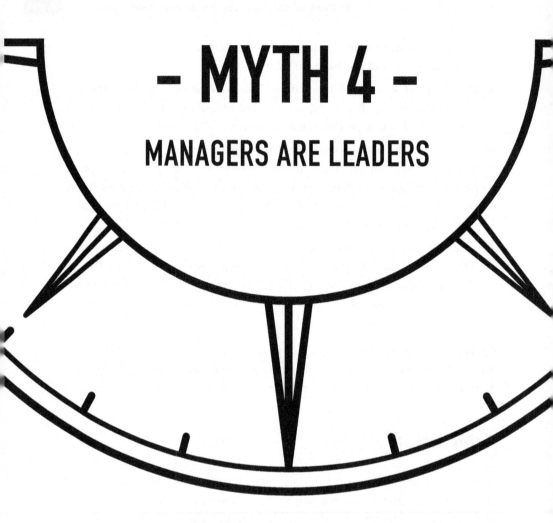

Leaders may change the world, but managers run the world.

The nature of the myth

We live in a world of word inflation. If you get one song into the charts, you get billed as a global megastar. The old Personnel Department has become the Strategic Human Capital Division. Sales people are now Relationship Managers. Traders at banks become vice presidents with no one reporting to them. And nowadays, all managers are told that they are really leaders.

The debate about the difference between a leader and a manager can quickly become a matter of opinion, which generates more heat than light.

Fortunately, I have discovered that there is one statistically proven difference between leadership and management. The difference between leadership and management is that leadership sells more books. I have written books on leadership and management. Books with 'Lead' in the title outsell books with 'Manage' in the title by about five to one. This is true across all business books: mentioning the word 'leader' instead of 'manager' boosts sales dramatically. We all want to be leaders, not managers.

Why this myth matters

At one level, there is no harm in title inflation; it is a cheap way of recognizing people who work hard and make a serious contribution. But at another level, it does matter because the cult of leadership undervalues both leadership and management, and is a source of mismatched expectations.

Undervaluing leadership

One major retail chain is proud of the fact that its new graduates on the shop floor act like real leaders: they have to find solutions to staffing shortages, they have to keep maintaining high standards on store cleanliness and stock availability, and they have to deal with an endless variety of customer situations. There is no doubt that this a highly demanding set of tasks for a recent graduate, but is it leadership? If that is what leaders do, then what are all the top management doing?

This is where the Kissinger definition of leadership helps: 'Leaders take people where they would not have got by themselves.' This makes it clear that much of what is deemed to be 'leadership' is not leadership at all: it is highly effective management.

Revolutions provide an insight into the nature of leadership. Revolutions need revolutionary leaders who will upset the old order and bring in the new world of hope, prosperity and fairness – although some revolutions seem to bring gulags and dictatorship. But before and after the revolution you need countless managers who make sure that the trains run on time and that the bread gets delivered each morning. If your revolution is all leaders and no managers you have chaos. Leaders may change the world, but managers run the world.

By assuming that all managers are leaders, we undervalue leadership. Leadership is a high bar to jump.

Undervaluing management

The modern fetish with leadership means that no one wants to be seen as a 'mere' manager. Why be a manager when you can be a leader? This seriously undervalues both the importance and challenge of being a great manager.

As we have seen with the revolutions analogy, you need managers to run the world before, during and after the revolution. Managers enable great leaders to lead; without good management, a leader can talk much and achieve little.

The challenge of management is, if anything, even greater than the challenge of leadership. Managers lack the control and clarity available to leaders:

- Leaders normally have control over the resources they need to achieve their goals; every year managers find that their budget goes down but their targets go up.

- Leaders have the authority to match their responsibility; standard operating practice for managers is to have responsibilities which exceed their authority. They have to find ways of influencing people over whom they have no control to make things happen. Staff functions often seem to help the CEO, but hinder other managers.

- Leaders have control over their direction: they decide where to go. Managers in the middle often find themselves facing conflicting demands from different parts of the organization. They have to resolve the ambiguity that is inherent to the middle of any firm.

Managers have to make things happen through other people. It is seriously hard work. Success is not natural because events always conspire against managers: staff leave; suppliers let you down; customers want more for less; the taxman just wants more and top management bring forward deadlines and come up with bright ideas for you to act on.

Instead of pretending that all managers are leaders, we should celebrate managers for what they are: the backbone of success in any organization.

Mismatched expectations

Graduate recruiters will always hype up their offering. A standard part of the hype is to show that they expect their newly minted employees to act like leaders from the start. These new leaders then find themselves consigned to doing boring grunt work which is the staple of all people learning a new trade. The expectations mismatch is a major source of frustration and helps to drive large turnover of staff in the early years of their career. Cheap talk can be very expensive.

Lessons for leaders

- **Do a reality check: are you really leading?** If you are a manager, celebrate that. Your work is the bedrock of success for any firm.
- **Celebrate and value your managers.** You are only as good as your management team. They are the people that will turn ideas into reality.
- **Set expectations clearly.** Not everyone can be leading all the time. Even the best leaders spend most of their time on management tasks: making things run and avoiding disaster, rather than changing the world. If you value management properly, then no one will have a problem being called a manager and they will understand what they have to do. If you pretend everyone is going to be a leader from day one, you will find you have many frustrated and disappointed managers who will look for greener pastures elsewhere.

Conclusion

A myth which manages to devalue both leadership and management deserves all five unicorns. We should value management more, and understand how leadership is different.

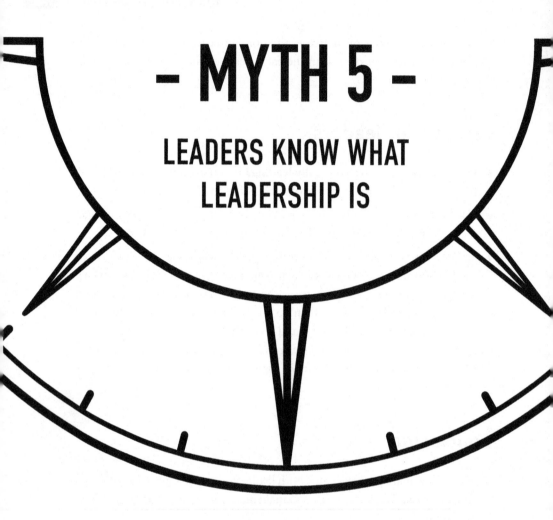

– MYTH 5 –

LEADERS KNOW WHAT LEADERSHIP IS

*Leadership is like a game where you do not know the rules,
but the rules and the referee keep on changing.*

The nature of the myth

The good news is that leaders know exactly what leadership is. And many of them have no hesitation in telling you or in making speeches about it.

The bad news is that they all disagree with each other. Individually leaders offer clarity, collectively they offer confusion.

Here is what leaders said about leadership in original leadership interviews conducted for the start of Teach First:[1]

- Baroness, House of Lords: 'It's service. If you regard it as getting to the top it is something very unpleasant: hubris, pride and ambition.'

- CEO, recruitment firm: 'A leader is someone everyone wants to follow.'

- Head of government agency: 'A leader is the person who goes first. You need a sense of where you are going and you have to motivate people to follow you.'

- Head of major university: 'It is about problem solving and finding solutions. Many people can analyse problems, but leaders find solutions.'

- Major search firm: 'Leaders have a combination of humility, the ability to really listen, be inquisitive and open minded and to set a course of action.'

- CEO, global law firm: 'Leaders convey a clarity of purpose and a vision and enthusiasm for their business.'

- CEO, global media firm: 'Lots of types of people can lead in lots of different sorts of situations...'

- CEO, financial services firm: 'The stereotype of a leader is the larger-than-life, off-the-scale extrovert, but the truth is the opposite: most leaders are quiet but effective.'

All of these definitions have three things in common:

- They are all true, up to a point. They may not be complete definitions of leadership, but they all capture some aspect of what some leaders do.

- They are all different.

- They all reflect the character of the speaker. These were leaders I knew directly or indirectly. In each case they were not describing leadership; they were describing how they aspired to lead. Given that they were all successful leaders in their own contexts, this implies that there is more than one formula for successful leadership.

If you read the media, there are as many definitions of leadership as there are leaders.[2] Here are some of the things CEOs say leadership is about:

- having a selfless heart;
- setting your team up for success;
- inspiring others to become better people;
- being bold enough to have a vision;
- listening, inspiring and empowering;

- understanding that true leadership comes from influence;
- stepping out of your comfort zone and taking risks.

Each one of these is entirely valid. Each soundbite can be converted into a powerful set of values and beliefs which can drive their respective firms. But collectively, the list is overwhelming; it means you have to be superhuman to lead. It does not tell you what you have to do to succeed in your context.

Why this myth matters

If leaders disagree on which is the best rock band, that does not matter. If leaders disagree about what leadership is, that matters for two main reasons.

Developing the next generation of leaders

If you cannot agree what leadership is, it is hard to develop new leaders. It pays to know what you are building before you start building.

Even more dangerous is when leaders believe their own rhetoric about leadership. That implies they want the next generation to be a series of mini-me leaders cloned from their own leadership DNA.

Hubris

Leaders who think they know the answer are setting themselves up for a fall. Success in one context is no guarantee of success in the next context, or if the current context changes. The problem is most acute with the most successful leaders: they become prisoners of success. One success model has delivered huge success to them, and they do not take kindly to academics or gurus suggesting that it is not the only way to succeed. When people find success, they naturally keep doing the same thing. They see changing their success model as risky. In the short term, it is risky to change what you do; in the longer term, it is fatal not to change what you do. You cannot win in the future with yesterday's formula.

Lessons for leaders

Leadership is contextual

You have to find out what works in your context. Do not believe the gurus who claim to have the universal formula for success in three easy steps.

Learn and grow

Throughout your career your context will change: you will be promoted, you will face new challenges and the world around you will change. Leadership is like a game where you do not know the rules but the rules and the referee keep on changing. This puts a premium on being able to grow and learn fast. Employee handbooks tell you all the rules, except for the one you need: how do I succeed? The important rules, you have to find for yourself.

Discover and build the core skills and mindsets of success

There are some universal truths about leadership. If you fundamentally do not like other people and you are lazy, cynical and unambitious then you will struggle to be a leader. You need your own success theory: it may be wrong, but at least it gives you something to work with. And if you learn and grow fast, then you can adapt your success theory in response to experience. Start with the principle that leaders take people where they would not have got by themselves and work back from that. If that is the goal, what are the skills and mindset you need to achieve it? Normally, you will require some combination of motivating and influencing people, having a clear and compelling idea, and communicating well and making decisions.

Conclusion

If leaders cannot agree on what leadership is, that is a fundamental challenge to the nature of leadership. Five unicorns.

Endnotes

1 These are transcribed from video interviews leaders did for the author in 2005. Teach First is now the largest graduate recruiter in the UK.

2 http://www.businessnewsdaily.com/3647-leadership-definition.html. This provides 33 CEOs' definitions of leadership, and they all conflict.

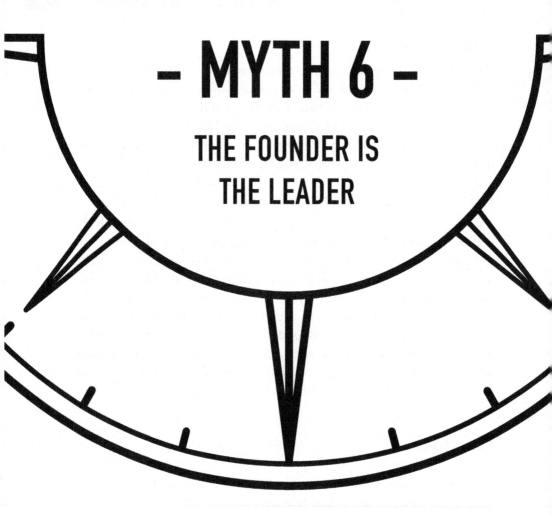

– MYTH 6 –

THE FOUNDER IS
THE LEADER

*The job of the founder is not to be the smartest person on the team;
it is to get the smartest people onto the team.*

The nature of the myth

The essence of this myth is based on a simple reality: the easiest way to lead something is to start something. The question is whether the founder is the right person to lead, and for how long.

You don't have to found a firm to be a founder. Within a firm, if you start a new initiative, you are the founder of that idea. If you found something within a firm, then the idea of the founder as leader principle works well.

The founder as leader is more natural when founding a new firm, but like volcanoes, crocodiles and hurricanes, what is natural can be very dangerous.

Within a firm, if you have an idea you will normally get first shot at making the idea happen. First mover advantage is very powerful. Once you are leading the new project, or developing the new product, all sorts of people will come on board and make a difference. But they are all fine-tuning the big idea you started with. Within the firm, you have to keep on earning the right to lead your idea. If you start to struggle you will first receive support and then you will be replaced. The founder's rights are strictly limited; you get a chance to lead, but you do not get freehold leadership rights for your idea.

The challenge arises with founders of firms and not-for-profits, who will often have a stranglehold on governance through shareholdings or through the membership structure of the not-for-profit. The normal checks and balances that exist within the firm do not apply to the founder of the firm. They can go on until they are making billions or until they go bust.

The problem gets worse as a result of survivor bias. We all read the tales of brilliant entrepreneurs who start in the mythical garage and land up jetting around the world meeting presidents and addressing the World Economic Forum. This gives the illusion that the founder is always the person who has to lead the firm to success. We never hear about those who do not survive; they started in the garage, built up a small business and then went bust. For every founder who becomes a billionaire there are countless thousands of founders who do not make the grade. The job of the founder is not to be the smartest person on the team; it is to get the smartest people onto the team.

Why this myth matters

This myth matters because the founder is not always the right person to lead their business, but they often find it very difficult to let go. When you start a new venture, it is your baby; you put all your time and effort into making it succeed. The thought of handing over to someone else is anathema; they might kill your baby or turn it into a monster. And for many entrepreneurs, the joy is in the journey. It is not just about making money, although that helps; it is about the joy of turning an idea into reality.

There is magic in creating something out of nothing, and no founder wants to give up that magic. At a more prosaic level, founders know that they have limited options. They know that trying to start another successful start-up is hazardous at best. And they also know that they cannot return to working for someone else. Founding a firm is a one-way leap: once you have tasted the freedom and terror of starting your own business it is emotionally impossible to return to the gilded cage of employment. The petty rules, the politics, the indignity of working for someone you do not respect are hard to deal with.

Founders often struggle to lead their start-up to maturity for the same reason that young leaders within a firm find it hard to become middle and senior leaders. Whether you work inside a firm or you have started a firm the rules of leadership success change as you progress. Within the firm, you are likely to move more slowly and receive more support. When you start a new firm, growth can be dramatic and you lack the support infrastructure to help you learn and lead.

When you start a new business, you are your own sales force, customer management, head of operations, IT help desk, HR department and facilities manager. You have to do everything, and it is massively inefficient. Transitioning from there into a large organization which has its own IT, operations, finance and accounting, HR, legal, sales and marketing is a huge leap. If you are doing all these things yourself, you are a founder but not a leader. As a leader, you have to build the team which will turn your idea into reality. If you do that, you will have succeeded as a leader and entrepreneur, regardless of what title you give yourself. Never confuse your title and your role: you do not have to be the CEO to be the leader.

Lessons for leaders

Move first, move fast

Founders within a firm benefit hugely from first mover advantage. You will normally get the chance to lead your idea if you are first to move. This is true of moments of crisis and ambiguity when no one is quite sure what to do, or all the options seem too risky. First mover advantage also applies to start-ups, many of which are team efforts. Be part of the founding team, which normally means getting involved before there is a website, name or legal entity. If you are involved that early, you have the chance to shape your destiny. If you join later, you will find that your destiny is shaped by the first movers: the founding team.

Know where you add value

As a founder you will bring some magic sauce to the firm you start. You will have the inspiration, passion and vision. This makes you the natural cheerleader-in-chief in dealing with customers, investors and partners. You may also have some specific talent to bring. As founder, you have the right to shape your role as you want it, and that does not mean you have to be CEO.

Build your team

Focus on what you can do well, and bring in other talent to support you. You would not consider doing all your own book keeping as the firm grows because other people can do that better: apply the same principle to all the management and leadership tasks of the firm.

Learn and grow fast

If you want to lead the firm to scale, you need to learn and adapt fast. See Myth 9 for how the skills of leadership change at each level of the firm. You will not be progressing in terms of seniority, but you will be progressing in terms of scale. Scale is a good proxy for seniority: the larger your business, the more your leadership role looks like a senior role.

Conclusion

Starting something is the easiest way to lead something, which means that this is in danger of being reality, not myth. But many founders fail because they are not good leaders. All good myths mix truth and fantasy. This is no exception. Three unicorns.

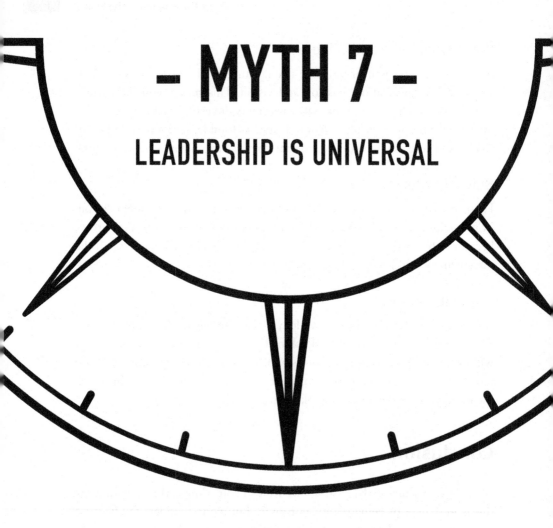

- MYTH 7 -

LEADERSHIP IS UNIVERSAL

Instead of trying to build cultural knowledge, build cultural intelligence.

The nature of the myth

At the last count, Amazon offered 58,217 books with the word 'leadership' in their title. With this one, you can add one more to the total. Happy reading.

Like latter-day alchemists, the majority of these books attempt to find the elixir of leadership. Most of them offer some useful insight into leadership, but the quest for universal truth is as pointless as the medieval quest for the elixir of eternal youth, or the formula for turning base metal into gold. There is no universal formula; there is only what works for you in your context. One of the critical dimensions of context is global; different cultures lead and manage in different ways.

Because most of the leadership literature is written in English by writers from the English-speaking world, there is a heavy bias towards assuming that the Anglo way is the right way. In the era of American hegemony, there was some justification to this. It meant that globalization was the code word for spreading western practices around the world. The rise of Japan and its decimation of various western industries was the first wake-up call. The second wake-up call is the rise of China and the rest of Asia.

Despite this, leadership still has a strong western bias. As one Japanese manager put it: 'We read many business books by American authors, but how many Americans have read business books by Japanese authors?' The Japanese understand America better than Americans understand Japan. Indeed, the greatest success of Japanese management was the deployment of the Quality Movement. They had learned the principles of quality from an American, W Edwards Deming,[1] but America only adopted Deming's methods when Japan started its onslaught.

The world understands the West, but does the West understand the world? There is a huge knowledge gap between East and West, which is not to the advantage of the West.

Why this myth matters

Leadership varies around the world. You cannot assume that what works in one culture will work in another.[2, 3]

Table 7.1 highlights a few of the differences between a few of the cultures. Research has shown that even when you make the very short trip by train under the Channel Tunnel from the UK to France, all the rules change.[4] The following vignette makes the point.

ANGLO-FRENCH COLLABORATION AND CONFLICT

Bertrand was chef de cabinet: he led a large government ministry in Paris. During our interview, he mentioned that the British are very pragmatic decision makers. That sounded like a compliment, but he is French and I am British, so it had to be an insult. I asked Bertrand to explain:

In France we are very rigorous in decision making. We take an intellectual approach, so when we arrive at a decision we know it is right and we stick with it. But you are more pragmatic: you do what makes sense today, but tomorrow you might change your mind. And because you don't use body language, we don't know what you are thinking. So we don't know what you think but we do know you will change your mind. So that is why we find it hard to trust the Brits.

I probably looked crestfallen, because then he added helpfully: 'But don't worry, the Germans are worse…'

Lessons for leaders

Build your cultural intelligence

There is a huge amount of literature out there which maps the cultural differences between nations, but no one can master all the cultural nuances of the world. Your job is not to be an anthropologist; your job is to lead.

The principles are easy, even if the practice is hard:

- **Don't assume that your way is the right way.** One reason for global working is to find the best talent and best solutions in the world.

- **Be quick to observe, learn and adapt.** Stay curious: try the local foods, music and ways of doing things. Working globally is a great chance to broaden your experience and capabilities, so make the most of it.

- **Recognize that you are the one with the exotic culture and habits.** See the text box on page 36.

- **Have positive regard.** On global teams, misunderstandings arise more easily and are harder to fix. When this happens, assume the other side is professional and wants to do a good job. Avoid suspicion and the blame game.

- **Communication starts with understanding.** This means listening more than you talk.

Table 7.1 Leadership and business styles in four cultures

Factor	UK	Japan	Traditional societies	France
Decision processes	Pragmatic, well communicated	Consensual	Communal, open	Top down, well thought through
Hierarchy	Call boss by first name	Respect-based language	Age and sex	Tu, vous, title depending on relationship
Networks	Based on profession	Based on keiretsu	Family based	Academic background
Education focus	Liberal arts	Maths, science, engineering	Informal, oral, generalists	Maths and science
Key industries	City, services, media	Engineering, manufacturing	Subsistence	Engineering, luxury goods
Values	Ethics, spirit of the law	Honesty and trust, outside law	Respect for the community	Honesty, letter of the law
Delegation	Responsibility exceeds authority	Collective responsibility	Compartmentalisation of roles	Responsibility requires authority
Feedback	Indirect, often positive	Avoided	No	Direct, often negative
Body language	Hidden, appears devious	Formality, ritual	Open	Open and direct
Openness	Wimbledonization of London	Closed	Binary	Closed: revolution not evolution
Law	Common law, flexible	Avoid using law	Tradition, personal	Roman law, highly prescriptive
Thinking	Pragmatic	Practical	Tradition	Theoretical, based on principles
Meetings	Make decisions	Confirm decisions	Social	Air views, defend position

WHO HAS THE EXOTIC CULTURE?

It was late and we were drunk. That is the point in the evening in Japan when you can tell the truth and still be forgiven in the morning. The senior executive leaned over to me and said, 'Jo-san: there is something I need to ask you'. I leaned in towards him: we were clearly getting down to business.

'How do you shake hands?' he asked.

We think Japanese bowing is impenetrable. It is not. Meishi (business cards) give you all the information you need to know who should bow first, deepest and longest: that is why meishi are always exchanged immediately on first meetings.

By comparison, shaking hands is a mystery. What are the rules? When do you know to shake hands and with whom? How hard and how long do you shake? Are the rules the same everywhere? And let's not even get onto the French habit of kissing…

Now you try to explain the rules of shaking hands.

Conclusion

This myth is widespread and dangerous at every level. Individuals think that their success formula is unique, and then fail when they are in a new context. The West thinks it has a monopoly on wisdom, but is being challenged by leaders who think differently. Five unicorns.

Endnotes

1   W Edwards Deming (2000) *Out of the Crisis*, 1st edn, MIT Press.

2   This is based on original research for Jo Owen (2016) *Global Teams*, Pearson FT.

3   The table is based on original research which first appeared in Jo Owen (2007) *Tribal Business School*, Wiley.

4   The comparison between the UK and France was also original research reported by CNN, http://edition.cnn.com/2007/BUSINESS/04/30/execed.anglofrench/.

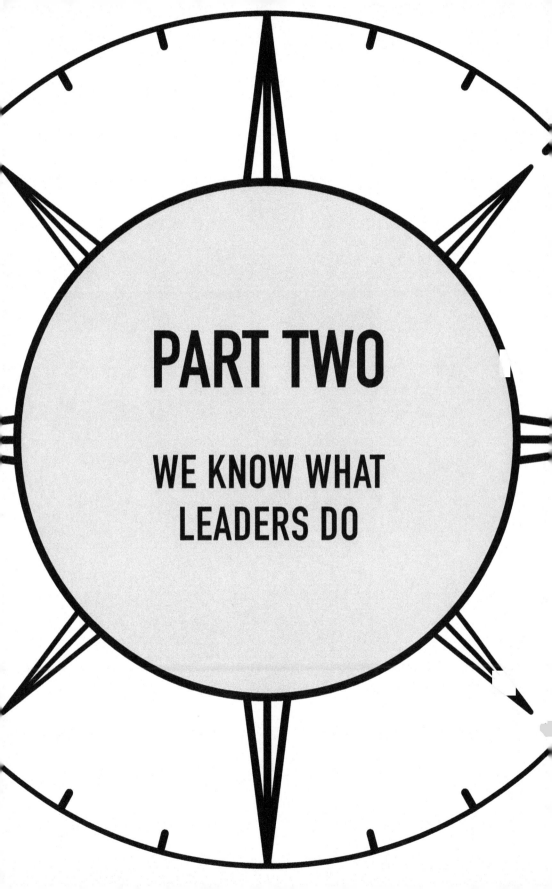

PART TWO

WE KNOW WHAT LEADERS DO

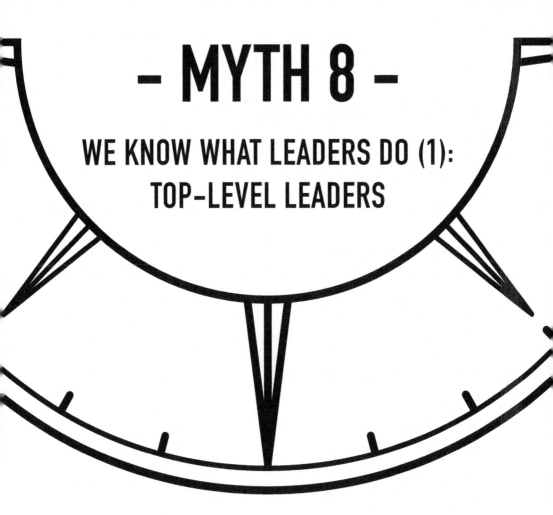

– MYTH 8 –

WE KNOW WHAT LEADERS DO (1): TOP-LEVEL LEADERS

Leader is contextual. There is no one-size-fits-all leader.

The nature of the myth

At one level we know exactly what leaders do. They talk to people, they listen, they do e-mails, have meetings and read documents. But that is what anyone does in an office job. We can also see that leaders breathe: true, but useless. The real question is: 'Do we know what leaders do, that no one else does?' There is no single, simple answer to that question. In different contexts, leaders have to do different things. For instance, leaders who grow the firm and leaders who cut costs are very different beasts: they have different skills and will do different things.

This means that leadership is contextual. There is no one-size-fits-all leader: you need different leaders for different challenges.

Why this myth matters

This matters for two reasons:

- appointing leaders;
- managing your leadership journey.

Appointing leaders

When the board is looking for a new CEO, they are not just looking for a person with leadership qualities (however those may be defined): many people have leadership qualities. The board will be looking for a solution to whatever they think the major challenge is for their firm. This leads them to find someone who has already solved that problem before. For instance, the challenge for the firm may be about:

- going global;
- restructuring and generating growth;
- simplifying operations;
- generating faster growth;
- accelerating innovation and time to market.

There are countless other challenges, and each one requires a very different skill set from the leader of the firm. It also means the leader and the firm will be engaged in very different sorts of activity. If the challenge is about going global, the leader will be spending more time on flights than if the challenge is to restructure domestic operations.

The same logic applies to appointing leaders at all levels: you look not just for the right person, but for the right solution. You need someone who will deliver the outcome you want. At more junior levels, the stakes are lower so you can take a risk and develop people in role. The more senior the appointment is, the higher the stakes become, and there will be lower risk appetite for taking a chance on someone without the right experience developing in role.

This has major implications for how you develop your leadership career.

Managing your leadership journey

It is not enough to develop broad 'leadership' capabilities. You need to be excellent at something: you need to have a signature strength which will keep you in demand. This is not how many HR systems work: they identify your weaknesses and encourage you to work on them. But no one succeeds by working on their weaknesses. You will succeed by working on your strengths. Fortunately, leadership is a team sport and you should build your team to support you in the areas where you are not so strong.

BE CAREFUL WHAT YOU SUCCEED AT

As a new employee, Debbie drew the short straw at assignment time. She was asked to develop the business case for implementing a new IT system at a European life insurance company. It was vital work, but dull: not exactly what she had hoped for. However, she was keen to make a good impression, so she pulled out all the stops and by the end of the project, she was being praised for an outstanding contribution.

Shortly afterwards, another European life insurance company also needed a business case for a new IT system, and Debbie was the natural choice to lead that work. With the experience gained from her first business case, she did an even better job in about half the time. A star was born. She was now the official maestro of business cases for IT systems in European life insurance companies. She was the first port of call for all such work, and was in great demand.

Success was a curse: she did not like the work, which was not the sort of work which would get you promoted, and she was not broadening her experience. She had successfully backed herself into a career dead end.

Lessons for leaders

Build your claim to fame

As a leader you need a portfolio of skills and experience. But you also need one or two claims to fame, where you are recognized as being best in class at doing something. In other words, you need both breadth and depth of experience.

Keep learning, keep growing

In practice, you cannot predict what skills and challenges will be dominant in 20 years' time at your firm. Instead, build capabilities which you know will be in demand somewhere all the time: cutting costs, growing revenues and improving operations are capabilities which never go out of fashion. Even if your skill is not top of the agenda at your firm, it will be top of the agenda somewhere else. If you want to control your future, your employability is more important than your employer.

Conclusion

Misunderstand what leaders do and you can find yourself appointing the wrong leader (end of firm) or acquiring the wrong experience (end of career). So this slightly dull and technical myth is very dangerous. Five unicorns.

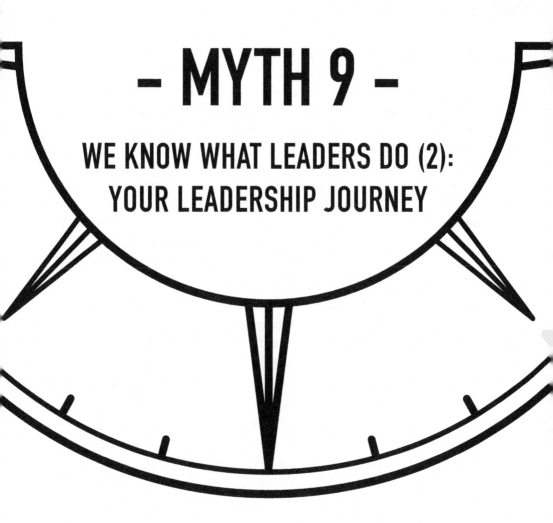

- MYTH 9 -

WE KNOW WHAT LEADERS DO (2): YOUR LEADERSHIP JOURNEY

Keep on growing, keep on learning, keep on changing.

The nature of the myth

Leadership is a journey, not a destination. There is no single concept of 'leadership' which we can bottle, label and sell. Leadership means different things in different contexts. When your context changes, the nature of leadership changes. This is particularly true when you gain promotion.

This myth is implicitly recognized in most firms' appraisal and development processes: you are expected to perform differently in different roles and at different levels.

Why this myth matters

Increasingly, we cannot rely on employers for our careers. The median job tenure in the United States is now down to 4.2 years,[1] implying most people will change employers many times in their careers. Increasingly, career is becoming a verb, not a noun; we career from role to role, rather than having a career for life with a benevolent employer.

If we have to manage our own leadership journey, it pays to have a map of where we are heading. Google may have mapped most things on our planet, but they have not yet produced a reliable leadership map, nor has anyone else. Opposite is a simplified map of a typical leadership journey.

Here are a few of the main changes that happen on most leadership journeys, from emerging to senior leader:

- Time horizon goes from short term to long term. As a new graduate, you will be given tasks that need to be completed in a few hours or days. By the time you are the CEO, you will be planning years ahead.

- The key skills go from technical or craft skills to people and political skills. When you start your career, you will learn a craft such as accounting, law, teaching, or preparing PowerPoint presentations. By the time you reach the top, you will be getting other people to do these things for you.

- Financial skills become increasingly important over time. At the start of a career, most people have no budget other than their own time; at board level there is relentless focus on financial performance and presentation.

- Staff go from being the enemy who stop you doing things, to allies who help you make things happen

Leaders who fail to learn and grow become marooned: they hit a career ceiling which they cannot break through. If you want to keep moving along your leadership journey, keep learning.

Lessons for leaders

There is a very simple message for leaders at all levels: keep on growing, keep on learning, keep on changing. No matter where you are on your leadership journey, you will find that your context keeps on changing. That means you have to change as well. Three examples will make the point.

Table 9.1 The leadership journey[2]

Leadership level	Managing self: new employee	Managing others: front-line supervision	Managing a function: several teams	Managing a business with P&L	Managing a group of businesses
Time horizon	A day or a week	A week to a quarter	A quarter to a year	Over a year	Long-term future
Main task	Doing: quality, speed, craft skills, work planning	Managing: coach, motivate, performance manage, delegate	Optimizing: improve how things work	Integrating and changing	Leading
Who you value	Self	Your team	Other functions	Staff support	External stakeholders
Financial skills	N/A	Cost management	Budget management: negotiate and control	P&L management: revenue generation, cost allocation	Financial accounting: tax, reporting
Traps and challenges	Disenchantment: dull, boring work	Not changing your game	Not managing politics	From impostor syndrome to hubris	Losing touch

The emerging leader

Your first promotion is often the most hazardous step on your leadership journey. If a new graduate does a good job, promotion will ensue. The graduate will then naturally do more of the same: when you have a success model, stick to it. The graduate then gets fired, not because they have become incompetent but because they have not realized that the game has changed.

The new graduate is like the great footballer who is promoted to coach. The increased responsibility does not mean that the player has to play harder or better: the player has to learn a new role. The job of the coach is not to score all the goals, make all the tackles and play beautiful passes. The job of the coach is to select and develop the right team and to decide the right tactics. The same is true for the graduate: they no longer have to do all the work themselves, but they have to help the team do the work effectively. New leaders must make the crucial transition from asking 'how do I do this?' to 'who can do this?' Moving from 'how' to 'who' changes everything.

The entrepreneurial leader

The classic entrepreneur always seems to start in a garage or a bedroom, or occasionally at the kitchen table. This is when you discover or develop new talents, because you have to be able to do everything. You are your own personal assistant, IT help desk, sales force, product development team, financial controller and book keeper. It can almost make you nostalgic for the days when you were enabled and imprisoned by the corporate life support systems of most large firms.

As you succeed, you can start to hire staff. This means you can focus your role where you make the most difference. Your context is changing, so you change. Your role continues to focus as the firm grows. But many entrepreneurs struggle with the change, because they do not want to give up direct control. They interfere where they should delegate, which demoralizes the team and overworks the leader. They become the classic overbearing entrepreneurial leader: 'my way or no way'. Success proves to them that they are right; failure proves to them that they cannot trust other people. Inevitably, the firm becomes highly dependent on them. This is not sustainable.

Even when you are the founder of the firm, you have to keep growing and adapting if you are to build a sustainable firm.

All leaders

Think of your favourite movies and music. What age were you when they were first produced? Many people believe that there was a golden era when they were in their late teens and early twenties: anything earlier is old fashioned, and anything since then is just not as good. We get stuck in our own cultural time warp. At a personal level, that is not a problem. At a professional level, it is a big problem. We have to cultivate a mindset which is open to new ideas, new experiences and to learning new things. If the best is always in the past, we cannot move forward.

Conclusion

This myth cuts to the heart of your career: leadership is a journey, not a destination. This means you have to keep learning and growing because the rules of survival and success keep changing. If you believe leadership is a journey, not a destination, then you are right. Zero unicorns.

Endnotes

1 Bureau of Labor Statistics, September 2016, https://www.bls.gov/news.release/pdf/tenure.pdf.

2 This first appeared in Jo Owen (2015) *Mindset of Success*, 2nd edn, Kogan Page.

– MYTH 10 –

LEADERS MOTIVATE THEIR FOLLOWERS

There is a huge reality gap between the perceptions of leaders and their followers.

The nature of the myth

When you ask followers what they want from their leader, two factors stand out from the rest. A good leader must:

- have a vision;
- be motivational.

The good news is that leaders themselves recognize the importance of this. The even better news is that 67 per cent of leaders think that they are good at motivation. The bad news is that only 32 per cent of their followers agree.[1] There is a huge reality gap between the perceptions of leaders and their followers. You may think you are good at motivation, but what does your team really think?

'Leaders motivate their followers' is true in theory, but largely false in practice. It qualifies as a practical, but not theoretical, myth.

Why this myth matters

The nature of leadership has changed. In the past, leaders expected compliance from their teams. They had the power and authority to enforce compliance. Given that most work was routine and easy to measure, compliance was enough. But the nature of work has changed, which has forced leaders to change how they lead. Work is now much more ambiguous: what does a 'good' report or meeting look like? How much time and effort should go into each piece of work? Professional work is, by its nature, ambiguous. The growth of the professions means their productivity is more important. But how do you measure the output of a consultant, psychotherapist or health and safety officer? It is not like measuring quantity and quality on a production line.

In this new world of work, compliance is not enough. You need real commitment from the team to deliver quality which is more than 'good enough'. Time and cost pressures mean that there is a real squeeze, so leaders rely on their team to keep on going the extra mile to make things happen.

Clearly, motivation does not come only from the leader. Motivation also comes from four other sources:

- **Internal motivation.** Each team member has to find their own sources of motivation: most professionals take pride in their work and want to do well. Ultimately, we are all responsible for ourselves and our feelings. Depending on others to feel good or bad is a classic victim mindset.

- **Job structure.** There is widespread literature on how jobs can be structured to make them more fulfilling. Typically, the more autonomy and variety there is in a job, the more motivational it is.

- **Reward systems,** which are tricky. Formal rewards will encourage people to hit the target, if necessary by gaming the system. Meeting targets and being motivated to do a good job are different concepts.

- **Organization culture,** which the leader of the organization influences but rarely controls. Organizations develop a life and culture of their own. The civil service and nuclear engineers are rightly risk averse. Asking them to become entrepreneurial is dangerous, inappropriate and like asking a leopard to change its spots.

Clearly, the leader can influence the culture, job structure and reward systems of the firm and the team. But the leader also has a huge direct role to play in motivating the team. Gallup research[2] shows that 70 per cent of the variance in employee engagement is attributable to the quality of the boss. Gallup defines engagement as being enthusiastic and committed to work, as opposed to being indifferent and sleepwalking through the working day. If a team is to be high performing it has to be engaged, and the leader has a vital role in making sure of this. The same research also showed that roughly 50 per cent of employee attrition is driven by staff wanting to get away from their boss. As a leader, you have a huge impact for better or for worse on your team.

Lessons for leaders

It is one thing to say that leaders need to be motivational; it is another to know how to be motivational.

The good news is that you do not have to be like Mr Motivator at the company conference who delivers inspiring keynote speeches. The same research clearly shows how leaders can motivate their teams well. None of it is rocket science. Here is what you can do:

Set clear expectations

This is not about telling people what to do. Expectations are genuinely two way. You need to hear and understand what each of your team members wants. This does not come from a formal meeting to exchange expectations. It comes from endless small and longer conversations where you discover the real hopes and fears of each follower.

Have a vision

A good vision is motivational in its own right, especially when each team member sees that they have a valuable role to play in getting there. But goal setting is not enough: you have to take time to explain the context: why the vision is important, to whom and what the main risks and opportunities are. Only then will each team member fully understand what is expected of them.

Set clear goals

It is not enough to say, 'Produce this report by this time...' As with the vision, you have to set the context. And you also need to involve team members in setting their longer-term goals. By letting them influence their own goals you not only motivate them, you also increase accountability and ownership for the goal.

Communicate more

George Orwell wrote, 'Seeing what is in front of your nose requires constant struggle'.[3] Communicating is obvious, but requires constant struggle because most leaders are swamped with fighting the noise of day-to-day leadership challenges. Communication gets lost in the noise. A crucial part of communication is regular feedback: no one wants to wait to year end to find out how they have done. Critically, communication is about listening more than you talk.

Be positive

No one likes working for a grump. Being positive means focusing on your team members' strengths, not their weaknesses; focusing on what can be done in the future, not on what went wrong in the past; finding things to praise, not to criticize. Being positive makes you more approachable, which means you can communicate better.

Finally, there is one statement which is an unerringly reliable predictor of whether your followers will think that you are a good boss or not:

My boss cares for me and my career (agree/disagree).

Followers who thought their boss cared for them and their career rated their boss positively on nearly all other criteria; bosses who scored low on this question scored low on everything else. Showing you really care takes time and effort: it is an investment of time which pays rich dividends.

Conclusion

Leaders should motivate their followers, so that is not a myth. But leaders usually fail to motivate well. The myth exists in practice, if not in theory. The theory would earn no unicorns, because it is reality; the practice earns four unicorns because so many leaders fail to motivate well. We will compromise and award this two unicorns.

Endnotes

1 Author's original research with over 500 leaders and followers, first published in Jo Owen (2015) *How to Lead*, Pearson.

2 Jim Harter and Amy Adkins (2015) Employees want a lot more from their managers, Gallup [online] http://www.gallup.com/businessjournal/182321/employees-lot-managers.aspx.

3 George Orwell (1946) In Front of Your Nose, essay first published in *Tribune*, London, 22 March.

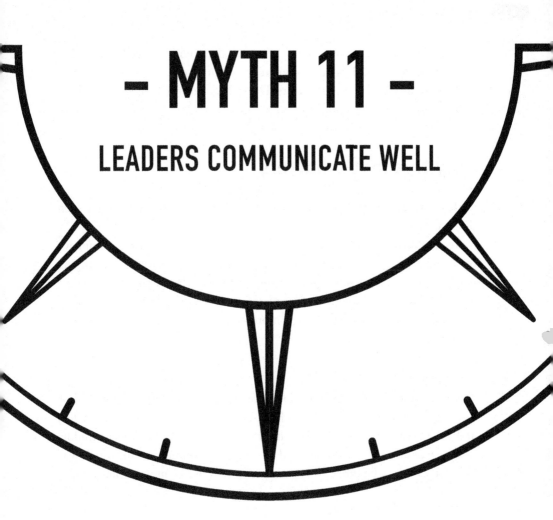

– MYTH 11 –

LEADERS COMMUNICATE WELL

*We communicate more than ever, but understand
each other as little as ever.*

The nature of the myth

The birth of democracy in Ancient Greece also saw the birth of rhetoric. If you aspired to lead in a democracy, you had to acquire powers of persuasion. Great orators became influential. It was said of Socrates that if he lost a wrestling contest, he would get up and persuade the crowd that he had actually won the contest. In those days, education of leaders was both intellectual and physical because a small democracy surrounded by tyrants knew that it would have to fight for its existence.

Since then, leaders have been expected to communicate well. But reality is different. Most leaders are not great communicators, and many business leaders are abysmal communicators. Death by jargon is as ugly as death by bullet point.

Why this myth matters

Technology means we communicate more than ever, but understand each other as little as ever.

Technology improves efficiency of communication; it does not improve the effectiveness of communication. More is not always better. The changing nature of technology and organization means that the way leaders need to communicate is changing. Leaders were not very good in the old world of communication, and struggle even more in the new world. There are three main reasons to communicate:

Communicate to control

This is the traditional form of business communication in a hierarchy: orders flow down and information flows back up. Maintaining integrity of orders and information is essential. This used to rely on ranks of diligent middle managers, but it now relies on good IT systems. Communication which was indirect, can now be direct: this puts a premium on communicating well.

Communicate to persuade

This is where leaders go back to the future. The art of communication was the art of persuasion in the ancient Greek democracy. It is also the future of communication in firms where traditional hierarchies are slowly eroding. Better-educated staff now expect to be involved more; matrix organizations mean that you no longer control all the resources you need to succeed. In other words, you can no longer rely on authority to make things happen: you have to use persuasion.

Communicate to understand

Communication has traditionally been seen as finding ways of broadcasting your message as effectively as possible. That takes us back to the traditional view of leadership where the leader has all the answers, and communication is about spreading the message. But today communication is a two-way street. Business is so complex and changing so fast that you cannot know it all. You need to listen to understand.

Lessons for leaders

Listen more

Effective leaders and sales people have one thing in common: they all have two ears and one mouth, and they use them in that proportion. Leading is not about dominating the airwaves. It starts with understanding, and that requires listening at least twice as much as you talk. Observe a meeting with a very senior person: often the senior person says little other than asking one or two sharp questions. They are building their understanding. When they do speak, they command attention because they speak so little.

Listening well is an art form as much as speaking well. A good listener knows that it is better to offer smart questions than smart answers. A good first step to becoming a good listener is to learn the art of paraphrasing. When you hear someone say something, say it back to them in your own words. This achieves several goals at once:

- It helps you understand their position without having to agree to it. You can only influence their thinking when you know what they are thinking.
- It helps you remember what they said.
- If there is any misunderstanding, you discover it fast and can deal with it.
- It encourages the speaker to shut up. People often make the same point repeatedly because they fear that they have not been heard. When you paraphrase back to them, they build confidence that they have been understood and they can move on.

Less is more

Inflation applies to speech: the more you talk, the less each word is valued. If you speak little, each word carries more weight and more value.

THE VALUE OF WORDS

The Fulani[1] elder sat down outside his hut and thought for a while before speaking. He then quietly said:

> Words are like gods. Words create whole new worlds in people's minds. Words make people do things and change things. So we should value each word. We should carve each sentence like a mason and polish each word like a silversmith.

Having made his point, he fell silent again. Can you make each word count?

Choose the right medium

Good communication and high trust go together. We communicate more openly with people we trust. And trust is only built face to face. Technology helps with transactional communications ('what time will you arrive today?') but you do not build trust or motivate people by e-mail.

E-mail is a plague on modern business. It eats up the day, is a constant distraction and it is a poor form of communication. It is a good way of leaving an electronic audit trail to prove that you were right and they were wrong; it is a good way of copying everyone in on a 'just in case' basis. E-mail confuses efficiency with effectiveness: it is an efficient way of spreading messages, but it is not an effective way of doing so. There are two much more effective communication technologies:

1 Phone (or video call). This is real time and allows both sides to adapt to each other and find common ground. If there is disagreement, you will discover that quickly either directly or indirectly by hearing the tone of voice at the other end of the phone.

2 Shoes. Walking to another desk and talking face to face is the most effective form of communication, even if it is the most inefficient. You can see all the non-verbal cues which tell you how the other person is reacting; you can avoid misunderstandings before they arise; you can build trust and move to agreement and action fast.

Present well

Leaders have to present to large and small groups, without having the benefit of an education based on rhetoric. You do not need a professional speech writer to be able to speak well. A good presentation will make one point very clearly: anything more just dilutes the message. And then focus on how you present. This is where it helps to remember the three E's of presenting:

- **Enthusiasm**: if you are not enthusiastic, do not expect anyone else to be enthusiastic for you. You will be remembered for how you are more than what you say, so present as you wish to be remembered.

- **Experience**: the more you present, the more comfortable you become. But you have to learn from each experience: there is no point in making the same mistakes 30 times. And experience also means rehearsing and preparing.

- **Expertise**. If you have been asked to speak, it is because someone thinks you know something.

Write well

None of us can aspire to the heights of Shakespeare, or even a Hollywood screen writer. But we can follow a few basic rules to raise our game. Below are the five rules which my editor always tripped me up on. If you can follow these rules consistently, you will be seen as an effective writer:

- Write for the reader. What is the point you need them to hear; what is it they want to know from you? Make it relevant, personal and practical.

- Tell a story. Your message needs a simple narrative: here's the challenge, here are the options and here is the solution. Make it easy for your reader to follow.

- Keep it short. Short words and short sentences aid clarity.

- Keep it positive. Avoid the passive tense and the impersonal.

- Support assertions with facts. If you say something is important, urgent or strategic then that is just your opinion. Show why it is important, urgent and strategic to the reader of the message.

These are simple rules which are very hard to follow all the time.

Conclusion

In an ideal world, leaders would be great communicators. In an ideal world, there would be no famine, war or disease. But we do not live in an ideal world. In reality, many leaders are not good communicators, and that inhibits their ability to lead. In theory, this myth should get no unicorns (because it is true): in practice it should get five (because leaders often communicate poorly). The obvious compromise is three unicorns.

Endnote

1 The Fulani are a farming tribe in Mali. This story comes from the author's original research which featured in Jo Owen (2007) *Tribal Business School*, Wiley.

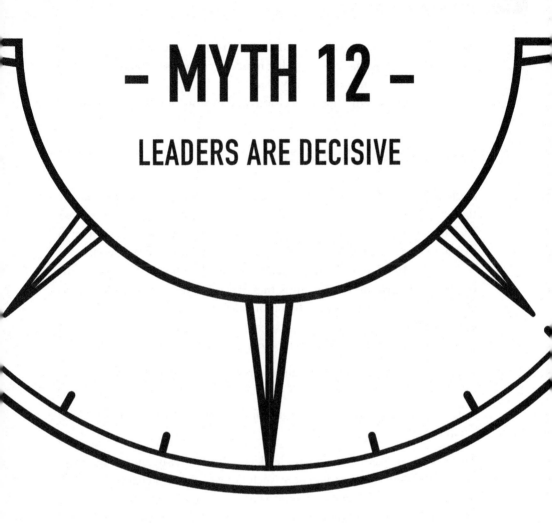

– MYTH 12 –

LEADERS ARE DECISIVE

You cannot know the answer if you do not know the question.

The nature of the myth

The decisive leader conjures up images of generals on horseback issuing orders and leading their army to victory: you never see paintings of the losing general fleeing on horseback. It is an image which finds echoes in 1950s photographs of leaders looking very stern as they hold a phone in their hand, ready to bark orders at hapless middle managers.

We want leaders to be decisive. One of the top five expectations that followers have of their leaders is decisiveness. The alternative is a nightmare. Indecisive leaders mean that the team has to spend half its time trying to guess what the leader will do, and the rest of the time re-working things after the leader has changed his or her mind. Decisiveness creates clarity and focus and gives the team what they want.

Decisiveness is better than indecision. End of story. But is it end of story?

Why this myth matters

Decisiveness is part of the Great Man theory of leadership (see Myth 37). Only the Great Man can be trusted to make the right decisions, so everything flows back to the general on his white horse issuing orders to his army. This is a myth that both leaders and followers happily subscribe to, with adverse results.

Leaders often like to be the general on the white horse. The person the leader trusts most on their team is themselves, so they are often comfortable making the big decisions. Teams are also more than happy to delegate upwards. When things go wrong, it absolves them of all responsibility. Seen in this light, decisiveness is more of a vice than a virtue because it shows:

- the leader lacks trust in the team and is not prepared to delegate decision making;
- the team wants to avoid responsibility by delegating decision making upwards.

There is an alternative. In Japan, leaders will often issue quite vague and apparently contradictory directions such as 'we need to increase profitability and we need to increase market share'. Sometimes this is because the manager is weak and does not know what to do, but often it is a deliberate decision by a good leader. They know that in a hierarchical society like Japan, if they give instructions then the team will follow them literally: the team will have no discretion. So the best way to find the best solution is not to give specific instructions, but to give broad priorities. That leaves the team free to find the best solution.

The great leader does not need a white horse, and does not need to make all the decisions.

Lessons for leaders

Leaders have to be able to make decisions: you cannot avoid it. The decisions which really matter are often high risk and have high uncertainty. The trap for leaders is to regard decision making as an intellectual exercise to which there is a right or wrong solution. That may have been true at school where you were set clear exam questions. In business, often the greatest challenge is to find out what question you need to ask, and what questions you can ignore. You cannot know the answer if you do not know the question.

Even when you have found the right exam question, the solution is not just an intellectual exercise. Organizations are full of people, and that makes them political. Good decision making is both logical and political.

The only good decision is one which leads to action. In the old world of command and control, that meant issuing orders. In today's world that means there has to be fair process around decision making. The decision must engage people so that they accept, own and will act on the decision. The lessons for leaders are about the logical and political aspects of making decisions.

Logical decision making in uncertainty

The intellectual principles for making a decision are:

- **Recognize the pattern.** Business sense is simply pattern recognition. You should be an expert in your area, so you should recognize the pattern and be able to make a decision accordingly. Back yourself. If you do not recognize the pattern, find someone who does and consult them.

- **Follow the strategy and the values.** At moments of uncertainty and ambiguity, with limited data, how do you choose? This is where a clear strategy and strong sense of values will guide you in the right direction. The strategy and values may not tell you what to do, but they can tell you what not to do. That is valuable.

- **What does the data say?** This is where you can use formal decision-making methods to weigh the pros and cons of each path of action. Evidence-based decision making is better than guesswork. But for many leaders, evidence-based decision making is code for 'find me the evidence to support my decision'. Leaders often use data like drunks use lamp posts: for support, not illumination.

- **Who does this decision matter to?** Different stakeholders will be affected unequally by your decision. Look at the decision through their eyes and understand what options will not work and will be highly resisted. Identify the solutions which are most likely to gain support. You do not want an intellectually brilliant decision which dies on first contact with political reality.

- **Drive to action.** Formal decision-making tools like Bayesian analysis, or perhaps mind maps, fishbones or SWOT analyses can help but can also be excuses for inaction: 'analysis paralysis'. The problem with analysis is that there is always another fact to be found, another analysis to be run. The perfect solution does not exist in an imperfect and changing world: the perfect is the enemy of the good. At some point, you have to make your mind up.

Political decision making: fair process

An effective decision is one which leads to action. That requires fair process in how you make the decision. You have to involve your team and other stakeholders appropriately. If you can delegate the decision, delegate it. Like the Japanese, you can set the broad priorities and let the team decide on how best to get there. By doing this you are not just delegating the decision. You are also delegating the responsibility and ownership for the decision. The result is that you will have a team which is committed to making the idea work. People rarely argue with their own idea, so let the idea be theirs.

If you cannot delegate the decision, then fair process remains important. You can at least consult your team and others before making the decision. This is a process the Japanese called *nemawashi*: building agreement in private one by one. In private, all the influencers and stakeholders can say what they really think, and you can align all their agendas and gain their tacit support. The subsequent meeting is not to make the decision, but to confirm in public the agreement that has been reached in private: it is a commitment process, not just a decision process. This process is highly political: welcome to the real world.

When communicating the decision, fair process requires more than just the decision. For the team to understand the decision properly, they need the full context: why the decision was made, what the alternatives were, and the pros and cons involved. It is not enough to communicate the decision, you have to sell it.

Conclusion

Leaders need to be decisive, so this should earn no unicorns. But it earns one unicorn because leaders who are too decisive are control freaks, which is not leadership. It earns a second unicorn because in practice, making decisions in uncertainty and making decisions stick in an organization is very tough and is rarely done well. Two unicorns.

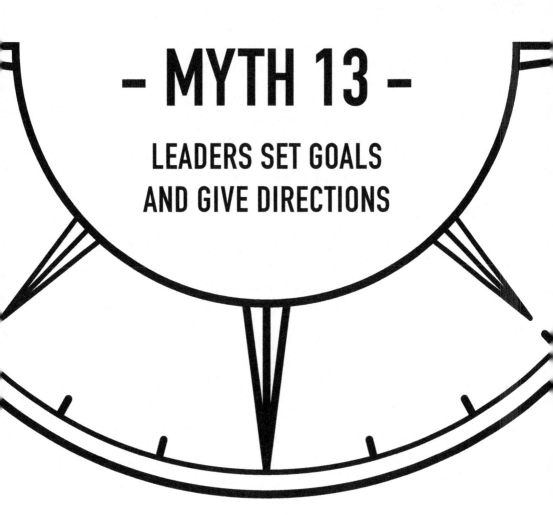

– MYTH 13 –

LEADERS SET GOALS AND GIVE DIRECTIONS

Clear goals are of no use unless they are shared goals.

The nature of the myth

This myth is, in fact, a truism. All leaders set goals and give directions: if they don't set goals and give directions they have no chance of taking people where they would not have got by themselves.

Case closed.

Pause for a moment before you file this case away in your number one file, the waste basket. What makes sense at first does not always make sense on closer inspection. This is a regular discovery for anyone who has a bright idea in the bar one evening, and wakes up the next morning to discover that their idea is not quite as bright as the dawn.

This apparent truism contains two fatal flaws.

The minor problem is that it does not differentiate between leaders and managers. Both leaders and managers need to set goals and give directions. Teachers set goals and give directions. Supervisors set goals and give directions. Sports coaches set goals and give directions. Teachers, supervisors and coaches may be supremely professional and good at their tasks, but that does not necessarily make them leaders. So setting goals and giving directions is part of leadership, but it does not define leadership. It is like breathing: necessary but not sufficient to lead, and it fails to separate leaders from the rest.

The major problem is that leaders are not very good at setting goals and giving directions. Research on the effectiveness of global teams found that they face big challenges around trust, communications and culture. But 65 per cent of team members said goal setting was a problem.[1] This was a surprising finding. Setting goals is Management 101: how on earth could high-flying, globetrotting leaders be so poor at goal setting?

As with many of the myths of leadership, the practice of leadership often struggles to keep up with the theory. This does not show that leaders are fools: it shows that leadership is exceptionally hard. Even getting the basics right is hard. This is true, not just for leaders, but for top sports people and musicians. We can all kick a football, but try controlling and kicking it in the right direction when moving at high speed and under huge pressure from the opposition. What looks simple can be very hard, and this is true of goal setting.

Why this myth matters

If leaders struggle to set goals and give directions well, then they struggle to lead. Doing this well is fundamental to your success as a leader.

Lessons for leaders

Process matters

Leaders often make the mistake of thinking that goal setting is about clear goals. That is only half the story. Clear goals are of no use unless they are also shared goals. Your team has to own the goals. Leaders will spend a huge amount of time thinking about their goals and how to frame them, because it is genuinely difficult to fix the right goals. Too often, they then expect their team or firm to internalize months of thinking as a result of a brilliant 40-minute speech. That is never going to happen.

If you want your team to own your goals, you have to take them on your journey. The best way to do that is to involve them from the start. If your team believes that the goals are their idea, they will be committed to them: people do not argue against their own ideas. If they have been involved from the start, they will understand the context, the thinking and the trade-offs. They will understand how to act in ambiguous situations.

Involving the team from the start is ideal but not always practical. It means you will have to invest heavily in selling and explaining your idea after the event. After a two-year turnaround, one CEO remarked: 'Figuring out what to do was easy. That took 5 per cent of my time. Thirty-five per cent of my time was spent working on the plan. Sixty per cent of my time was spent selling it and then selling it again. I could not believe it took so long.' Taking people where they would not have got by themselves means you have to persuade them and keep on persuading them.

Context matters

When talking about goals, leaders often focus on the what, who, when and where questions. They will then explore the 'how' question at length as required. The one question which is easy to forget but is the most important is 'why'. Your team wants to know not just the goal, but the context for the goal: why did you pick this goal and what were the other options? What are the trade-offs and how should they be handled? They will only understand the context properly if you have managed the process of goal setting properly.

Manage the trade-offs

The two best moments of owning a boat are the day you buy it and the day you sell it. The same is true of goal setting: the best two days are the day you set the goal and the day you achieve the goal. The time in between is a struggle. The day you set the goal you have clarity and hope. The next day, reality sets in. You face three challenges:

Sacrifice If you ask for one thing, others tend to slip. Focus on profits and customer service slips; focus on efficiency and you lose flexibility; reduce risks and innovation is reduced. There is no free lunch. Bold leaders are ready to make these sacrifices. Weaker leaders go for the balanced scorecard approach which ensures that they get a little of everything: that is good management but not good leadership.

Game playing   The good news is that everyone will want to achieve the goals you set. The bad news is that they will play games to get there. Cheating doesn't just happen in sports with drug taking and professional fouls; it happens in every walk of life. In education, governments keep on setting new goals, and even trustworthy teachers cheat the system. For instance, what is wrong with requiring that all 16-year-olds show they are numerate and literate? Here is how a school could react:

- By narrowing the curriculum to focus on literacy and numeracy. Out go important things like becoming employable, sports, music and drama, and all the other academic subjects get squeezed as well.

- By focusing all efforts on children on the pass/fail margin. Ignore the high achievers because they can look after themselves; ignore the low performers because they will fail anyway.

- By teaching to test. Focusing on drilling students on how to answer the exam questions, which is separate from helping them to become literate or numerate. The dull drills put children off education for life.

All of this can help the school look good on exam results, but at the cost of not giving the students a good education. Game playing is normal: manage it.

Competition and teamwork   There is real tension between collective and individual goals. This cuts to the heart of how far your team is a team or just a group of individuals with separate goals; it also cuts to the heart of the accountability and collaboration challenge. Collective goals are good for collaboration, but weak on individual accountability. Individual goals encourage each person to retreat into their own silo and you lose cooperation. There is no magic answer. Recognize that your leadership team is only a team for some challenges, and is a group of individuals for others. Know which is which and set goals accordingly.

Conclusion

This problem appears repeatedly: the theory is a truism (zero unicorns), but the practice of leadership does not live up to the theory (up to five unicorns). The response is the same in each case: three unicorns.

Endnote

1 Jo Owen (2016) *Global Teams*, FT Publishing, pp 121–42.

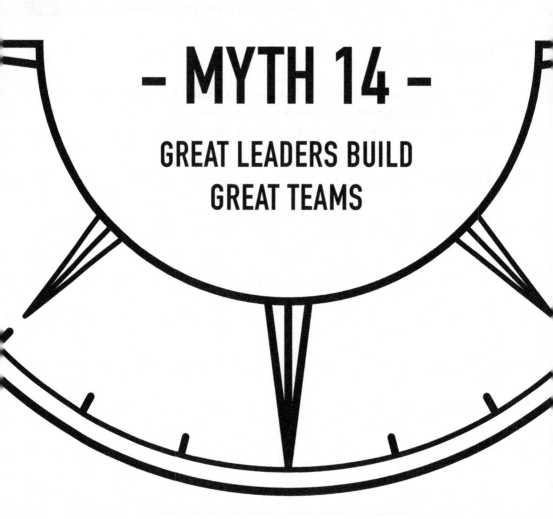

- MYTH 14 -

GREAT LEADERS BUILD GREAT TEAMS

Teams, like firms, constantly slide towards the chaos of entropy.

The nature of the myth

This is another modern myth which is set against the Great Man theory of leadership. Its main ally in the fight against the Great Man theory is the theory of distributed leadership (Myth 40). If leadership is no longer about the lone hero, then by default you need to have a great team to achieve great things.

Why this myth matters

Unless you happen to be a great man or woman, you will need a great team to achieve great things. Your power lies in the power of your organization, not just in your personal power and brilliance. This is a cruel lesson which many senior executives discover too late in their careers. As they progress through their firm, they get used to the trappings of power. Doors open for them, both literally and figuratively. They have easy access to decision makers. Hubris is when you believe that you can only turn left at the aircraft door.

And then the time comes for the senior executive to move aside for a younger generation. Suddenly, they find that doors no longer open for them either figuratively or literally, and that you can turn right at the aircraft doors without dying. Decision makers no longer return your calls, and you have no one to chase up for you. A horrible discovery looms: no one wanted to talk to you because of who you were, but because of who you represented. This is when the value of the team and the firm comes home: any leader is only as good as the followers they have. If you have no followers, you are not leading and you have no power.

Lessons for leaders

In theory, great leaders need great teams. In practice, leaders often struggle to build the team that will fulfil their ambitions.

The team you inherit is not the team you need for the future

It is common for new leaders to shake up their teams. There are three reasons you may want to do this:

- **To take control.** Reorganizing is often a political act as much as a rational act. It is a way of removing power barons and blockers, and putting in people you trust and can depend on. It sends a signal that you are ready to move people around and make difficult decisions.

- **To upgrade performance.** The legacy team may well have found its comfort zone, enabling it to perform well without breaking sweat.

- **To set a new direction.** The legacy team was there to address a legacy challenge: your predecessor's legacy. If you are to lead people where they would not have got by themselves you need a new and clear agenda.

A new agenda means you probably need new skills and a new balance in the composition of your team.

The alternative is to live with the legacy team. The longer you live with it, the more you will be acquiescing in the old agenda, the old team and the old ways of working. It becomes harder to justify reorganizing the longer you leave the legacy team in place. Moving fast helps.

Keep on refreshing your team

Teams, like firms, constantly slide towards the chaos of entropy. Team members leave for good or poor reasons: to pursue their ambitions elsewhere, to make more money, because of illness, incompetence or stress, or for better work-life balance. The natural churn of your team is mirrored by the churn of events. Stuff happens. Yesterday's challenge and priorities will not be the same as tomorrow's. External pressures of technology, competition, customers and regulation force change as well as the never-ending internal pressures of new initiatives which have to be dealt with. Teams, like milk, can go off fast. Keep your team fresh.

Leaders value loyalty over competence

Most leaders have this blind spot. As one put it: 'Most sins are forgivable, but disloyalty is not one of them.' She was speaking the truth. Contrary to the popular image of bosses, most bosses are forgiving and for good reason: replacing team members takes time and effort and is risky. There is no guarantee that the replacement will be any better. Loyal team members are the last to be fired, although if you have a gold medal in incompetence then nothing will save you. This is useful knowledge when you are following: overt loyalty never does you any harm, while failing to support your boss fully at critical moments is a career limiting move. As a leader, you need to balance your desire for loyalty and continuity with your need for performance.

Recruit to values, not just to skills

Research consistently shows that values and attitudes are better predictors of performance than raw skills.[1] For instance, Met Life decided to test its life assurance sales recruits for skills and optimism. As a test, it decided to take on candidates who had just failed the skills test but scored high on optimism: the unskilled optimists outsold the skilled recruits by an average of 70 per cent. You can teach skills, but not optimism or values. Your team also needs skills. But skills without values is a recipe for disaster. As one leader put it: 'I find I always hire for skills and fire for values.'

RECRUITING TO VALUES: THE SHOE REPAIR SHOPS

Timpson is a large chain of shoe repair shops in the UK. Repairing shoes is not glamorous. The stores tend to be pocket sized and wages are modest. And yet these workers have huge responsibility: they run the entire shop and have to be able to repair shoes, inscribe trophies and do all the chores of any small business. So how do you find the right people to make this business a success?

Initially, Timpson hired cobblers. If you want to repair shoes, then you need cobblers to repair shoes. What could possibly go wrong?

Everything can go wrong. Cobblers do not always have great customer management or business management skills, and these shops are all about managing customers and managing a business. But to find anyone who has all the required skills is impossible, unless you pay uneconomic salaries.

Timpson realized that you can train skills but you cannot train values, so they started to recruit to values. To make the point, they replaced the normal assessment forms with one page of Mr Men cartoons. On one side it had 'good' Mr Men like Mr Honest, Mr Keen and Mr Helpful. On the other side it had Mr Men from the Dark Side: Mr Fib, Mr Idle, Mr Grumpy. Store managers had to circle which Mr Man each candidate was most like. Candidates from the Dark Side were turned down, however much skill they had. The system worked well. It worked even better when they introduced some female alternatives.

Conclusion

It is true in theory that great leaders build great teams, but it is rarely true in practice. Most leaders could do better in building the dream team. Like all myths which are true in theory but not in practice, this earns three unicorns.

Endnote

1 Martin Seligman (1998) *Learned Optimism*, Pocket Books. This research has been replicated in other industries and geographies.

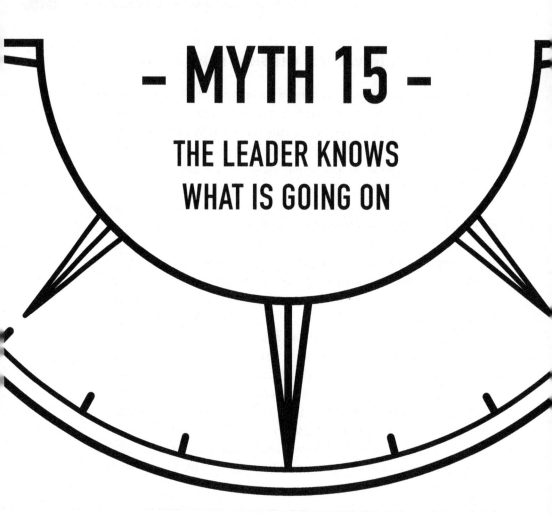

- MYTH 15 -

THE LEADER KNOWS
WHAT IS GOING ON

*The information you get is about the past. The information
you need is about the future.*

The nature of the myth

If you don't know where you are, you are unlikely to know where you are
going. Leaders have to know what is going on. But they can never know all
that is going on.

Leaders, like governments and businesses, have an insatiable appetite for
knowing more and more. Dictators down the years have resorted to all sorts
of ruses to know who is doing what, and where real or imagined treachery
might lie. Today, we give away more information about what we do and

what we think than any dictator of the past could have dreamed of finding. Businesses may know more about us than our loved ones know.

In the age of hyper information, leaders should be able to know exactly what is going on. In practice, the information leaders have and the information they want is not the same. Information is about the past, but leaders need to know about the future. Failing that, they need information which can guide them to their future perfect. But driving to the future by looking in the rear mirror is a recipe for disaster.

Why this myth matters

Trust and control

The old saying is that 'knowledge is power'. The current equivalent is 'information is control'. Given that leaders are meant to be in control, they want information. And if more control is better, then that implies more information. Or to put it the other way around, more information allows leaders to be in more control, so clearly more information is always more desirable. But is it?

Trust is inversely proportional to control and information. The more information we demand and the more control we exert, the less trust we show in our teams. This is a dilemma for leaders. More professional and educated staff expect to be trusted more. But the deluge of hyper information is a temptation which few leaders can resist.

The challenge for leaders is to know what information they really need, and how far they can avoid micro-managing through micro-information.

Lessons for leaders

Separate information from intelligence

The information you get is about the past. The information you need is about the future. We all wish we knew the future: that would be a short cut to making a fortune at the bookies.

Since you cannot know the future, however, you need an alternative which does not involve reading tea leaves and throwing chicken bones. As a leader, you will have a few projects which will help you shape and change the future. These are the projects where you need good information, which leads to rapid action.

The best way to start your information and reporting system is with a blank piece of paper. Write down what you really want to know, under the headings of budgets, people, customers/markets and projects. Then start to fill it in. The chances are that most of what you currently receive is not relevant and about half of what you do want is unavailable. But at least you have converted the unknown unknowns into known unknowns.[1]

To gather the intelligence, you need a balance between formal and informal information systems. Most leaders have limited trust in formal reports where evidence is used to support a position, not to illuminate the truth. You have to get out and meet customers, meet people on the front line and form your own opinion of reality. But do not be blinded by what you see: balance what your eyes see and what your information systems tell you. Neither is perfect, but together they give you a better chance of controlling what matters and shaping the future successfully.

Focus on priorities

An old-fashioned watch has three hands: the hour hand, the minute hand and the second hand. Front-line staff watch the second hand: they are dealing with the here and now. Managers watch the second hand and the minute hand. The minute hand is about all the near-term goals and initiatives which they have to plan and execute. The leader watches all three hands. The hour hand is about the longer-term direction of the team and the firm.

As a leader, you need information about all three hands: if the second hand is not moving smoothly, then neither of the other hands can move. Most corporate reporting systems focus on the second hand, but although this generates huge amounts data, not much is of use. It is useful mainly to manage risk: it shows what is not working and allows you to intervene on an exception basis.

You can manage your information on the same basis as the watch. The second hand generates huge amounts of data. It can be a black hole which sucks you in: one piece of data generates demand for another piece of data to explain it. There is no escape. Avoid getting sucked in. Use this data on an exception basis: you only need to intervene where it shows that things are going materially off track, or are at risk of doing so. Materiality is key: if it is not material, delegate the challenge down and trust your team to deal with it.

The more you step back from micro-information management, the more trust you show in your team. It also allows you to focus your time on building your future. Ultimately, you have to recognize you cannot know and control everything and nor do you need to. But for leaders, letting go is often the hardest thing to do.

Respect different perspectives

As a leader you may see the world from the top of the mountain, which allows you to see into the far distance. But never forget what it was like at the bottom of the mountain: in the farmyard you could see the chickens running around and the children playing in the street. These things are invisible from the top of the mountain. Your reporting system may tell you how many chickens and children there are, but it will not tell you what it is really like down in the farmyard.

You have to bridge the gap between the top and the bottom of the mountain. Climb down the mountain to find out what is really going on, and speak to people. You will discover what reporting systems can never tell you: what people think; what they see as the challenges and opportunities; and what are the obstacles they face in making your agenda work.

In the past, middle management were your Sherpa guides: they conveyed your orders to the bottom of the mountain and passed information about what was happening at the bottom back up to you. This meant that top management were often remote: they were stuck on the executive floor, with their executive dining room, executive toilets and executive parking spaces. To be effective, you need to be your own Sherpa. That means not only seeing life at the front line yourself, but also explaining the view from the top. The people in the farmyard cannot see your view and you need to explain what you see and how it affects them. Your vision is meaningless without context, and you are the best person to share that context.

Conclusion

Leaders can never know all that is going on, and above all they can never know the future. But the availability of information provides an irresistible temptation to meddle, micro-manage and demand even more information. This myth drives leaders to behave in the wrong way, so it rates a solid four unicorns.

Endnote

1 'There are known knowns' is a phrase from a response given by former US Secretary of Defense Donald Rumsfeld to a question at a US Department of Defense (DoD) news briefing on 12 February 2002 about the lack of evidence linking the government of Iraq with the supply of weapons of mass destruction to terrorist groups.

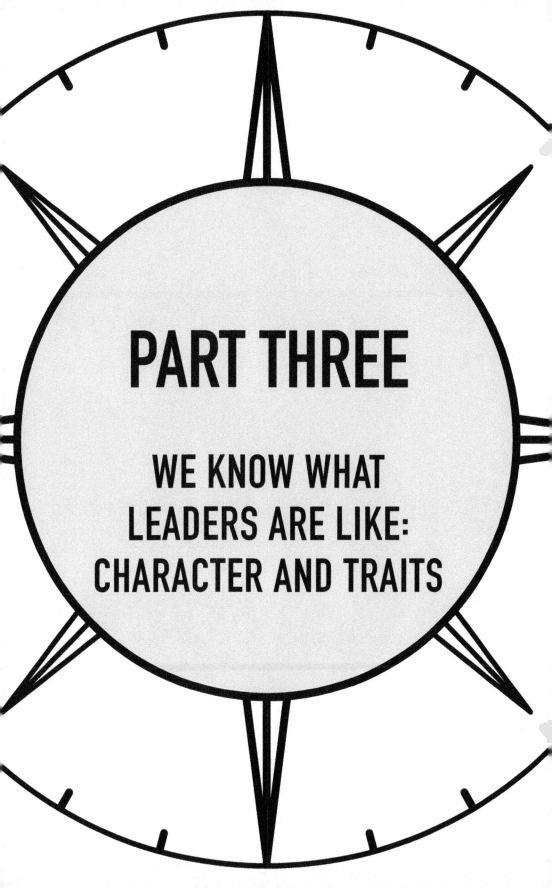

PART THREE

WE KNOW WHAT LEADERS ARE LIKE: CHARACTER AND TRAITS

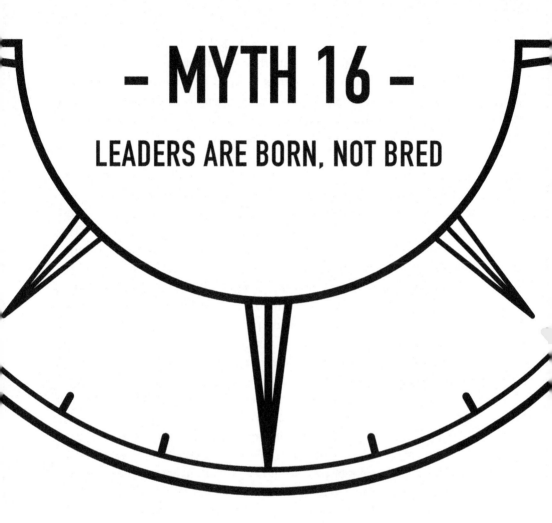

– MYTH 16 –

LEADERS ARE BORN, NOT BRED

*If we do believe that leaders are born, not bred, then
most people may as well give up.*

The nature of the myth

The nature versus nurture debate has been going on for decades, and possibly for millennia.

Fortunately, we have some hard evidence about the debate. In fact, we have several thousand years' worth of data to look at.

For at least a thousand years, Europe ran an experiment in which leaders were born, not bred. If you were born into royalty, you might get murdered or you might get to rule your country. If you were born a peasant, you got to dig mud throughout the winter until you died of some vile medieval disease. Everyone was pretty much born into their station of life.

The result was that most countries were led by a mixture of murderers, incompetents, adventurers and psychopaths along with the odd genius who would become a national hero and make up for all the others. As leadership selection methods go, it produced pretty mixed results. There is no indication that the best leaders are born.

The reason that this myth gets four, not five stars is that there is an element of truth in it. Research shows that if you come from the right social background you are far more likely to succeed: this is less about talent and more about having an advantageous upbringing, socially and educationally. Two economists – Guglielmo Barone and Sauro Mocetti of the Bank of Italy – looked at tax returns in Florence for 1427 and 2011.[1] They found that the occupations, income and wealth of families in 1427 were good predictors of the occupation, income and wealth of the same families nearly 600 years later. This shows that having the right parents loads the dice in your favour in terms of wealth; however, it says nothing about whether you are a good leader or not. You can win the lottery and become rich, but that does not mean you can lead.

Finally, there is some evidence that choosing the right DNA helps you reach the top. Research shows that the average height of a Fortune 500 CEO is 1.83 metres, versus an average for American males of about 1.77 metres.[2] There are two question marks about this research. The first is that it is based on what CEOs claim to be their height: 183 cm just happens to be six feet tall and a suspiciously large number claim to be six feet tall, not 5'11" or 5'10".

US Presidents show the same height pattern: here are the heights of the last few presidents:[3]

- Ronald Reagan   185 cm
- George H Bush   188 cm
- Bill Clinton   188 cm
- George W Bush   182 cm
- Barack Obama   185 cm
- Donald Trump   191 cm

The more important objection is that being a CEO, or even being president, does not mean that you are a leader; it means that you are very good at career management or at getting elected, which are different skills altogether. It is for you to decide which US Presidents have been effective leaders, and whether height has anything to do with it.

So if you want a stellar career, it helps to choose the right DNA or bolster your shoes to gain height. It also helps, overwhelmingly, to be white and male to succeed in a European or American context. If you want to succeed in a Japanese firm, it helps to be male and Japanese; in a Chinese context, it helps to be Chinese and male. The pattern is obvious.

It appears that social background and DNA will help you succeed in your career, but it says nothing about whether you will be a good leader once you reach the top.

Why this myth matters

If we do believe that leaders are born, not bred, then most people may as well give up. You can go back to the modern equivalent of digging mud unless you can show that you made a smart choice of parents and have the right DNA.

Believing that leaders can be bred is more constructive. It means that we all have a chance of becoming a leader. And in reality, we all can learn to lead. Learning to lead is like learning to play the piano. A little effort and rehearsal will make us better than most people who never even try. We may not have the patience, dedication and talent to become a famous soloist playing at Carnegie Hall, but we can all learn to lead better.

Inevitably, this raises the question of how we can learn to lead: that is the subject of the next myth.

Lessons for leaders

We can all learn to lead, and we can all learn to lead better even if we never become a global star in terms of leadership. To do this, we have to work out:

- What we have to learn: what are the skills and aptitudes we need to build to be an effective leader? (See Myth 9.)

- How we can learn it: what resources do we have to help us on our leader-ship journey? (See Myth 35.)

Conclusion

The second paragraph of the American Declaration of Independence states: 'We hold these truths to be self-evident, that all men are created equal.'[4] Ideally, this would be true. The evidence shows it is false: your social background has a huge influence on your success in later life. But being successful and being a leader are different ideas. Anyone can be a leader, but getting into a leadership position is affected by your social background. For this reason, the myth does not get a full five unicorns: four unicorns are enough.

Endnotes

1 Josh Zumbrun (2016) The wealthy in Florence are the same families as 600 years ago, *Wall Street Journal* [online] http://blogs.wsj.com/economics/2016/05/19/the-wealthy-in-florence-today-are-the-same-families-as-600-years-ago/.

2 Bisi Daniels (2016) Why many CEOs are tall people? The heart of the matter, *Premium Times* [online] http://www.premiumtimesng.com/arts-entertainment/naija-fashion/203429-many-ceos-tall-people-height-matter-bisi-daniels.html.

3 Wikipedia, Heights of presidents and presidential candidates of the United States [online] https://en.wikipedia.org/wiki/Heights_of_presidents_and_presidential_candidates_of_the_United_States. Note that Donald Trump's height is disputed.

4 To be fair to the founding fathers, they probably did not intend to say that all people are born with equal life chances, but that they are equal before the law and equal as human beings.

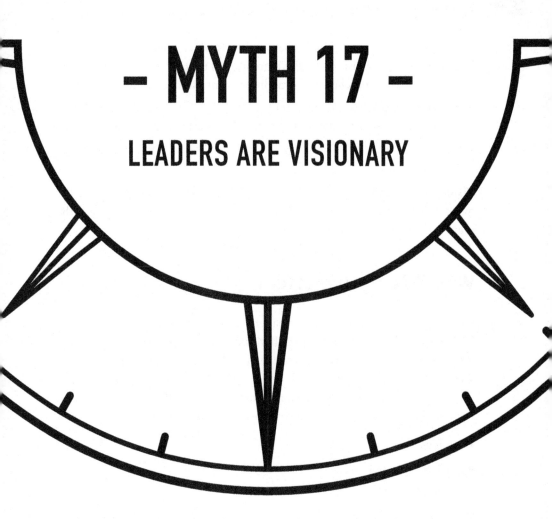

– MYTH 17 –

LEADERS ARE VISIONARY

Leaders are peddlers of hope.

The nature of the myth

Research shows that the most important thing followers expect from their leader is a clear vision.[1] And when we think of all the great leaders, they all have great visions. Kennedy sent man to the moon for the first time; Martin Luther King had his famous 'I have a dream…' speech. So it seems to be case closed: leaders need to be visionary.

But we should pause before we walk away, for two reasons:

- First, grand visions are dangerous. Every mad dictator down the ages has had a crazed vision. Some want to conquer the world, others want to conquer the enemy within. These are visions which have led to millions of deaths. For every visionary who marches you to the Promised Land, there is another who marches you straight back into the desert and to death.

- Second, if you are leading a team it is hard to have a grand vision. If you feel the urge one Monday morning to stand on your desk and announce to your team, 'I have a dream…' your team may wonder what you put in your coffee.

Visions are problematic for normal leaders. The greater the visions, the more dangerous and less credible they become to your team. But what is the point of a small vision?

Why this myth matters

Having a vision matters for all leaders. Leaders take people where they would not have got by themselves. If you don't know where you are going, then you will not get there and your team will be confused at best. Without a vision, you cannot lead.

This means we have to understand what a vision really means for leaders. For a team and its leader, an effective vision has three parts:

- an idea;
- a promise of hope;
- a call to action.

These three elements allow you to craft a compelling vision which is relevant and credible to your situation.

Lessons for leaders

Here is how you can build your vision based on the three elements.

An idea

It is hard to have a vision, but we can all have ideas. A visionary idea is no more than a story in three parts, as follows:

- this is where we are;
- this is where we are going;
- and this is how we will get there.

We can all tell a story, and that is all we need to do. We can dress it up as a strategic initiative if that makes people feel better about it. But at the heart of any strategy, vision or idea is a simple story which you can tell about how you will make a difference.

Big ideas beat small ideas, because they excite and energize people more. If you have an idea about rationalizing the use of paper clips in your office, that is worthy but you will not get many people excited about it. Big ideas are noticed across the organization; they are ideas where you make a difference. They will attract both support and opposition. Dare to be bold.

A promise of hope

Leaders are peddlers of hope. Cynical and junior team members tend to stay that way: cynical and junior. No leader succeeds by peddling gloom. Even in Britain's darkest hour, when defeat to the Nazis looked likely, Churchill peddled hope, not gloom. He reached his rhetorical heights: 'Never in the field of human history has so much been owed by so many to so few... this was their finest hour... we will fight them on the beaches...' He did not resort to the middle management blame game: 'I warned you in my e-mail that this would happen.'

Every vision must have a promise of hope. Your idea has to show how things will be better in the future, both for the firm and for the individual. This makes your vision far more than a plan or a budget. Meeting a budget is not a promise of hope: it is a requirement to be met. Your idea has to show how things will be different and better in the future.

A call to action

Your vision may be important to you, but that does not mean it is important to anyone else. If your idea is to transform the supply chain, that could be very good for the business, but your team may not be impressed. Some will think that it has nothing to do with them; they will shrug their shoulders and focus on what they need to buy for dinner that evening. Others may wonder if your vision means that they will lose their job; are you going to march them to the Promised Land or to the desert? Do not expect your team to fall in love with an abstract idea.

To make your vision meaningful, you have to make it personal to each team member. You have to answer the two questions each team member will have:

• How will this affect me? New ideas provoke both fear and hope. Fears are natural: will this mean more work, will I have to learn new skills, will this affect my pay and promotion prospects? Show how your idea will help your team members grow and develop.

- What is my role? If you can paint a picture which shows that each team member has a vital role in helping the vision become reality, then you increase their commitment. Giving your team members a sense of control, involvement, relevance and purpose is highly motivational.

Your vision will mean different things to different people. Each person will be asking the WIFM question: 'What's In it For Me?' Help them answer that positively. Remember that visions are not just about ideas: they are about people.

Conclusion

Leaders do not need to be visionary like Martin Luther King, but they do need to have a vision or idea of what they will achieve. Being visionary is about style; having a vision is about substance. If the idea is that leaders have to be visionary, this merits five unicorns. If the idea is that you need a vision, then that is true and it merits no unicorns. Split the difference: three unicorns.

Endnote

1 Author's original research with over 500 leaders and followers, first published in Jo Owen (2015) *How to Lead*, Pearson.

– MYTH 18 –

LEADERS ARE CHARISMATIC AND INSPIRATIONAL

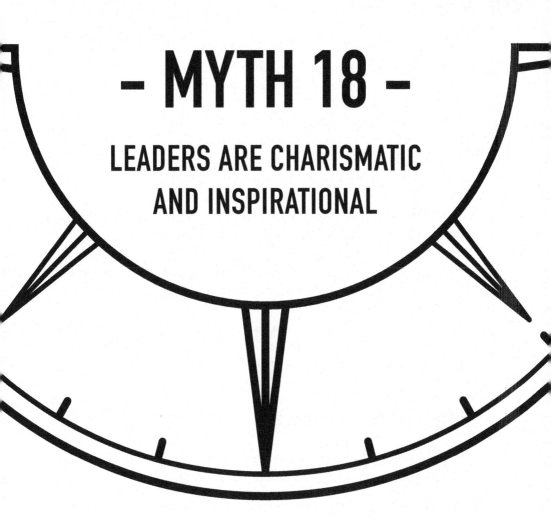

The need for heroes runs deep.

The nature of the myth

Charisma and inspiration are part of the hero myth. Down the ages, people have looked to the great leader who will take them to the Promised Land. The great heroes of history live on in books and as statues in main squares. The really great ones have movies made about them. Each country is selective about its heroes and its heroic stories. The English remember Henry V defeating the French at Agincourt a mere 600 years ago, and Shakespeare wrote a play about it (*Henry V*). But the English get very vague about how Joan of Arc beat the English in return, whereas the French celebrate her as a heroine.

The statues, history books and movies all reinforce the message that great people achieve great things. These heroes are always larger than life. Even if they were modest in their day, stories and mythology attach to them over time like barnacles to a ship.

The need for heroes runs deep. Hollywood lives on the backs of heroes who save the day and save the world. The need for magical solutions has always been there: priests would pray for divine intervention, wizards would cast their spells, and the king was the divinely appointed saviour of the nation.

We want leaders who can transform our fortunes, or at least transform our working day so that we can do better. Our leaders may not be able to cast wizards' spells; instead they reach out for the latest miracle medicine being peddled by consultants and academics who claim to have found the solution to your strategy, operations, processes, leadership or teamworking. The desire for magic is still there and we keep on buying the medicine bottle, in a triumph of hope over reality.

The charismatic and inspirational leader offers the hope of a better future. It is an offer we all want to believe in, which makes us ready to believe the charismatic leader.

Why this myth matters

The myth is both dangerous and useful. It is dangerous because charisma and inspiration are largely unattainable and are not necessary:

- **Effective leaders are rarely charismatic.** Think of the leaders in your business, from team leaders to the big boss at the top. How many of them would you rate as charismatic and inspirational? I have interviewed thousands of leaders: many of them are exceptional, but very few were charismatic and inspirational. The most charismatic one is currently under investigation for fraud.

- **Charisma and inspiration are not always forces for good.** Like the Force in *Star Wars*, it has a dark side. Genghis Khan, Mao Tse-tung, Adolf Hitler, Mussolini and Pol Pot were all charismatic and inspirational in their own ways. Psychopaths are often charismatic: they are very good at reading people and manipulating them.

- **You cannot teach charisma and inspiration.** That means you are born with charisma or you are not, in which case we may as well select leaders at birth based on finding the charisma gene. So far, medical science has not invented the charisma transplant operation.

- **Charisma is not the solution.** Modern business is so complicated that it cannot rely on the inspiration of one person. Breakthrough ideas can come from anywhere, and implementation can be a huge team effort.

The myth is useful because it points to two requirements of leaders today. Charisma and inspiration are founded on the twin pillars of hope and motivation. Effective leaders have to offer hope, and they have to engage their team. Leaders need willing and motivated followers.

Lessons for leaders

If charisma and inspiration are a dead end, what is the alternative? Research shows that followers expect five things from their leaders.[1] Here they are, in order of priority:[2]

Vision

Give your team a clear sense of purpose, direction and hope. This is not an abstract vision about improving shareholder returns, because your team may well not care about shareholder returns. It is a concrete vision which shows how each member of your team can make a difference, how their future will be better and how they are contributing to something worthwhile and meaningful.

Ability to motivate

Part of motivation is about structure: ensure each team member has a balanced set of tasks. Inevitably there will be some dull and routine work, but there should also be challenging and interesting work. Leaders motivate most by doing one thing: they show that they care about each team member and their future. That means taking an interest in them, giving them honest and constructive feedback regularly, assigning them the right tasks, recognizing their contributions in public, and even saying 'thank you' once in a while.

Decisive

If you really want to demotivate and annoy your team, make decisions slowly and then keep on changing your mind. This will ensure that your team will endure the maximum of uncertainty and the maximum amount of rework. Teams crave clarity, so give it to them. Even if the situation is uncomfortable, clarity and decisiveness create a way forward and offer the hope of a solution.

Good in a crisis

A crisis is what separates a leader from the rest. It is the moment leaders take control and shine. Crisis management is about what you do and how you do it. What you do means looking forwards, finding solutions and driving to action rather than analysing the past to find who to blame. Even more important is how you carry yourself. If you are positive, professional and constructive then you will leave the impression that you are in control and you know what you are doing (even if you have huge doubts yourself). If you run around like a headless chicken, then your panic will spread across the team.

Honesty

The research asked about honesty, and it scored highly. Most of us want to work for an honest person but the evidence is that many people are very happy to work for crooks, psychopaths and dictators. So the research dug into the honesty question and found that followers really want something even more powerful than honesty: they want trust. No one wants to work for a leader they do not trust. How you build trust is the subject of Myth 19.

If you can deliver on these five expectations, you will be a highly effective leader and very professional. You will have a vision of hope and the ability to motivate which will make people want to follow you. There is even a risk that your team will see you as being charismatic and inspirational.

Conclusion

The charismatic and inspirational leader is not only a myth, it is a dangerous myth. Charisma and inspiration are unattainable and unteachable for most of us, and are not necessary; leaders who have charisma can turn out to be dangerous demagogues and fraudsters. This would give us five unicorns, but occasionally you do find a great leader who is charismatic and inspirational. The exceptional leaders who are charismatic mean that only four unicorns appear here.

Endnotes

1 Author's original research based on interviews with successful leaders, originally published in Jo Owen (2015) *How to Lead*, Pearson.

2 Each of these leadership requirements is covered in detail in this book, with a separate myth for each one.

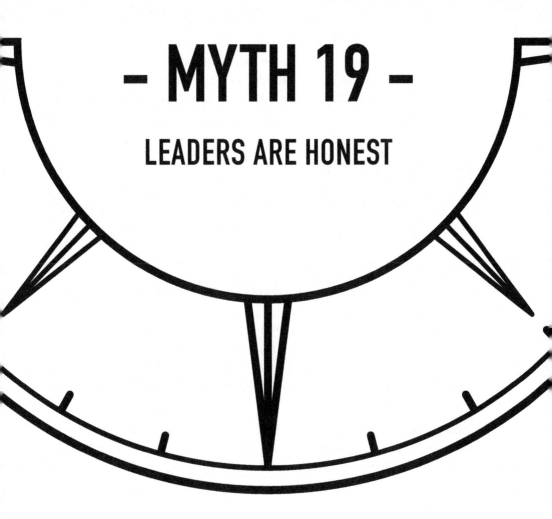

– MYTH 19 –

LEADERS ARE HONEST

It is not enough to be an honest leader; you have to be the trusted leader.

The nature of the myth

From an early age, children are taught that honesty is good and dishonesty is bad. It is a principle that pervades everyday life, and is at the heart of the law and a civilized society. We expect our fellow citizens to be honest and we certainly expect our leaders to be. The repeated failure of our political leaders to be honest is the source of endless scandal and media headlines.

Research[1] on leadership showed that honesty was one of the top five expectations that followers had of their leaders. It was also the most divisive expectation. Leaders either scored very high or very low: there was no middle ground. Leaders who were rated high on honesty had a chance of doing well on other leadership criteria. Leaders who scored low on honesty were trashed on every other criterion. No one liked working for a dishonest boss.

Why this myth matters

Given that honesty is so important, it is worth understanding what people mean by honesty. An implausible interview with a senior investment banker revealed the essence of the challenge. I sat down in his plush office with the fake antiques and here is our conversation:

Banker: 'Honesty has nothing to do with ethics or morality.'
Me: '??!!#?!'
Banker: 'It is far more important than that. Honesty is about trust. If my team does not trust me, then they will walk across the road tomorrow. If my clients don't trust me, then I will have no clients. A banker with no team and no clients is no use. Trust is everything.'

Trust requires hard-form honesty: it is not just the absence of lies, but the ability to say it as it is, all the time. It is not enough to be an honest leader: you have to be the trusted leader.

Lessons for leaders

Leaders need to be trusted. Over the years, a simple formula has shown the way to building trust. Here it is:

$$t = \frac{(i \times c)}{(s \times r)}$$

Where:

t = trust

i = intimacy

c = credibility

s = selfishness

r = risk

This is how you put the trust equation into practice, so that you can become the trusted leader.

Intimacy

This is about having common values, common experiences, common outlook and a common agenda with your counterpart. It is both style and substance.

In style terms, we all find it easier to work with someone like ourselves, because we understand how they think and operate. One of the challenges of global teams is that there is too much distance between team members who do not understand how the other members think. This is one reason why people often appear to waste time gossiping about trivia when they first meet. The gossip has a purpose: they are trying to find common ground in terms of experiences and outlook. It is the first building block of building personal trust between strangers.

In terms of substance, intimacy means sharing a common agenda and common goal. This should be self-evident. We will find it easier to cooperate if we have a common need, or even a common enemy, than if we are working on competing agendas. In practice, it is often hard to find out what the mutual need is. In particular, when selling or negotiating, a large part of the art is to discover the other side's agenda. When you know what their needs, wants and fears are it is much easier to find the win-win solution.

Credibility

Most of us have friends who would score highly on intimacy, but we would not trust them to do anything important. They score low on credibility. Credibility is about always doing what you say, 100 per cent of the time. Credibility is hard to build and easy to lose. Like a vase, once it is broken it is very hard to put back together and is never quite the same.

Most of us like to believe we do as we say. Perhaps we do. But what we think we say is not the same as what other people think they hear. Messages always get scrambled. We may say things like:

- 'I hope to...';
- 'I will try...';
- 'I will see if...'

What the other side hears is 'I will...' When we then come back and say we tried (but did not deliver) we will have lost trust. There is no point in arguing about what was or was not said. Perceptions may be false, but the consequences of perceptions are real. This means that we have to be brutally clear in what we say and we have to make sure that we have been understood.

Credibility requires 100 per cent delivery and very clear communication.

Risk

Risk is like kryptonite to trust. The riskier the situation, the more trust is required. I may trust a stranger to tell me the way to the post office. I would be unwise to trust the stranger with my life savings. Risk matters. You can manage risk two ways: reduce the risk or raise the risk.

Reducing risk is obvious, up to a point. Risk is not the abstract risk that exists in risk logs. It is personal risk: will I be able to do this, will I look like a fool if it goes wrong, will I still have a job at the end of it? This is the sort of risk you need to manage as a leader. Reduce the challenge into bite-sized chunks which make it less risky and provide the right support. De-risk the future.

The less obvious route to managing risk is to raise it. Show that the risks of doing nothing are greater than the risks of change. This is where leaders often create the 'burning platform' story. They show that the business is burning down and that without radical action everything will be lost.

Selfishness

We are all heroes of our own life story, and the universe revolves around our own reality. But the more we put ourselves first, the less other people will want to work with us and for us. Even the best leaders ultimately put themselves first. But they also have an ability to understand and respect the needs and wants of others.

Conclusion

This should be a unicorn-free zone: honesty is vital as part of trust. The problem is that trust is asymmetric: we know others can trust us, but we are not sure we can trust others. This means that in practice many leaders fall at the trust hurdle. This myth earns one unicorn, to recognize that leaders are (mostly) honest, but struggle to build trust.

Endnote

1 Author's original interviews with leaders and their teams.

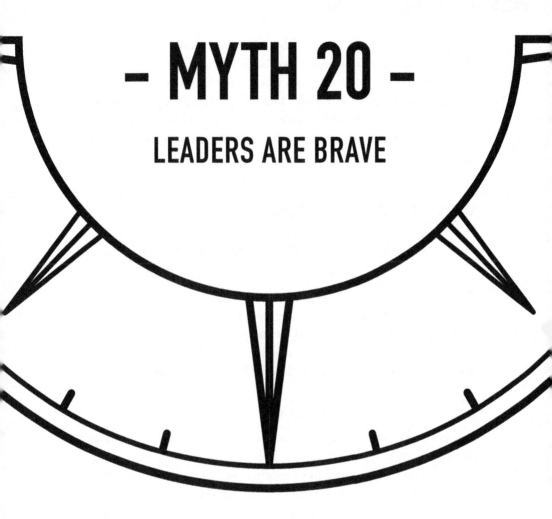

– MYTH 20 –

LEADERS ARE BRAVE

If you want to lead the crowd, not follow the crowd, you take risks.

The nature of the myth

Throughout history, leaders have had to be brave. The leader leading his (and once or twice, her) troops into battle was not a metaphor: it was reality. But history has moved on. The last English king to lead his troops in battle was George II at the Battle of Dettingen in 1743.[1] In tribal areas, leaders still need physical bravery to deal with increasingly well-armed rivals, and to deal with the ever-present threat of wild animals.[2]

But most leaders today are not like the kings of old or the tribal leaders of today. Competitive warfare may be intense, but it is not violent. The brave leader would seem to be a reality that has passed into myth.

But research shows that courage is as important as ever for leaders. However, the nature of courage has changed.[3] Courage is consistently identified as one of the seven mindsets which separate the best leaders from the rest. This makes sense. If a leader takes people where they would not have got by themselves, then that involves taking risk. And taking any sort of risk requires courage because risks can lead to failure. That means you can only lead if you are brave.

Why this myth matters

Courage stands at the heart of what modern leaders have to do:

Making decisions

The problem with making a decision is that it might be wrong. That is why most organizations are addicted to committees and long decision-making processes. If everyone is implicated in making the wrong decision, then there is no one to blame. But that is followership, not leadership.

Having difficult conversations

Leading people means that you have to have awkward conversations with them from time to time. No one likes dealing with under performance, lowering expectations around promotions and pay or giving negative feedback. But if you fail to do this, then when the news finally comes out in the year-end review it is a surprise: you will no longer be trusted because you failed to deal with the truth early. If you can have these difficult conversations early and positively, you build trust.

Stepping up, not stepping back

In any firm there are crises and moments of uncertainty when no one knows what to do. The easy way out is to quietly step back into the shadows and see what happens. No one got fired for missing an opportunity; many get fired for taking a risk and missing. Leaders have to be prepared to step up at the right moment.

Taking risks

If you want to lead the crowd, not follow the crowd, you take risks. This is not risk taking as most firms think about it. Firms try to capture risks in a risk log, complete with a heat score and mitigating actions. This is all logical risk, which can be managed with enough insight and resource. The sorts of risks that leaders have to take are personal. Leaders know the adage that success has many friends, but failure is very lonely. When a risk goes sour, the blame game soon finds a victim: the consequences can be embarrassing or career limiting. Risk for leaders is personal and emotional. If you never want to look foolish, you will avoid taking the sorts of risks leaders have to take.

Lessons for leaders

At first, it would appear that there are no lessons for leaders: you are either brave or you are not brave. You can't learn to be brave, can you?

Both the Royal Marine Commandos and the Fire Brigade show that you can teach bravery. They require their teams to do things which most of us would consider to be brave or even foolhardy. Would you want to go into the office if it was on fire and full of smoke? For fireman, that is their workplace from time to time. Both the Royal Marine Commandos and the Fire Service use the same basic approach to helping their recruits do brave things. They take it in easy steps.

For the Fire Service, this means that the raw recruit first learns how to wear their kit and look after it properly; then they might learn how to extinguish a fire in a chip pan; then they can learn how to climb a small ladder safely. Slowly, the fires get bigger, the ladders get longer, the situations get more hazardous and the kit gets more sophisticated. Eventually, they are doing things that you or I would think are crazy brave.

The Fire Service chief highlighted the reality behind much modern bravery when he was asked how he gets his firemen to be so brave: 'I never want a brave fireman, because a brave fireman is soon a dead fireman and that is no use to me.' To you or me, the firemen appear to be doing brave things. For the firemen, they are dealing with familiar situations which they know how to handle. Your office may be alight with gossip; theirs is alight with fire.

Leaders, like firemen, can acquire bravery in small steps. Learn to take small risks: don't make your first public speech in front of 2,000 key managers at your firm's global conference. Start with a small talk to a small group of trusted colleagues on a familiar topic. Work up from there.

As with firemen, much of what appears to be bravery is simply pattern recognition; once you have seen a situation enough times, you know what to expect and you will have the confidence to deal with it.

The Royal Marine Commandos teach us one more lesson about bravery. Bravery is relative to your context. The commandos may, at some point, literally risk their lives. That is extreme bravery, which takes more than training. It takes indoctrination of core values, which are reinforced through rewards, sanctions, teamwork, culture and stories. At the opposite extreme is the classic machine bureaucracy where changing the coffee machine might be seen as a bold move. Inevitably, both extremes will recruit candidates with the basic aptitudes they require, including a higher or lower appetite for risk and adventure.

As a leader, you do not need to put your life on the line. You do not need to be as brave as a commando or a fireman; you just need to be braver than your peers.

If you want to cultivate the bravery of a leader, your keys to success are:

- **Take small steps.** Take small risks first and work up from there.

- **Gain experience.** Keep putting yourself in situations where you can learn patterns of success and failure. This will give you the confidence to deal with such situations in future.

- **Be relatively brave.** You only need to be braver than your peers, and braver than you were last year. You do not need to put your life or your career on the line every day.

Conclusion

Leaders today have to be brave, but the nature of bravery has changed since the days of history. So this myth is in fact reality: you have to be brave. But the nature of leadership bravery is widely misunderstood, so this myth earns just one unicorn.

Endnotes

1 The Battle of Dettingen took place outside Frankfurt as part of the War of Austrian Succession. An alliance, including the British, Austrians and Hanoverians, defeated a French force. King George was in command of the army, but he was smart enough to lead from the rear, not the front. When his horse bolted towards the front, an ensign duly brought him back. He was brave, but not suicidal: smart leadership.

2 See Jo Owen (2008) *Tribal Business School*, Wiley.

3 See Jo Owen (2015) *Mindset of Success*, Kogan Page.

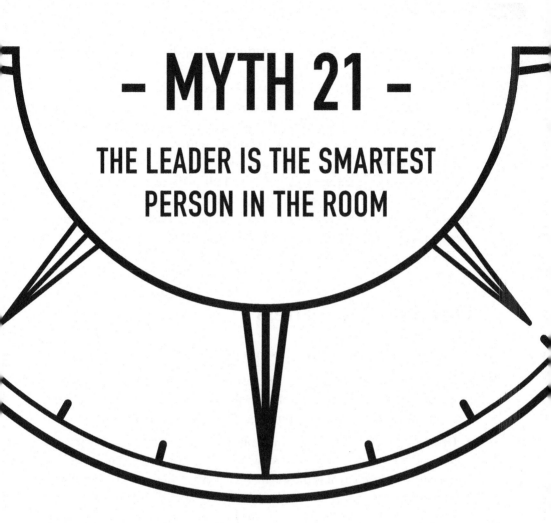

– MYTH 21 –

THE LEADER IS THE SMARTEST PERSON IN THE ROOM

If you want to be a leader, trust your team to take on every challenge.

The nature of the myth

Hierarchy replicates the parent–child relationship:[1] the boss is the parent and the team member is the child. This creates unhealthy tension in the team. In practice, it means that many teams are very good at delegating: they like to delegate all the problems up to the leader. This relieves them of accountability for the solution. It also allows them to complain that the boss has made the wrong decision in the wrong way, and that the boss is really a complete idiot, just like teenagers complaining about their gormless parents. Inevitably, the boss is the last person to hear of these complaints. To your face, the team will be polite and supportive because they know their future is in your hands.

The boss is complicit in this game. The boss may be a benevolent or abusive parent, but the dynamic is the same. The boss often feels the need to prove their worth. They want to show they can handle the toughest problems; they want to be seen to be smart and in control. They want to be the adult in the room and they want to look good.

This is a game which gets played out in all parts of the firm, even at the highest levels. The essential child–parent script never really changes. Inevitably, 40-year-old adults resent being treated like children, but that is the role that the script of the hierarchy forces on them.

This myth is closely related to the idea of the leader as the lone hero.

Why this myth matters

The parent–child script is highly dysfunctional, because it:

- **Disempowers.** By letting delegation flow up to the parent boss, the team is disempowered. If it does not take decisions, then it cannot be held accountable. That makes performance management extremely hard.

- **Disables.** A high-performing team is one that is challenged and stretched, not one which lives life in the slow lane. By letting the team delegate upwards, the team avoids the toughest challenges. In the short term, this is often the easy way out. If the boss knows what to do, then let the boss do it. But in the long term it is the road to under-achievement: the team will never learn and never develop.

- **Demotivates.** A team which is disempowered and not developing will lose motivation, even if in the short term life in the comfort zone is comfortable. Lack of delegation from the boss shows lack of trust and confidence in the ability of the team. This then sets up a vicious circle. As the team loses motivation, confidence and performance go down. This signals to the leader that the team cannot be entrusted with vital work, so the leader takes on an increasing burden. This then further disempowers, disables and demotivates the team.

- **Overwhelms.** By delegating everything upwards, the team leader takes on an increasing burden which is eventually overwhelming. If you want to be heroic, take on every challenge yourself. If you want to be a leader, trust your team to take on every challenge.

Lessons for leaders

Here are the top six lessons for leaders from this myth.

Know your role

The role of the leader is not to be the smartest person in the room. The role of the leader is to get the smartest people in the room. The coach of a sports team is very rarely the best player; the coach is the person who finds and develops the best players for the team. Once you do this, you can value each person for their unique talents and contribution and you can start to move away from the parent–child script.

Change the script

Change the script with your team. Move from the parent–child script to the adult–adult script. At the heart of this is a revolutionary idea: ignore the hierarchy. Instead of thinking like boss–team member, simply think of the team where each person has a different and vital role to play. The team leader has a role to play in coaching, setting direction and managing resources, but each team player has a vital role to play as well. You all have an equal contribution to make and no one is better than anyone else: each contribution is simply different.

Enforce accountability

Do not let your team delegate upwards to you. Delegation should work the other way around. You should be finding ways in which to stretch and challenge your team with meaningful work. In a parent–child script, the leader always lands up with all the accountability. This leaves the team members disempowered and resentful. In an adult–adult script, everyone is equal and everyone has different roles and accountability: each person is empowered. This normally raises morale and performance, and it makes performance management easier because it is clear who is accountable for what.

Pay more attention to your team

As a manager and leader it is natural to spend most time thinking about how to manage your boss. We spend more time looking up, not down, the hierarchy. This makes sense, because your boss can control your fate. Bosses do not come with a user manual, so it takes real effort to work out how to influence your boss. But the result is that leaders often do not spend as much time thinking deeply about how to influence each team member. But if you are the coach of your team, you can only get top performance if you act like a coach who is dedicated to helping each team member improve.

Trust your team

Failure to delegate reflects lack of trust in your team, and your team knows that. Show confidence in your team, and your trust will normally be repaid handsomely. Most people want to do well and want to show that they can be trusted with important challenges. Don't let the buck stop with you: pass the buck down. Let your team rise to the challenge, and then watch them grow in confidence and capability.

Be humble

The graveyard is full of indispensable executives. The reality is that when we go we will disappear without a ripple. As a leader, your role is not to become indispensable; your role is to make yourself dispensable. Build your team and your firm so that it has the strength to thrive without you.

Conclusion

This myth runs deep. It means that many leaders struggle because they fail to delegate or trust their team properly. But it is not 100 per cent fatal to a leadership career. Leaders can limp along with this belief, if it is true: sometimes the leader is the smartest person in the room. This is a myth which cripples rather than kills the leader. It merits four unicorns.

Endnote

1   This section is based on Transactional Analysis. See Eric Berne (1964) *Games People Play: The psychology of human relations*, 1978 reprint, Grove Press.

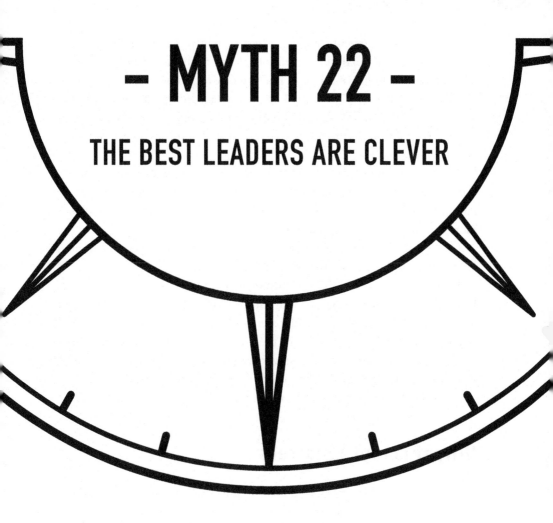

– MYTH 22 –

THE BEST LEADERS ARE CLEVER

Being academically clever and being smart are not the same thing.

The nature of the myth

As with all myths, this myth is lost in the mists of time. From time immemorial, communities have craved the wise leader who could dispense justice and uphold the law.

The advent of the industrial revolution took this idea forward. New-fangled factories needed to be organized by smart leaders and run by workers who were essentially unreliable cogs in the machine. Ideas had to flow out of the heads of the bosses and into the hands of the workers: bosses had the brains and workers had the hands. This was made explicit in the rise of Scientific Management, the high priest of which was Frederick Taylor.[1] He spent his career analysing operations down to the last detail and working out how to improve them. In one famous experiment, he managed to get workers to handle 47 tonnes of pig iron a day, up from 12 tonnes before he intervened. Behind the time and motion studies of scientific management was an assumption that workers were too stupid and too idle to maximize their own productivity.

Total quality management (TQM) is the heir to scientific management, but with a crucial twist: TQM recognizes that workers are not simply brute labourers: they are now better educated, which means they can achieve more but they expect more in return.

Given that the workforce is now more educated than ever, this implies leaders need to be smarter than ever. But is this true?

Being academically clever and being smart are not the same. Academic leadership is an oxymoron: a room full of PhDs will generate debate, not leadership. No one ever accused Einstein of being a great leader. If you turn to today's top billionaires, most of them are an MBA-free zone and about half of them did not complete university. But it would be unwise to call Zuckerberg, Gates or Brin dumb: they are clearly very smart.

Smart leadership is different from the past.

Why this myth matters

If you are to succeed as a leader, it helps to know what skills and capabilities you need for success. The 19th-century requirement of being the one smart person among a dumb workforce is clearly no longer the recipe for success. In a world where everyone is better educated, education is a necessary but not sufficient condition for success.

The nature of leadership is changing fundamentally, because the nature of the firm and the workforce is changing fundamentally. The two major changes are:

1 The workforce is smarter than ever, and will only get smarter in the future. This has two implications for leaders:

   - What sort of smartness do you need to lead when everyone else is also smart?

   - How do you lead people who probably want less management but have higher expectations than ever before?

2 Firms are outsourcing, downsizing, flattening out and specializing like never before. This means that leaders no longer control either all the people or all the resources they need to succeed. So how do you lead when you no longer have direct control?

Lessons for leaders

The smart leader today requires three sets of skills, which we can label IQ, EQ and PQ.

IQ: Intelligence Quotient

An intelligent leader is likely to do better than a dumb leader. But management intelligence is different from academic intelligence. Academic intelligence is about slowly accumulating a body of knowledge over time. Management intelligence has two elements:

- **Recognizing patterns fast and reacting to them**. This is experience on steroids. A lawyer who has handled 499 divorce cases will know what to expect when she sees her 500th case; a salesperson who has made thousands of sales calls will recognize how each buyer reacts and will know what to do. A crisis management specialist will recognize what to do when a client has a crisis: for the client it is unknown territory but for the specialist it is familiar. Leaders have to identify patterns in all the ambiguous situations they encounter and learn from them, so that next time they encounter a similar situation they know what to do.

- **Learning and adapting to new situations fast**. Pattern recognition does not always work, because you will inevitably encounter unfamiliar situations. When faced with crises, uncertainty or ambiguity, managers will step back and leaders will step up. This is when you learn fast and grow as a leader. The more often the leader steps up, the more they learn about how to step up successfully: pattern recognition surfaces again.

EQ: Emotional Quotient

Given that the workforce is now better educated than ever, leaders have to lead differently. It is not enough to be the leader that people have to follow. You need to be the leader that people want to follow. This means treating people as people, not as cogs in a machine. Smart EQ is about motivating, building balanced teams, developing talent and managing yourself and your own emotions well. EQ requires understanding how you affect other people and adapting appropriately: this was never a requirement of leadership in the 19th-century factory.

PQ: Political Quotient

You can find plenty of nice (high EQ) and smart (high IQ) people who languish in the backwaters of the firm. They are used by more ruthless colleagues as doormats on the path to success. Clearly, something is missing in the success formula. In the 21st century, the nature of leadership has changed. Firms have hollowed out and flattened. Leaders no longer control all the resources they need. Instead, they have to:

- persuade colleagues;
- build networks of influence and trust within and beyond the firm;
- align agendas and find allies for their projects;
- fight for resources, which means that your real competition is not in the market: it is sitting at a desk near you;
- find the right bosses, projects and experiences to succeed.

These 21st-century skills are deeply political. They are about making the organization work with you and for you. Leaders with these political skills have high PQ: political quotient.

Leaders may still need to be smart, but the nature of smartness is changing, and they need other skills as well. Today, leaders need IQ, EQ and PQ skills. The performance bar rises all the time.

Conclusion

In the 19th century, this would have rated one unicorn because it was reality, not myth. In the 20th century, it would have rated three unicorns because leaders needed EQ as well as IQ. In the 21st century, this myth earns five unicorns because being smart is not enough: you need EQ and PQ as well.

Endnote

1 Frederick Winslow Taylor (1911) *The Principles of Scientific Management*, Harper & Brothers.

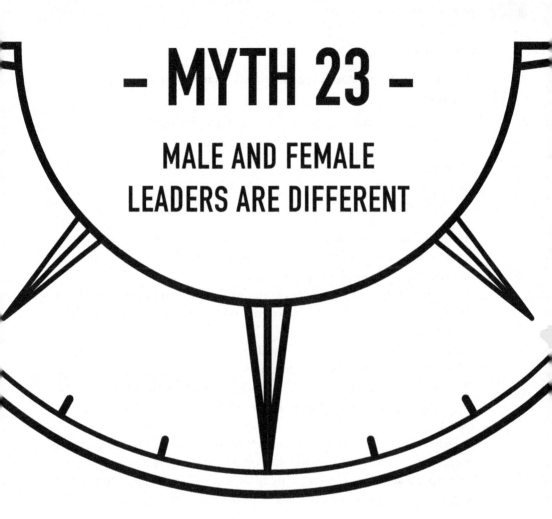

– MYTH 23 –

MALE AND FEMALE LEADERS ARE DIFFERENT

Respect people for who they are, not for their DNA or chromosomes.

The nature of the myth

A good way to sell books and get media attention is to show that men and women lead in fundamentally different ways: 'Men are from Mars and Women are from Venus'[1] is not just the message; it is also the title of a best-selling book.

Research may be more boring, but is also more useful. Even in a post-truth world, it can pay to act on the basis of evidence as opposed to belief. The research is nuanced.[2] There are differences, but not as dramatic as the popular press might want to show. An early landmark meta-analysis by

Table 23.1   Male and female leadership stereotypes

Female leadership stereotypes	Male leadership stereotypes
People focus	Task focus
Participative/democratic	Directive/autocratic
Cautious	Risk taking
Less assertive	More assertive
Emotionally aware	Focus on the facts

Professor Alice Eagly found that in real organizational life, the differences between male and female stereotypes were small.[3] In laboratory conditions, the stereotypes became more pronounced.

The standard stereotypes between male and female are shown in Table 23.1. You can add or subtract your own views of gender stereotypes to the table.

A different way of looking at the debate is to ask how far the genders differ on each factor. The two diagrams below show how you can think about gender differences. Figure 23.1 shows how the popular press like to portray the differences: men and women are literally from different planets.

Figure 23.2 shows how the research portrays the differences between genders. It shows that there are differences, but they are not a clean split on gender lines. You can find plenty of men who have more of the female stereotypes, and plenty of women who have more of the male stereotypes.

Figure 23.1   Stereotypical view of gender differences

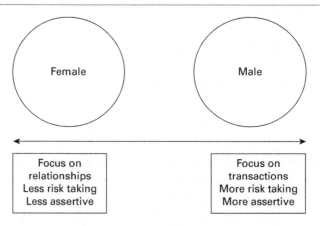

Figure 23.2 Research-based view of gender differences

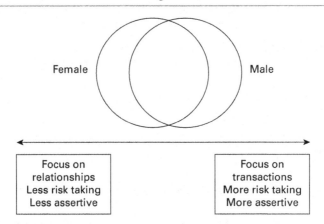

Why this myth matters

Gender differences, or lack of them, matter from at least three perspectives.

Building a balanced leadership team

Clearly, if the popular view of gender differences is accurate than that has major implications for picking and developing leaders. It would mean that some leadership roles should be the sole preserve of women, and others should be the sole preserve of men. Some roles require high risk taking (male) while others require excellent interpersonal skills (women).

If the reality is more nuanced, you will still need a balanced team in terms of styles. The gender stereotypes illustrate a few of the major style differences, but they are not the only ones.

Developing leaders of the future

If there are gender differences, then one-size-fits-all leadership development can lead to very unequal outcomes, as illustrated by the experience of Future Leaders (see below).

BUILDING LEADERS OF THE FUTURE

Future Leaders was a project designed to fast track outstanding talent into leadership of schools in the toughest areas. Its intake broadly reflected the population of middle managers in schools: it was 50/50 female/male.

After about five years, we found that 80 per cent of the people who had been promoted to head teacher were male. This was not the outcome we expected or wanted.

We looked at what was going wrong. Unsurprisingly, we found women faced significant hurdles:

- conscious or unconscious sexism from selection panels;
- the buggy in the hallway: women were still finding that they were doing most of the home making and child minding.

We also found the genders living up (or down) to their stereotypes. Typically, men would start applying for posts even when we knew they were only 40–50 per cent ready. They would try to blag their way through, confident that if they got the job they would rise to the challenge. If they were rejected, their view was that the selection panel had made a mistake. They ignored the feedback from each panel. This meant they would keep on trying, and eventually they would land a role.

In contrast, the women waited until they knew they would be able to do the job. Even when we knew they were 80 per cent ready (and no one is ever 100 per cent ready to step up to a new role), they had to be encouraged to apply. If they were rejected, they would take the feedback from the selection panel seriously, meaning they would not apply again until they felt they had addressed the weaknesses the selection panel claimed to have found.

Men were pushing themselves forwards; women were holding themselves back. In the following five years, the programme was adjusted to reflect the different approaches of each gender and eventually the promotions to headship achieved a gender balance.

Public policy

The gender debate will continue for many decades. It is for you to decide how far the stereotypes are true and what should be done about them: this book focuses on the implications for you as a leader.

Lessons for leaders

Below are four lessons we can draw.

Build a balanced team

The different stereotypes highlight the need to achieve a balanced leadership team. If the whole team is made up of risk junkies, it may succeed fast but it is also likely to crash fast. Achieving a balance of talents and styles is vital.

Understand your own style

Regardless of your gender, it is worth thinking about how far you are task focused or people focused; democratic or autocratic; risk taking and assertive; or cautious and supportive. It is usual to say that there is no wrong or right style, but that is misleading. Universally, there may be no wrong or right style, but in your specific context there will be a style which works better than others. You have to find a context to work in which your style succeeds.

Promotions do not go to the meek

The story of Future Leaders (above) shows that you have to be prepared to push yourself. Don't wait until you are 100 per cent confident you can step up, because you can never be 100 per cent ready for your next role.

Respect people for who they are

Perhaps the most important lesson for leaders is to respect people for who they are, not for their DNA or chromosomes. How far we should discriminate in favour of one group (and by implication against another group) on the basis of their DNA is a public policy matter on which everyone will have their views.

Conclusion

We live in a post-truth world where people believe what they want to believe. There clearly are gender differences, but there is disagreement about how great the differences are, whether they matter, and what should be done about it. You have to make your own mind up on this one. You decide how many unicorns to award here.

Endnotes

1 John Gray (1992) *Men Are from Mars, Women Are from Venus: A practical guide for improving communication and getting what you want in your relationships*, HarperCollins.

2 A good review of the research can be found here: http://www.ciitlahore.edu. pk/pl/abrc/Proceedings/All%20papers/Gender%20Differences%20and%20 Leadership%20An%20Empirical%20Evidence%20(Dr.%20Mahmood%20 A%20Bodla).pdf.

3 Alice Eagly and Blair Johnson (1990) Gender and leadership style: a meta-analysis, *Psychological Bulletin*, **108** (2).

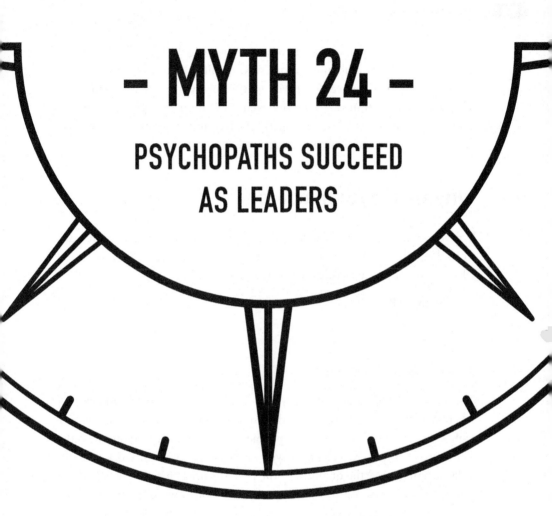

– MYTH 24 –
PSYCHOPATHS SUCCEED AS LEADERS

*Being charming, violent and lacking empathy
are all part of the same package.*

The nature of the myth

Psychopaths are generally seen as mad, bad and dangerous to know. Psychopaths are regular customers of prisons around the world. They are 25 times more likely to land up in prison than the rest of the population.[1] At first sight, this is not the obvious profile of a leader.

Research estimates that about 1 per cent of the population (mainly male) is strongly or moderately psychopathic.[2] Between 3 and 21 per cent of senior corporate officials are rated as psychopaths.[3] The wide divergence of estimates reflects ambiguity about who qualifies as a psychopath. There are many varying degrees of psychopathy: everyone has an element of the psychopath within them. In any event, it is clear that psychopaths are disproportionately good at getting themselves into trouble; they are also disproportionately good at getting themselves into power.

Why this myth matters

If psychopaths succeed as leaders, then there must be things we can learn from them about the nature of leadership. So it makes sense to understand what the main characteristics of a psychopath are:[4]

- bold and self-confident;
- stress tolerant;
- risk taking;
- charming and charismatic.

These are all good qualities for any leader to have. If you are to take people where they would not have got by themselves, you have to take risks, endure high stress, be bold, and engage people enthusiastically in your mission. These are also traits which work well in particular types of work. Traders at large banks need the qualities of the psychopath as listed above. Perhaps if investment banks test for psychopaths, it is not to weed them out but to select them in. The film *Wall Street* and subsequent scandals would indicate that some investment banks may have been selecting on this basis, accidentally or otherwise.

So why do psychopaths get such a bad name? Because they also have traits from the dark side. They are:

- amoral;
- lacking in any empathy;
- manipulative;
- violent.

Not all of these traits appear to be consistent; how can someone lack empathy but be charming? The answer is that psychopaths are very good at reading people. They will find your motivations, hopes and fears fast, and then they will play on them. This can appear empathetic, but it is a performance; they turn their show of interest on and off like flicking a switch. They appear to be charming, but they are simply manipulating. The less educated psychopaths have less ability to manipulate through charm or to intimidate through words. Instead, they will seek to manipulate and intimidate through violence: that is how so many land up in prison. Being charming, violent and lacking empathy are all part of the same package.

The ability to manipulate enables psychopaths to work their way up through an organization. Their self-confidence to take risks and make bold decisions can help them become leaders who make a difference. But their success comes at a price: they are often divisive, destructive and amoral. They are natural dictators within your firm, and natural dictators of nations.

THE PSYCHOPATH IN ACTION

Lee did not care for working for bosses he regarded as weak and foolish. So he told the partners that he would start a new practice based on advising oil and gas companies. Since none of the partners worked in this area, they let him get on with it.

Lee was very ambitious. He worked hard and soon got clients eating out of his hand. He could charm them, and he made sure they got high-quality work by building a devoted team. He demanded 100 per cent loyalty from them, but he gave 100 per cent loyalty in return. In return for working all hours, Lee consistently delivered outsized bonuses and promotions to his team. Anyone who showed just 99 per cent loyalty was ejected and trashed. Anyone who dared opposed him was squashed: no one dared to stand up to him.

In effect, Lee had set up his own business which played to its own rules: Lee's rules. There were dark stories about how success was achieved, but as long as the profits flowed the questions were not too searching.

Lessons for leaders

Seek to understand, not to judge

Moral indignation is a natural reaction to finding that psychopaths succeed. But what is natural is not always good: floods, earthquakes, death and disease are all quite natural. Instead of judging psychopaths, understand them. That way you can learn from them, you can learn how to spot them, and you can learn how to deal with them or avoid them.

Look in the mirror

We all have psychopathic tendencies, both good and bad. At times of great pressure and stress, even decent people will put themselves first. It is easy to appear amoral, to be trying to manipulate people, facts and events, and to have less empathy than is ideal.

Beware psychopaths

They are highly manipulative. They know how to lie and how to fight, because they have plenty of practice. You are unlikely to win a fight against them because you have less experience. So you have a choice. Either you can sign up and support them: the best psychopaths know they need a good team and will be very loyal to you... for just as long as they have use for you. Alternatively, steer well clear of the psychopath and find better colleagues to work with.

Avoid labels

Calling someone a psychopath is an easy insult, but insults do not help. Leave the diagnosis to the medical world, although even they struggle to agree on who qualifies as a psychopath.

Beware your firm

Most firms have the character of a psychopath: they have no empathy and, by themselves, they are quite amoral. Constant corporate scandals show how firms can be amoral. Normal working and environmental conditions in many emerging economy firms show that morality and empathy do not rate highly. Firms, like psychopaths, will support you and be loyal to you in return for your loyalty and commitment... until they decide they no longer need you.

Conclusion

This myth is built on a large dose of reality. Being a psychopath is good for getting into leadership positions, but does not necessarily make you a good leader. Two unicorns.

Endnotes

1 Kent A Kiehl and Morris B Hoffman (2011) The criminal psychopath: history, neuroscience, treatment, and economics, *Jurimetrics*, Summer, **51**, pp 355–97.

2 Paul Babiak and Robert D Hare (2007) *Snakes in Suits: When psychopaths go to work*, HarperBusiness.

3 The estimate of 21 per cent comes from forensic psychologist Nathan Brooks in a study of 261 corporate officials, *Washington Post* [online] https://www.washingtonpost.com/news/on-small-business/wp/2016/09/16/gene-marks-21-percent-of-ceos-are-psychopaths-only-21-percent/?utm_term=.9ef69bf1477b.

4 R D Hare and C N Neumann (2006) The PCL-R assessment of psychopathy: development, structural properties, and new directions, in C Patrick (ed), *Handbook of Psychopathy*, Guilford, pp 58–88.

– MYTH 25 –
LEADERS ARE REASONABLE

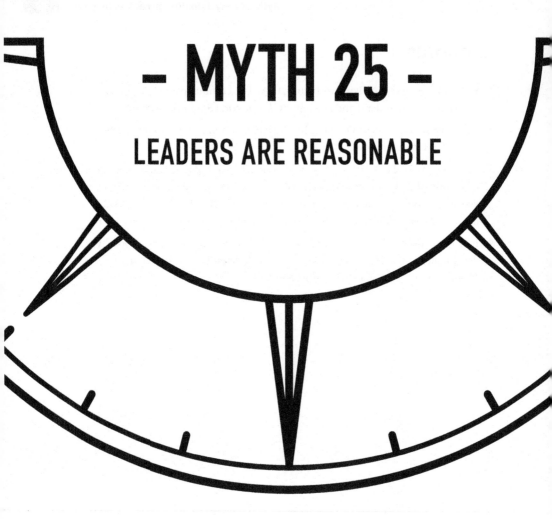

The world was never changed by reasonable people.

The nature of the myth

To tell someone that they are being unreasonable is an insult. As a society, we value reason. The 18th century witnessed the Enlightenment, which was also called the Age of Reason. It was the era when scientific method finally displaced religious belief as a way of explaining and exploring the world. It was the moment when Europe started to make huge progress in knowledge and technology, paving the way for the industrial revolution and transforming society. Reason was the mark of civilization. Leaders were meant to be well educated and able to command reason. Reason stood at the heart of society and of leadership.

The power of reason moved directly into business with the rise of Scientific Management, with Frederick Taylor in the vanguard of the movement. Nowadays his methods are seen as being little more than time and motion, but that is unfair. He always took account of the human element in a very logical way, and his methods transformed productivity. They found expression in Henry Ford's revolutionary moving production line for cars which transformed the auto industry.

Leadership is still based on reason. IT systems become more powerful all the time and produce more data than ever before. There is an insatiable appetite for data to help leaders gain insights and make more informed decisions. Strategy consultants produce volumes of data to justify their findings. An age of hyper data is also an age of hyper reason.

So it looks like case closed: leaders need reason and logic and they need to be reasonable. Anyone who is unreasonable is seen to be wild, unpredictable and very difficult to work with.

No leader wants to be unreasonable, do they?

Why this myth matters

The best leaders are not reasonable. They understand that when you accept reason, you accept failure: there are always reasons why something cannot be achieved, why a deadline must be put back, why a target should be lowered. There is always a reason you should not chase your dream.

The world was never changed by reasonable people. Great empires are not built on reason, whether they are territorial empires or business empires.

ALEXANDER THE REASONABLE?

Alexander the Great was born in a tin pot state on the edge of (Greek) civilization. If he had been reasonable, he would have fooled around in his state and pretended to be civilized: his father had hired Aristotle, the rock star philosopher of the day, to educate Alexander in an attempt to gain admission to the civilized world.

Alexander may have been tutored in logic and reason, but he was not reasonable. From his tin pot state he conquered the entire civilized world and beyond by the age of 30. As with endless conquerors since, he met his match in modern day Afghanistan.

> Since then, he has always been known in the west as Alexander the Great. Meanwhile, who has ever heard of his cousin Alexander the Reasonable? Greatness and reasonableness do not sleep together.

In business, no one in their right mind would try to take on entrenched multi-billion-dollar businesses which have a monopoly on technology and market access. But people who have more belief than reason will do that, and they can succeed. In each case in the table below, the incumbents would never have imagined that they would be threatened by today's challengers: either the challengers did not exist, or they were too small to worry about (Table 25.1).

In many cases, the new challengers did not start with a detailed business plan. Ryanair started with one plane and an idea: it is now the largest European carrier in passenger numbers.[1] In every case, reason took a back seat to ambition.

The tension between reason and ambition is now reflected in strategic thinking. The traditional approach to strategy was dominated by pointy-headed analysts who would crunch data. This was the world of Michael Porter's five competitive forces,[2] and the BCG growth/share matrix. It was a world of charts and two-by-two matrices, where analysis would yield an insight into the future. It was a world Isaac Newtown would have recognized: predictable action and reaction. Such a rational world might help slow-moving legacy firms; it did nothing to help disruptive upstarts who wanted to change the nature of competition itself.

Table 25.1 Challengers and incumbents

Challengers	Incumbents
Ryanair	British Airways
Sky/Fox	BBC/CBS
Toyota	Ford, GM
Dyson	Hoover
Amazon	Barnes & Noble
Spotify, Deezer, Tidal	Warner, Universal, Sony
Uber	Taxi firms
Google	Encyclopaedias, map-makers, classified ads, printed media

C K Prahalad and Gary Hamel led the revolt against reason with their ideas of strategic intent and core competences.[3] They encouraged leaders to be bold, set audacious targets and then build the capability to achieve those goals, while fundamentally changing the terms of competition. They learned from David and Goliath: don't fight on the terms of the giant.

Leaders hate being called unreasonable or ruthless, but even the nicest leaders can be ruthless in achieving their goals. They might call it being 'hard edged' but if you are on the receiving end of the hard edge, it feels pretty ruthless.

HARD EDGED OR RUTHLESS?

Sarah and Anne had joined the school teaching staff at the same time, straight from university. They both progressed through the school, taking on ever-greater responsibilities. Over 20 years, they became firm friends. Their families would go on holiday together and they often had Sunday lunch together.

Eventually, Sarah was appointed head teacher. It was a popular appointment because the staff liked Sarah. Her friend Anne had been head of the English department for several years.

Sarah took stock of the school and realized that if it was to perform properly for the children it served, it needed to refresh the staff pool. Several staff members were not good enough and were holding the school back. Anne held a crucial role as Head of English, and was one of the key people holding back performance. Sarah fired Anne, as nicely as she could.

That was a quick end to a long friendship. But school performance improved dramatically and Sarah was confident she had done the right thing: hard edged or ruthless?

Lessons for leaders

Leaders need to be selectively unreasonable. Managers need to be reasonable. Below are three areas where you may forget to be reasonable.

Be unreasonable about your ambition

A leader takes people where they would not have got by themselves. That means you have to dare to stretch people and to challenge them. Most people rise to the challenge, and they grow as a result.

Be ruthless in pursuing the dream

One of the core tasks of the leader is to create the team which can deliver the result. Ultimately, survival of the organization is more important than survival of the individual. If you have to move people off your team, then that is what you must do.

Ignore excuses

Neither accept them nor deny them. Excuses are dangerous for two reasons: they look backwards, not forwards, and they create a reason for not delivering. Instead of focusing on the excuse, focus on what needs to happen next, if the original goal is to be achieved on the original schedule.

WHAT WOULD YOU DO?

Penicillin was discovered in 1928,[4] but it was hard to make in volume. It was only during the Second World War that the Americans finally worked out how to produce large batches of the life-saving miracle drug.

An early batch found its way to Egypt, where it posed a problem for the British commanders. They could use it on thousands of service men who had been fooling around in the pleasure palaces of Cairo and Alexandria: a small dose would cure them and get them back to the front. Or they could use much more of it on a few wounded war heroes: some might die anyway, others might have lived anyway but it could make all the difference and save a few of them.

They cabled back to London to ask Churchill what they should do. Your call: save the wounded war heroes, or get the troops who had been fooling around back onto the front line?

Churchill's choice was clear: 'Use it for best military advantage'. Use it to get as many troops as possible back onto the front line. The goal was to defeat the enemy, not save the wounded.

When leaders have a very clear goal, they become ruthless in chasing it.

Conclusion

We may want reasonable leaders, but leaders have to be selectively unreasonable and ruthless to achieve their mission. Reasonable people rarely believe in unicorns and rarely become leaders. This should make it a five-unicorn myth, but only four appear because the reality is that leaders are *selectively* unreasonable and ruthless. They may be reasonable for 90 per cent of the time, but are unreasonable at the moments of truth. Four unicorns.

Endnotes

1 Wikipedia, List of largest airlines in Europe [online] https://en.wikipedia.org/wiki/List_of_largest_airlines_in_Europe.

2 Michael E Porter (2008) The five competitive forces that shape strategy, *Harvard Business Review*, January, pp 86–104.

3 Gary Hamel and C K Prahalad (2005) Strategic intent, *Harvard Business Review* [online] https://hbr.org/2005/07/strategic-intent.

4 American Chemical Society, Discovery and development of penicillin [online] https://www.acs.org/content/acs/en/education/whatischemistry/landmarks/flemingpenicillin.html.

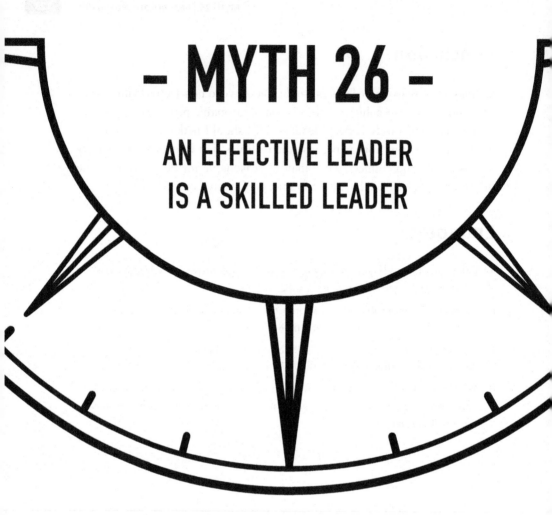

– MYTH 26 –

AN EFFECTIVE LEADER IS A SKILLED LEADER

The best leaders are not always the most skilled.

The nature of the myth

This myth permeates leadership development and leadership books. There are endless courses available which all deal with different aspects of leadership. At the heart of most leadership development is the belief that there are known skills and capabilities which can be defined, shared and learned by emerging leaders. The quality of these courses varies dramatically: some can be life changing. Others are a good opportunity to get up to date with your e-mail backlog.

On balance, a skilled leader is more likely to be effective than an unskilled leader. But as you look at leaders you have encountered, it is obvious that all leaders have weaknesses, and not all leaders are the most skilled people in the firm. This is partly the result of the goldfish bowl effect: leaders live life in a goldfish bowl where every movement and every defect is seen and commentated upon. Life in the backwaters is quieter and any minor flaws you may have are not so obvious.

If the best leaders are not always the most skilled, then they must have something else. Is there an x-factor which separates out the best leaders from the rest?

Why this myth matters

Skills are necessary, but not sufficient for a leader. If we are to find the leaders of the future and help them emerge, we need to know what leaders need in addition to skills.

Research has shown that the best leaders act differently because they think differently.[1] That much is obvious. More surprising is that the way the best leaders think is consistent and is different from the standard corporate mindset. The best news is that these mindsets are not part of your DNA. They are simply habits of mind that anyone can learn in the same way anyone can learn any skill: practice makes you better even if you never become a superstar.

Lessons for leaders

Here are seven (plus one) mindsets which separate out the best leaders from the rest.

High aspirations

The corporate mindset interprets high aspirations as excellence. Keep improving and become best in class. Excellence is fine as far as it goes, which is not far enough. Leaders look beyond excellence to see what they can change: can they change the rules of the game, or find a fundamentally different way of working? This is about making a difference, which implies taking far greater risks than the corporate mindset allows.

Leaders who are deeply committed to a mission they believe in quickly develop the other mindsets. They find the courage to take risks, the resilience to overcome setbacks, and allies with whom they can collaborate to succeed. They remain relentlessly positive about doing something they believe in and they will be prepared to make the tough decisions which appear ruthless.

Courage

If you are to take people where they would not have got by themselves, that means you will challenge orthodoxy, you will take people towards the unknown and you will meet resistance. It means taking risk, while the corporate mindset looks to manage risk. Leaders will take risks to start things and change things, to step up at crises when others step back, to challenge and fight battles where they have to.

Resilience

The nature of risk is that sometimes it does not succeed. If you have never failed, you have never taken enough risk: a risk which always works is not a risk. Most leaders succeed on the back of repeated failures and setbacks. This has a curious effect: the more you encounter setbacks, the better you become at dealing with them. If you never fail, you have no experience or resilience to fall back on.

Accountable

Corporate accountability is lopsided: take the praise and spread the blame. It is also limited to the formula where accountability = responsibility. Leaders see accountability differently in at least three ways:

- Seek responsibility beyond your narrow accountability. Build personal power through influence and networks of trust and support so that your power is not limited by your position.
- Spread the praise and shield the blame: the effect on team motivation and trust is transformational.
- Be accountable for your own feelings: wear the mask of leadership, not the mask of anger and frustration.

Positive

The corporate positive mindset is reduced on occasion to instructing staff to say 'have a nice day' while thinking 'please drop dead'. Being positive is not about telling people to have passion while you de-layer, right size, re-engineer and outsource operations. Being positive comes from within: find meaning in what you do; count your blessings; look to the future, don't dwell on the past; move to action, not analysis; see opportunities, not just problems.

Collaborative

The corporate rhetoric is about teamwork, but the corporate reality is that many managers find it hard to let go: delegating to the team and trusting peers is hard. The best leaders have the best teams. They are deeply collaborative because they have to be: they cannot do it all themselves. Having a great team enables each leader to focus their time and energy where they can most make a difference. Everything else can be delegated.

Growth

Leadership is a journey in which the context keeps changing and the rules of survival and success keep changing. This means leaders have to keep learning and adapting. It is not a craft skill like plumbing or the law where you have to master a known body of knowledge and skills (and then top them up over your career). You have to keep on refreshing your success model.

Ruthlessness

This is the 'plus one' mindset from the dark side. Making a difference requires a hard edge: making tough decisions; having difficult (but constructive) conversations; setting high and stretching goals; not accepting excuses; moving people in and out of the team. The easy life avoids these difficult moments, but leadership is not about the easy life. It is about making a difference.

Conclusion

It is true that leaders need to be skilled (zero unicorns) but it is not enough. The best leaders need the right mindset. If we call mindset 'habits of mind' then mindset can also be treated as learnable and the myth would still get zero unicorns. But leadership is more than just 'know what' skills. It is also 'know how' skills and mindset. Two unicorns.

Endnote

1 Jo Owen (2015) *Mindset of Success*, Kogan Page.

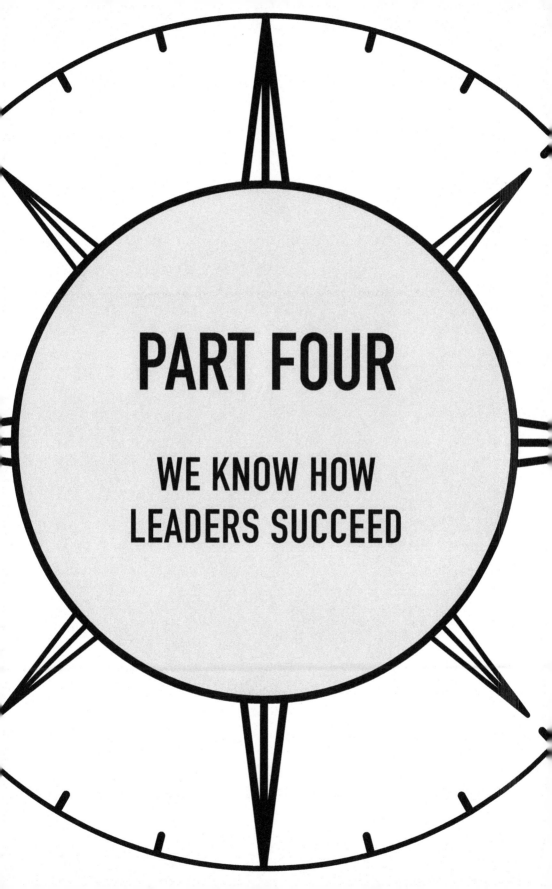

PART FOUR

WE KNOW HOW LEADERS SUCCEED

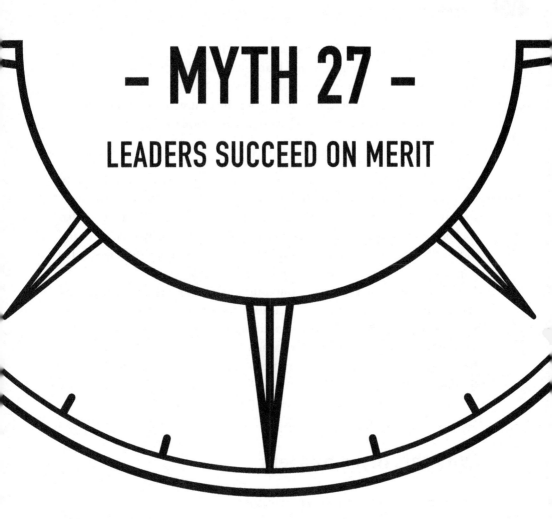

– MYTH 27 –

LEADERS SUCCEED ON MERIT

Leaders make their own luck.

The nature of the myth

Historically, merit had little to do with leadership. The main requirement to lead was to be born into the right family. Having the right parents still loads the dice in your favour, as seen in Myth 16. But the talent pool is much deeper nowadays, so the competition is far greater. So merit would seem to be winning the day. Most leaders support the merit principle: they like to believe that they have succeeded on the basis of merit, not luck.

But there is another view: luck matters. That is not just the view of the also-rans who nearly made it, and blame bad luck for their lack of success. More reflective leaders often say things like: 'Of course, I have been very lucky... but I have made my luck.' The difference between failure and success is often very small. A contract or a promotion can go one way or the other: success is on a knife edge.

Careers are like sport, where highly talented people compete against each other and the margin between success and failure is very narrow. Typically, the losing side will curse their luck in any one game. The solution is normally to play many games in a league (American football, baseball, soccer) so that the luck evens out over a season: the best side will normally become champions. That is why knock-out competitions are exciting: the unexpected happens, the underdog can win and luck plays its part.

A career is more like a knock-out tournament than a league. You cannot re-run your career endlessly, like a leadership version of Bill Murray in *Groundhog Day*. You have one shot at your career. You can take another shot at your career by starting at a new firm or starting a new business, but there is a limit to how many fresh starts you can squeeze into one lifetime.

So how much does success depend on luck or merit?

Why this myth matters

The merit myth is essential for two reasons.

Pay and rewards

Believing that success is based on merit is vital. If success is not based on merit, then there is no reason to pay top leaders outsized salaries, stock options, bonuses and deferred compensation. Without merit, leaders simply become lucky lottery winners.

Trust

If people believe that leaders are not there on the basis of merit, then the leaders will not be trusted. Why would you trust someone who succeeded through luck or through underhand means? The evidence is that trust in elites is evaporating fast: only 35 per cent of the population trust business leaders to tell the truth, and a mere 22 per cent trust government ministers to tell the truth.[1]

If leaders are not trusted, it becomes very hard for them to lead. Merit, trust and leadership walk hand in hand.

Lessons for leaders

Luck matters. Napoleon famously liked lucky generals, until he met Wellington. He was right. He understood that leadership luck is not random. Leaders make their own luck. So how do you make your own luck? Here is how you can become the luckiest leader alive – all you have to do is acquire the three Ps of leadership: persistence, practice and perspective.[2]

Persistence

Leaders, like entrepreneurs, get used to the feeling of failure. Except that they never see it as failure; each setback is just another step on the path to success. They have an unquenchable belief in themselves and their mission. Churchill was a serial political failure. He described the 20 years between the two world wars as his 'wilderness years'. Twenty years as an outcast would crush most people, but he kept going. In 1940, he became prime minister and discovered his finest hour at the age of 66. Often the difference between failure and success is as simple as not giving up.

PERSISTENT FAILURE... OR SUCCESS?

One leader started out as a door-to-door salesman, selling kitchen goods to homemakers. As a rule, you can expect to be rejected at 98 out of every 100 doors you knock on. How do you cope with serial rejection on that scale, day after day? Here is how he described it: 'Every time a door slammed in my face, I would just think, "I am one door closer to success."' With that sort of perspective, it is not surprising that he eventually succeeded, albeit in a completely different field: setting up and running large third-party data centres.

Practice

Legendary golf champion Arnold Palmer once remarked: 'The harder I practice, the luckier I get.'[3] This is true. An amateur might hole a five-metre putt 20 per cent of the time; with practice, the 20 per cent chance becomes a 40 per cent chance, and eventually the highly practised professional might succeed 90 per cent of the time. With practice, the lucky shot becomes the skilled shot.

Practice is more than persistence. Persistence means keeping going. Practice means learning from experience, both good and bad. It is not enough to have deep experience; you have to learn from experience as well.

Perspective

Try this exercise. Think of all the bad things that happened today: inconsiderate drivers, traffic lights against you, annoying e-mails; tedious meetings. So are you lucky? Now think of all the good things that have happened. Simply to wake up in a warm house, with hot and cold running water, largely free from the fear of war, disease and famine makes us lottery winners in the field of human history. Our ancestors would envy us. So are you now lucky or unlucky? Sometimes luck is simply a matter of how we choose to feel.

Perspective is also about spotting opportunities. The reality is that we are surrounded by opportunity, but we only see it if we are looking for it. In one famous experiment, viewers were asked to observe how many times a basketball was passed between stationary players on court. During the video, someone in a gorilla suit walked on, danced around the players and walked off. Fewer than one quarter of the viewers saw the gorilla: most refused to believe that there had been a gorilla there. They were too busy counting passes.[4]

Within any firm there are always crises, new opportunities and moments of uncertainty and ambiguity. If you are looking for them, you will find them. And for entrepreneurs, the world is full of opportunity, if you have the courage to take up the challenge.

Of course, all leaders are lucky, because they make their luck.

Conclusion

Leaders succeed on merit and on luck, but they create their own luck which means luck is also largely merited. This myth is true, but in recognition of the need for some luck it scores two unicorns.

Endnotes

1 Ipsos MORI veracity index 2016 [online] https://www.ipsos-mori.com/ researchpublications/researcharchive/3685/Politicians-are-still-trusted-less-than-estate-agents-journalists-and-bankers.aspx#gallery[m]/1/.

2 This section draws on the research of Richard Wiseman's 2004 book, *The Luck Factor: The scientific study of the lucky mind*, Arrow Paperback.

3 This is also attributed to Gary Player and Jerry Barber among many others. Regardless of who said it first, it remains a relevant comment.

4 There are many versions of this exercise, involving gorillas, storm troopers and moonwalking bears. For example: https://www.youtube.com/ watch?v=UfA3ivLK_tE.

– MYTH 28 –

LEADERSHIP IS ABOUT SURVIVAL OF THE FITTEST

To finish first, first you must finish.

Survival of the fittest is not one myth, but two. The two myths are:

- leaders are the fittest;
- becoming a leader is about surviving.

We will explore each myth in turn.

The nature of the myth (1): you have to be the fittest to be a leader

At one level, this is a tautology. If the person who becomes a leader is the one who best fits the role, then by definition the leader is the fittest person. But that is not the standard version of the myth. The standard version of the myth can be seen in sycophantic profiles of leaders in the business media. There is one group of leaders, normally male, who like to portray themselves as super-fit super heroes; they will usually get up three hours before everyone else wakes up and complete an ironman triathlon before dashing off to transform their firm.

Why this myth matters

This myth raises an important question: do you need to be fit to lead? Are the demands of modern leadership so intense, with a need to be 'on' 24/7, that only the fittest can survive the leadership marathon?

There is ample evidence you do not need to be an ironman athlete to lead. Winston Churchill was clearly fit in his youth; he took part in one of the last full cavalry charges in British history.[1] But by the time he became prime minister in 1940 he was 66 years old, fat and probably alcoholic and depressive. He was eventually joined by President Roosevelt. In 1944 Roosevelt, who suffered from polio, was found to have high blood pressure, atherosclerosis, coronary artery disease causing angina pectoris, and congestive heart failure.[2] Even the super-fit wonder kids of today might find fighting a world war to be quite testing, and yet neither Roosevelt not Churchill were pin ups for the fitness industry.

But there is one area where fitness does play a part in leadership performance: sleep.

The traditional view of sleep is that it is like lunch: it is for wimps.[3] Young graduates at top investment banks and consulting firms often go through rites of passage where they either pull an all-night session, or at least like to be seen to do an all-night shift by leaving their jackets at their desks.

This is a huge error. The same firms which value the commitment of people working all night would probably fire the same person if they arrived in the morning drunk. But research shows that drinking and lack of sleep have the same effect on performance: reaction times slow down and judgement gets worse.[4] Here are the effects of sleep on the likelihood of having a car crash the next day:

- 6–7 hours sleep: 1.3 times the crash risk;
- 5–6 hours sleep: 1.9 times the crash risk;
- 4–5 hours sleep: 4.3 times the crash risk;
- under 4 hours sleep: 11 times the crash risk.

Don't fool yourself: you cannot achieve peak performance on little sleep.

Lessons for leaders

The good news is that you do not need to be super fit to succeed. But you do need good health and good sleep. You really can sleep your way to the top.

The nature of the myth (2): leadership is about survival

Leaders do not have to be the fittest, but they do have to survive. The world is full of outstanding people who have crashed out, burned out or dropped out. The saying from the sailing world is apt: to finish first, first you must finish. There is no point in going fast and then capsizing.

For leaders, the difference between failure and success is as simple as giving up.

Why this myth matters

All leaders go through dark periods in their careers. These times can be very testing and very lonely. The temptation to seek a quieter life elsewhere can be overwhelming; the dream of the vegan farm in Vermont starts to grow. And if you want to chase that dream, you should. Leadership is an exciting and challenging journey, but it is not for everyone. But if you want to stay on the leadership journey you need to have or build the resilience to take you through hard times as well as good.

Lessons for leaders

Fortunately, there is a wide body of evidence about how to build resilience. Much of the work was done in the most extreme circumstances, from Nazi concentration camps[5] to Vietnamese prisoners of war.[6] If you can survive those sorts of conditions, you can probably survive the challenges of leadership.

Here are 10 ways to build your resilience:

1 **Find meaning in what you do.** As a leader, you should make a difference. That is a contribution worth celebrating.

2 **Take control.** The difference between pressure and stress is control. Most people react better to some pressure rather than no pressure. But when there is pressure and you have no control because you depend on other people and events, then stress soars. In practice, you can never control everything you need to control, so find those things you can control in your career and life, and make the most of those.

3 **Stay positive.** Focus on what you can do, and drive to action. There are always plenty of things you cannot do, so there is little point in worrying about them. If there is only one thing you can do, do that.

4 **Be adaptable.** The shortest way between two points may be a straight line, but if you are sailing against the wind then the quickest and only way is a zig zag. This means you always need a plan B for when things go wrong. As Mike Tyson elegantly put it: 'Everyone has a plan until they get punched in the mouth.'[7] What is your plan B?

5 **Find support.** Do not suffer alone.

6 **Count your blessings.** When things are bleak, it is easy to believe that everything is always bleak. Don't talk yourself down. Professionally and personally you will have much you can draw on. Professionally, you still have skills and experience that are valued; personally, we are all lucky to be living free from famine, war and disease for a start.

7 **Use perspective.** Everyone fails on the path to success. Here is basketball legend Michael Jordan: 'I've missed over 9,000 shots in my career. I've lost almost 300 games. Twenty-six times I've been trusted to take the game-winning shot and missed. I've failed over and over and over again in my life. And that is why I succeed.'[8]

8 **Use humour.** The Royal Marine Commandos understand extreme adversity, even in training. They do not talk about surviving adversity.

One of their four core values is cheerfulness in the face of adversity: 'How better to endure than with humour? One of the four Commando Spirit characteristics, cheerfulness in the face of adversity, is made possible only by humour, which, although not readily recognized as a quality anywhere else, is actually fundamental [*sic*] the way the Corps operates.'[9] Cheerfulness is the ultimate antidote to adversity.

9 **Embrace adversity.** Resilience is like your credit card: the more you use it, the more you are allowed to use it. As with courage, you can grow your resilience by exposing yourself to situations which test you and stretch you. If you always live life in your comfort zone you will never build the resilience required to sustain yourself in adversity. Push yourself.

10 **Enjoy what you do,** because you only excel at what you enjoy. To be excellent at anything takes dedication and commitment. You have to put in the hours and make sacrifices. As professionals, we can all do that for a month or two when there is a big crunch at work. But to sustain that level of effort for years and for decades is not possible if you dislike what you do. You have to find enjoyment and fulfilment in what you do, otherwise you cannot sustain your leadership journey, and your life will not be much fun. Enjoying your work is not a nice to have, it is a must have.

Conclusion

These myths are only half true. You do not need to be the fittest to lead, but you do need to be fit and alert. And although you need the persistence to survive, survival simply gets you into a leadership position. Surviving does not mean you are leading. It is a necessary but not sufficient condition of leadership. Half-true myths earn three unicorns.

Endnotes

1 Charge of the 21st Lancers in the Battle of Omdurman, 2 September 1898: 400 British cavalry charged 2,500 Mahdist infantry.

2 Wikipedia, Franklin D Roosevelt: declining health [online] https://en.wikipedia. org/wiki/Franklin_D._Roosevelt#Declining_health.

3 'Lunch is for wimps' is one of the classic lines from Gordon Gekko in the 1987 movie *Wall Street*.

4   AAA Foundation for Traffic Safety (2016) Acute sleep deprivation and crash risk [online] https://www.aaafoundation.org/acute-sleep-deprivation-and-crash-risk.

5   Logotherapy was developed by Viktor Frankl after his experiences in a Second World War concentration camp, documented in his 1946 book, *Man's Search for Meaning*, Beacon Press.

6   The Stockdale paradox is named after Admiral Jim Stockdale, who was held captive for eight years during the Vietnam war. See Stuart Rochester and Frederick Kiley (2007) *Honor Bound: American prisoners of war in Southeast Asia, 1961–1973*, Naval Institute Press.

7   Sun Sentinel (2012) Mike Tyson explains one of his most famous quotes [online] http://articles.sun-sentinel.com/2012-11-09/sports/sfl-mike-tyson-explains-one-of-his-most-famous-quotes-20121109_1_mike-tyson-undisputed-truth-famous-quotes.

8   As quoted in Robert Goldman and Stephen Papson (1998) *Nike Culture: The sign of the swoosh*, Sage, p 49.

9   Alpha Company Royal Marines Cadets: Aims, ethos and corps values [online] http://www.acoy.co.uk/page2.htm.

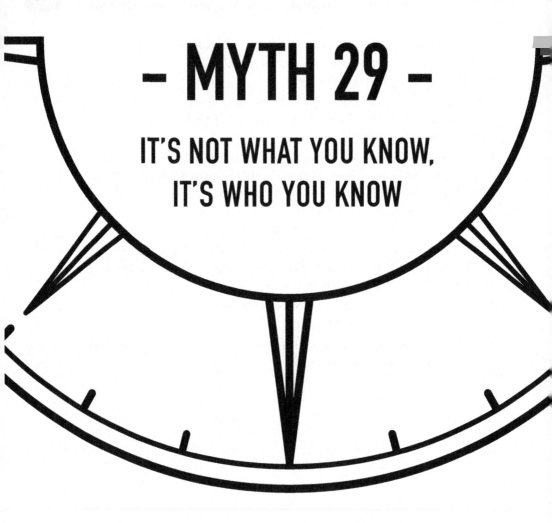

– MYTH 29 –

IT'S NOT WHAT YOU KNOW, IT'S WHO YOU KNOW

Leaders need both talent and networks on their leadership journey.

The nature of the myth

Throughout history there have been conspiracy theories which hold that the world is run by shadowy cabals: the Illuminati, Opus Dei and the Freemasons have all been fingered at some point. If an organization is closed, it attracts rumours. A cursory glance at the Freemasons would exclude them as masters of our destiny. If you hang out at a café near their Grand Temple in Holborn, London, you will see large numbers of ageing men dressed like superannuated butlers stopping off for a quick coffee on their way to the

Temple. They look like retired civil servants on a day out, rather than grand masters of anything. The conspiracy theorist would just say that proves what good cover they have for their sinister plots made by more senior and secretive Masons. You can never fully disprove a good conspiracy theory.

In business, there is a recurrent theme that jobs go to closed networks. The nature of these networks varies; sometimes it is referred to as the old school tie. If you went to the right school or college, then all the alumni will help each other to the top jobs; for others it is as simple as the all-male club conniving in the toilets to keep women out of top jobs. Others point to the tentacle-like networks of leading firms such as Goldman Sachs and McKinsey[1] which are able to parachute executives into leading roles in business and government. The assumption is that these alumni networks are self-serving; alumni will give business and jobs to their previous employer.

There is some evidence of a network effect. McKinsey alumni provide the CEOs for over 150 firms with a turnover of $1 billion or more. But correlation is not the same as causation. The innocent explanation for the success of McKinsey consultants is that they are all very smart, very driven, and have been trained to have good strategy skills. In other words, they are good raw material for becoming a CEO.

PERHAPS IT IS WHO YOU KNOW: ENA AND THE ENARQUES[2]

The École Nationale d'Administration was set up by France to make entry into the highest levels of government more open and more democratic. Entry into ENA is by a fearsome two-part examination, which is open to all. Up to 100 students graduate from ENA every year; it is truly exclusive compared to places like Harvard, Oxford and Cambridge which admit thousands of students each year. Anyone who graduates from ENA is called an Enarque, and is very bright and very privileged.

Since ENA was set up after the Second World War it has provided 10 presidents or prime ministers of France, 64 ministers or secretaries of state, and the heads of a complete alphabet soup of international organizations: UNESCO, the IMF, ECHR, European Central Bank, EBRD and the European Commission. It has also provided the CEOs for at least 20 of France's leading firms.

In research with the Enarques, it was striking that they all knew each other and how high they graduated in the graduation list. It is genuinely a close-knit community.

> The curious result is that although ENA was set up to make entry to the top of French society more open, it has had the perverse effect of making it more closed. If you graduate from ENA you are on the fast track to the top; if you graduate from elsewhere you will have to work even harder to succeed. Perhaps the old school tie really does matter.

Why this myth matters

Leaders need both talent and networks on their leadership journey. It is not a choice between one or the other.

Lessons for leaders

In practice, leaders need both talent and networks. Most of this book focuses on talent and what you need to do to succeed. This section will focus not on what you know, but who you know; build your networks.

Join the power network

If you really believe that the way to the top is through McKinsey, then join McKinsey. That is the point at which you will discover that talent is required to gain admission to the network. Talent and networks go together; what you know and who you know both matter.

If you believe that the Illuminati, Opus Dei or Freemasons are the way to the top, you could join them. But be prepared to be disappointed, unless wearing fancy regalia and following byzantine rituals gives you pleasure.

In practice, these networks are not magical. McKinsey alumni may have provided 150 CEOs of billion-dollar firms, but there are 1,922 publicly quoted firms with over $1 billion in sales[3] and many more that are privately held. If half the McKinsey alumni are still in post, that means that perhaps 75 out of 4,000 large firms are run by McKinsey alumni. That leaves you with 98 per cent of the market where McKinsey have not got a CEO. There is plenty of opportunity for you to succeed.

Build your own network

Your network is a powerful route to your next role. Estimates vary, but between 40 per cent and 85 per cent of jobs are found through networking. Even the lower estimate indicates that your personal network is a powerful tool.

Your most important network is in your current firm. Inevitably you will have a network of colleagues and team members who are at or near your level. This is a vital network to help you make things happen, but you also need a network which can steer you to the next opportunity. At a minimum, be nice to HR; they know what opportunities are likely to emerge. This allows you to position yourself appropriately for the opportunity ahead of time; you gain first mover advantage.

You also need one or two powerful sponsors in the firm. These are people at least two levels above you who understand the politics and can shield you; they can help you avoid the Death Star assignments and nudge you to the better opportunities. Senior people always appreciate flattery, always want information about what is really going on, and always need discretionary help on new ideas and challenges. Make yourself useful to them.

Finally, pay attention to your industry network and profile. Conferences are a great way to find out what competitors, suppliers and buyers are thinking and doing. They are also a great way to identify potential personal opportunities, to build your profile and extend your network. Sites like LinkedIn tell the world who you are, but you need to meet people face to face to build rapport and trust.

Conclusion

Is it what you know or who you know? You need both as a leader, so this is a semi-myth. Instead of five half unicorns, we have to settle for three whole unicorns.

Endnotes

1 Duff McDonald (2013) *The Firm: The story of McKinsey and its secret influence on American business*, Simon & Schuster.

2 This is based on original research by the author. A brief summary appeared on CNN here: http://edition.cnn.com/2007/BUSINESS/04/30/execed.anglofrench.

3 *Forbes*, The world's biggest public companies [online] http://www.forbes.com/global2000/list/#tab:overall.

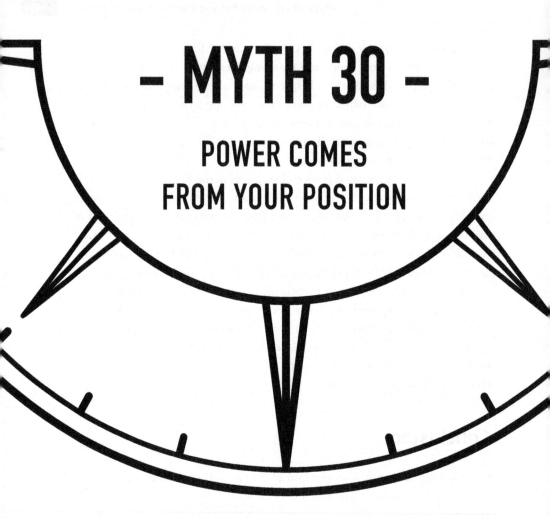

– MYTH 30 –

POWER COMES
FROM YOUR POSITION

The leader cannot achieve things by relying on formal authority only.

The nature of the myth

Traditionally, firms were organized on military lines. This made sense, because before the Industrial Revolution the only large-scale organizations were the church and the army. The army seemed to offer better insights into how to organize large numbers of people than the church, so from the start of our industrial age firms copied military models of management. To this day, we hear echoes of this military heritage when firms talk about competitive warfare, fighting battles, holding positions, divisions and officers of the firm.

The military heritage lives on as a command and control hierarchy. Even firms that are becoming flatter still rely on very clear schemes of delegation. Different sorts of authority are attached to different sorts of role. Some people have budget power, others may have approval power. Getting a decision made in a large firm can be a byzantine exercise where you discover many people have the power to say no, and no one wants to take the risk of saying yes. Most corporate approval systems are, in effect, disapproval systems. Success requires avoiding disapproval.

Once people have power, they guard it jealously. The less power they have, the more they protect it. Asking a security guard to use common sense instead of following an insane procedure is an exercise in futility. All they have is their procedure: take that away and you take away their job.

Why this myth matters

The world has changed since the Industrial Revolution, and the nature of the firm has changed as well. Large firms used to be like medieval walled cities: they contained everything they needed to survive. Famously, from 1928 to 1945, the Ford Motor Company even built the Fordlandia and Belterra rubber plantations in Brazil to secure their rubber supplies.[1]

The walls of the firm have come down, and firms have opened up to the world. Firms are specializing more and more in the activities they undertake, which means they become dependent on a complex web of suppliers, partners and customers.

Within the firm, the walls between functions and business units are also coming down. Functional silos were the hallmark of command and control firms; the matrix is the hallmark of many firms today.

In this new world, the leader cannot achieve things by relying on formal authority only, because no leader has enough formal authority. In the past, authority and responsibility were matched; now responsibility for a leader is routinely far greater than their authority.

The Industrial Revolution has finally succumbed to a leadership revolution. In the past, leaders made things happen through people they controlled. Now leaders have to make things happen through people they don't control, and that changes everything. It means leaders have to learn the art of leading without formal power. They need a new set of skills around influencing people, decisions and events.

Lessons for leaders

Leaders still derive power from their position, but that is no longer enough. Leaders need to build networks of trust and influence across and beyond the firm, and they have to be able to influence events and decisions.[2]

The topic of influence is too large to cover here, but all leaders should acquire the basic skills of building influence:

1 **Build trust.** Always deliver on your commitments. Find common ground with your colleagues: common interests, needs and priorities. Make it easy for your colleagues: remove risks and obstacles to them working with you.

2 **Create loyal followers.** Show you are genuinely interested in each member of your team and their careers: understand their needs; manage their expectations; build trust by having difficult conversations positively and early; always deliver on your commitments to them.

3 **Focus on outcomes.** Work to clear goals which have visibility and impact across the organization. Find your claim to fame, and then stake your claim; make sure people know about it.

4 **Take control.** Have a clear plan for your department, know what will be different as a result of your work, build the right team, and get the right budget and support for your plan. Do not accept the plan, team and budget you inherit as sacrosanct. You should build a legacy, not just inherit one.

5 **Pick your battles.** Follow Sun Tzu's three rules of warfare: only fight when there is a prize worth fighting for; only fight when you know you will win; only fight when there is no other way of achieving your goal.[3] It is better to win a friend than it is to win an argument.

6 **Manage decisions.** Understand the rational decision (what is the best cost, risk, benefit trade off?), manage the politics (what will the CEO and power brokers expect?) and the emotional decision (what do I feel most confident about and what will my team feel committed to?).

7 **Act the part.** Act like other influential people in your organization: be positive, confident and assertive; act like a peer to senior staff, not like their bag carrier.

8 **Be selectively unreasonable.** Dare to stretch yourself, your team and others; make a difference by going beyond business as usual and beyond the comfort zone. This lets you learn, make an impact and build influence.

9 **Embrace ambiguity**. Crises and uncertainty are wonderful opportunities to make a mark, take control and fill the void of uncertainty and doubt which others create. Ambiguity lets leaders flourish.

10 **Use it or lose it**. Control your destiny or someone else will; you only remain influential if you use your influence.

Conclusion

Clearly power does come from your position: the president of the United States has more power than a high school janitor in North Dakota. But for most leaders, formal power is not enough. You need to influence and lead people you do not control. Even the president has to persuade and cajole Congress and the public to succeed. This means that 'position comes from power' is true but incomplete and highly misleading: leaders need much more than position. Because it is so misleading and dangerous, this myth earns four unicorns.

Endnotes

1 Ford rubber plantations in Brazil [online] https://www.thehenryford.org/collections-and-research/digital-resources/popular-topics/brazilian-rubber-plantations.

2 The topic of influence is covered at length in Jo Owen (2012) *How to Influence and Persuade*, Pearson.

3 Sun Tzu (2009) *The Art of War*, paperback edition, Pax Librorum. Sun Tzu was a Chinese philosopher writing in the 5th century BC.

- MYTH 31 -

LEADERS NEED EXPERIENCE

Having experience is different to learning from it.

The nature of the myth

This myth pits the wisdom and discipline of age against the energy and creativity of youth. The evidence points to age winning against youth. In 2010, the average age of CEOs of S&P 500 firms on appointment was 53.[1] The average age of incumbent CEOs is higher. The youngest CEOs are Mark Zuckerberg and Larry Page, but they were not appointed to their posts. They created their posts by founding Facebook and Google, respectively.

Research also backs age over youth, even in start-ups.[2] Analysis of 500 engineering and tech start-ups found that the average age of the founder was 39, and founders were twice as likely to be over 55 than under 25. Zuckerberg appears to be the exception that proves the rule.

History gives a more mixed message about age versus experience. Henry VI of England came to the throne at the age of 8 months and 6 days. That was deemed slightly too young even by medieval standards, and a regent was appointed to rule until he came of age. Because lives were shorter, succession often meant rulers started young. To compensate, they were trained from birth to rule.

EXPERIENCE OR AGE: LESSONS FROM PAPUA NEW GUINEA

Far into the highlands of Papua New Guinea, the chief was explaining how he governed the village. I asked him who would succeed him. He stroked his beard for a moment and said:

> Well of course, the village will vote. The whole village will decide. And then they will elect my son to lead them. He is the only person they can elect. From the day he was born, he has been witness to all the arguments I have settled in the village. We have no paper and no records, so he is our living record of what has been agreed. And because he has seen me work all these years, he knows what to do and how to behave; he knows how to handle all the characters in the village and he knows how to deal with neighbouring village chiefs as well. If anyone knows how to avoid another village war, he is the one.

The chief had shown how democracy and the hereditary principle can exist together. He also showed why experience matters even more than age.

Why this myth matters

This myth contains three big traps.

Loss of leadership talent

If we believe in age over youth, then we exclude the bulk of the population from the leadership talent pool. We also make the fatal mistake of thinking that you only lead when you reach the top of the organization.

In practice, if you want good leaders at the top of an organization, then you need a strong pipeline of leaders lower down. Leaders are needed at every level. Looked at through this prism, there is no trade-off between age and experience. You can lead regardless of your age or experience.

Confusing leadership and position

The battle between age and experience applies to seniority and to position, but not to leadership. Being a CEO does not make you a leader; having a junior management title does not stop you leading and making a difference. Leadership is about what you do, not what your title is.

Confusing experience with learning

There are people who are in their fifties and who have worked for 30 years, but only have one year of experience repeated 30 times. This can be useful in technical experts; a plumber or a surgeon who has repeated a procedure countless times should be good at it. But if leaders really need experience, then that requires that leaders:

- are exposed to a wide variety of experiences, so that they are not repeating the same year of experience 30 times;

- learn from their experience; having experience is different to learning from it.

Lessons for leaders

Age is not a barrier to leadership. The earlier you start, the more experience you gain and the more proficient you will become. So the first challenge for any leader is to get the right experience. The 'right' experience is laid out in Myth 22; you need a mix of rational, emotional and political skills. The precise mix of skills depends on your role and seniority, but the most important skill is leadership. You can learn this by doing it at any level and in more or less any role. A leader is someone who takes people where they would not have got by themselves; set that as your challenge and you will hone your leadership skills fast.

The second challenge for leaders is to learn from their experience. It is easy to keep on repeating an exercise and never really learning or improving. Many people learn how to swim adequately and then never improve; they stick with what works for them, even if it is not very good. A leader has to keep on growing and developing. There is no such thing as 'good enough' for a leader, because improvement is always possible.

There is a very simple method of learning from everyday experience. After each key event, which might be a meeting, presentation or conversation, ask yourself two questions: WWW and EBI.

WWW

What Went Well? Most of us are very poor at learning from success. We learn vividly from the failures of others and ourselves but we take success for granted. But success is not natural or easy. Events are always conspiring to make things worse. Colleagues let us down, competition makes life hard, governments get in the way, key staff leave and random events happen. When something works well, pause for a moment and ask yourself what you did to make that happen. Catch yourself succeeding and then make it a habit. Even when things have gone awry, you may have done something to avert an even greater setback. Asking what went well is not just about making yourself feel good, although that helps. It is about discovering your leadership success formula and then applying it regularly.

EBI

Avoid WWW's evil twin: What Went Wrong? That is a recipe for misery. Ask yourself a more productive question: Even Better If... (EBI). However well or poorly an event went, there is always something you could do better.

The WWW and EBI habit can be applied in a few seconds as you walk down the corridor; you can use it to review the day or week as you travel back from work. It is also a very good discipline to use with your team to review events in the day. It creates the learning habit and accelerates team and personal improvement.

Conclusion

The ability to learn is more important than years spent in role. This makes the myth important and dangerous because many leaders have one successful experience and then become prisoners of that one success. They do not move on. Unsuccessful leaders do not learn from experience; successful leaders learn most from experience. So you need experience, but you have to learn from it. Three unicorns.

Endnotes

1 Spencer E Ante and Joann S Lublin (2012) Young CEOs: are they up to the job? *Wall Street Journal* [online] http://www.wsj.com/articles/SB1000142405297020 33158045772071310635011196.

2 Vivek Wadhwa and the Kauffman Foundation, reported in the *Wall Street Journal* article above.

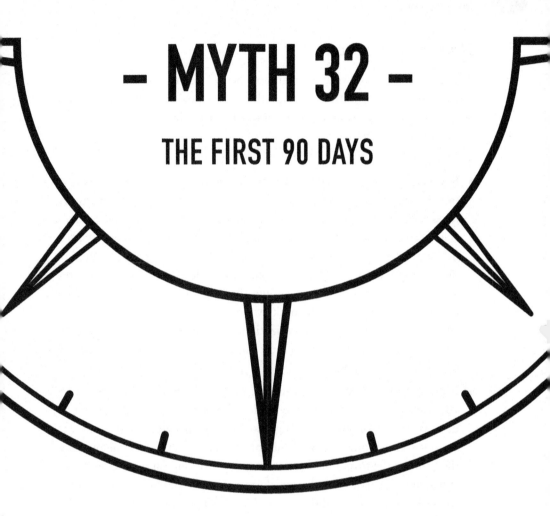

– MYTH 32 –

THE FIRST 90 DAYS

Starting a revolution is risky, and many revolutions eat their own children.

The nature of the myth

This myth states that the first 90 days in role are the make or break time for a new leader. At the end of the first 90 days (or 100 days, as you wish), everyone will have made their mind up about you. At its simplest it is a call to action. The challenge is that every adviser has a different idea about what action you have to take in those first 90 days. The two extremes can be characterized as follows.

Start the revolution

The first 90 days are your honeymoon period where you have the most freedom to act. Opposition to you will not yet have crystalized, and most people will want to make a good impression with the new boss. So this is when you have to act.

The revolution should have two main components:

- **Reorganize.** In theory, reorganizations are about improving the organization. But as you watch the carousel turn from customer focus, to functions, to geography and back again you realize that it is not moving forwards, it is just moving round. But reorganizing helps in two ways, especially for a new manager. First, it is a way of gaining control. Once you have fired or moved aside a few people and promoted people you trust, you have the team you want and you have shown that you are prepared to use your power. Troublemakers will think twice about making trouble. Second, you send a message to the organization about what is going to be important. That message should back up the second part of the revolution: a new strategy or vision.

- **A new vision or strategy.** The idea of the first 90 days is that the longer you leave things as they are, the harder they are to change. In the first 90 days, people are expecting change, so this is your golden opportunity to set a new direction. This works if you already understand enough about the team or the firm, but if you are simply working on instinct and past experience, it carries the obvious danger that you might be wrong. What worked in the past in a different context is not guaranteed to work today in a new context. Sometimes it pays to prepare.

Gain acceptance

This more modest version of the first 90 days is about embedding yourself into the firm and laying the foundations for future success. The main components of this are:

- Meeting all the key stakeholders inside and outside the firm, and understanding their motivations and agendas.
- Meeting regular staff and customers to get a better feel of what is really happening in the operations and market place of the firm.
- Reviewing and thoroughly understanding the strategy, finances and capabilities of the firm: people, technology and operations.

There is good reason to follow the more modest 90-day agenda. Starting a revolution is risky, and many revolutions eat their own children. Your revolution may lead to the Promised Land, or it may lead to the desert. Or it may simply fail to take off if you have not understood the politics and power properly. This means it makes sense to prepare for the revolution before launching it.

You can unite the two extreme approaches to the first 90 days. Here is how: spend the first 89 days gaining acceptance, understanding the business and laying the foundations for your revolution. Launch your revolution on day 90, when you are confident of success.

Why this myth matters

Clearly the first 90 days are important. But that is like saying leadership is important: it gives us no clue about what we should be doing.

In practice, many new leaders find themselves swamped. There is a deluge of day-to-day noise to deal with: crises, routine administration, e-mails, meetings, reviews and reports. Even finding out who is who and how the expenses system works takes time and diverts effort. And that is the real message of the first 90 days myth: don't let yourself drown in the noise of the day to day. You have to rise above the noise and develop a clear path forwards. If you are only dealing with the noise, then you will be managing but you will not be leading. You will not be taking people where they would not have got by themselves.

The message from this myth is clear: rise above the noise. Avoid getting caught in the swamp of the day to day and build your vision for the future.

Lessons for leaders

Here are three alternative perspectives on the first 90 days challenge.

The first 90 days, or the previous 90 days?

Generals believe that most battles are won or lost before the first shot is fired. One side is better prepared, with more resources and is in the right position. The same is true of new leaders: your fate may be sealed before you arrive.

This means you have to ensure you are set up for success before you take up your new role. Before you agree to a new role, your bargaining power is at maximum. Once you have accepted your new role, all your bargaining power evaporates. The previous 90 days are vital, and some of the keys to success include asking:

- Is this a firm which is going to succeed? Success is far easier in a growing firm than one which is retrenching. Is the firm in a growing market with a good competitive position? Do your homework.

- Does the role suit me? Is this the sort of challenge I can address, and is it the sort of culture in which I can thrive? Does the firm have the sorts of values I am comfortable with?

- Will I have the right resources? What are the capabilities of the team? Will I have sufficient budget? Will I have any sponsors who can help me and support me?

The first 90 days or the first 90 milliseconds?

First impressions matter. Research shows that we draw inferences about people after less than one second.[1] The same research shows that we become more confident about our impressions the longer we are exposed to someone, although confirmation bias means we tend to reinforce our first impression.

Leaders can put this to their advantage. If people will judge you by how you look and behave, then project the image you want them to see. Leadership is, in many ways, live performance art in which you act out the best of who you are. That takes continued practice and constant effort.

Make sure you act the part you want to be.

Back to basics: the art of taking control

As a leader, you have to take control. You know you are in control when the following three conditions are in place:

- **Idea.** You need a clear idea of how you will make a difference. This is your vision or strategy. Are you pushing your agenda, or simply following the agenda you inherited, with a couple of tweaks?

- **People.** You need the right team to deliver your idea. The team you inherited may or may not be the right one for the future. You also need the right network of support across and beyond the firm.

- **Money.** Any vision needs budget. Ideally, make sure you have this before you accept the role. The longer you stay in role the more you will be implied to have accepted the budget, agenda and team you inherited.

The first 90 days clearly matter for a leader. But for a good leader, every day matters and every minute matters.

Conclusion

There is nothing magical about the first 90 days. Of course the first 90 days matter (so no myth and no unicorns), but every day and every minute and the 90 days before you take up post also matter. So that nudges the first 90 days back into the land of myth, or more accurately into the land of a nice money-earning fad for gurus, coaches and advisers. Three unicorns.

Endnote

1 J Willis and A Todorov (2006) First impressions: making up your mind after a 100 ms exposure to a face, *Psychological Science*, **17**, pp 592–98.

– MYTH 33 –

YOU HAVE TO MANAGE BEFORE YOU CAN LEAD

The hierarchy in many firms resembles a Ponzi scheme.

The nature of the myth

Most firms operate as a pyramid. At the top there are a few senior executives who may or may not be leading. At the bottom are myriad workers actually making things happen. In between there are managers of varying seniority. It is no longer necessary to start at the very bottom before you get to the top. The journey from postroom to boardroom is rarely travelled, if only because a lifetime career is becoming as rare as hen's teeth.

The pyramid principle is epitomized by professional services firms which all operate on the basis of grinders, minders and finders. You start with the firm as a young graduate doing hard grunt work, or grinding. If you do that well enough, you may become a minder. Then your job is to manage the work of the grinders, ensuring quality and timely delivery on budget. If you do that well you become an exalted finder; your job is to manage client relationships and bring in the revenues. In other words, the apex of the professional services career is often to become a salesperson, although they always refer to themselves as partners.

Entrenched in the pyramid principle is the idea that you can only become a leader if you have been a manager first. The logic is that only when you have served your time will you really understand the nature of the business and be able to deliver to clients.

If you look at the classic corporate career, this is reality and not a myth; you have to manage before you can lead.

If you look at any entrepreneur, it clear that it is myth, not reality; you can lead long before you manage. Many of the world's top billionaires had no management experience, but that did not stop them from changing the world and making a fortune. Mark Zuckerberg, Bill Gates and Sergey Brin all lacked any management experience, but that did not stop them setting up Facebook, Microsoft and Google. They did not need management experience themselves, because they could hire the best management talent that stock options could buy.

You do not have to manage before you lead, because leadership and management are different skills. Success at one level does not mean that you will succeed at the next level. In professional services, minding (managing projects) is fundamentally different from finding (managing client relationships and selling work).

Nor is leadership related to your title; you can lead at any level of the firm.

Why this myth matters

The myth is a useful way of keeping junior people in their place. The implicit promise is that if you work hard and pay your dues you may eventually be admitted to the club of privilege at the top of the firm. Inevitably, this is a promise which can be kept for the few, not the many. But the 'manage then lead' myth is dangerous.

Loss of talent

Not all leaders are good managers; they are very different sorts of role. There is no reason that someone with deep expertise in managing the supply chain, or dealing with customers, or running IT projects can become a leader who changes the direction of the whole firm. In professional services, there is no reason why someone who is good at managing projects should be good at managing client relationships. The result is that people who could be very good in leadership roles never get there, because they are not good enough as managers.

Promotion of the wrong people

Not only do some good leaders never get discovered, but not all good managers are good leaders. In professional services, not all minders (managers) can become good finders (sales and client relations). The skills required are simply different.

Valuing the wrong things: wrong incentives

The hierarchy in many firms resembles a Ponzi scheme, in which a disproportionate amount of the rewards go to the people at the top of the pyramid. But seniority is not the same as value. Great sales people and traders can generate huge value for the firm. These people are fortunate because their contribution is visible and quantifiable. Other technical experts, in research, logistics, IT or operations are less fortunate. They may also be delivering huge value, but it is harder to isolate individual contributions and to attach a monetary value to them. But the message from the hierarchy is clear: technical skills are valued less than general management skills.

Lessons for leaders

There is a difference between leadership and career management. You have a choice to make between the two.

Career management

This requires that you follow the development steps of most firms. You have to keep on learning new sets of skills at each level. You do not need to lead; you need to manage very well. This is hard work to sustain over decades of a career, and means that survival is success. The people who reach the top are the ones who have the resilience to stay the course and the ability to avoid major career disasters. Taking large risks is rarely good for career survival.

Leadership

This is about taking people where they would not have got by themselves. It means you can be leading from the very start of your career. You may be leading in a smaller area when you start out, but you can still make a difference. By definition, leaders have to take risks and challenge the way things are if they are to take people where they would not have got by themselves. If you have never failed, you have never taken enough risk. By definition, not all risks can succeed. This means that leaders accelerate their careers: they succeed fast or they fail fast. In practice, all leaders are serial failures, but they have the resilience to pick themselves up and try again.

In reality, it is not a binary choice between leadership and career management. Even the most dedicated career manager will occasionally step up and take the lead; even the most ambitious leader will have to stabilize their career and their firm from time to time. Career managers will experience career as a noun; leaders experience career as a verb. Both choices are legitimate: you choose.

Conclusion

The myth is both widespread and damaging: all firms operate on the basis of this myth. At first glance it deserves five unicorns, but two unicorns go missing. One unicorn goes missing because the myth (and the unicorn) is completely ignored by entrepreneurs who just start leading anyway. The other unicorn goes missing because although the myth is damaging, it is not fatal to firms. They may lose future leaders who are not good managers, but that does not matter. There are enough good managers who can become leaders, which means that firms can have their cake and eat it in terms of leadership and management. Three unicorns.

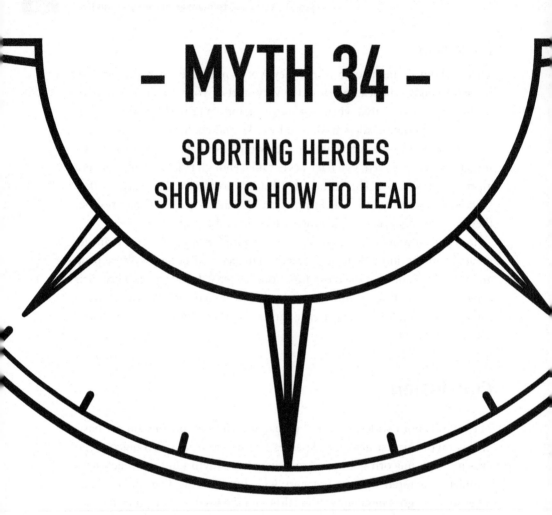

– MYTH 34 –

SPORTING HEROES SHOW US HOW TO LEAD

Unlike athletics, the leadership race never ends.

The nature of the myth

The centre point of most leadership conferences is the keynote speech. Frequently, this is given by a top sports personality, or perhaps by an explorer with tales to tell. The clear implication is that we can learn about leadership from people who have won plenty of gold medals.

But are sporting heroes good leadership role models? Table 34.1 shows a comparison of what it takes to win an individual sporting title and what it takes to lead well.

Table 34.1 What it takes to win as an individual and what it takes to lead

Individual sporting success	Leadership success
Work for own success; no followers	Lead others to success
Clearly defined goal	Multiple, conflicting goals: ambiguity
Clear rules of the game	Make your own rules
Compete for own benefit	Lead for benefit of others
Known competition	Multiple stakeholders, trade-offs
99% training; 1% competing	99% doing; 1% training

Sporting success and leadership success are completely different, as the table shows. At its simplest, most sports people are not leading because they have no followers.

One argument for listening to these speakers is that they are motivational. It is clear that you have to be highly motivated to win a gold medal at the Olympics. But it is not the same sort of motivation you need to be a leader. Athletes are working for themselves towards a clear and finite goal: if they win, then they get the gold medal and the glory. The winner takes all, which is far removed from the experience of corporate life. Leaders are not just working for themselves, and their goals are rarely clear or finite. They are normally working with an organization and there is no gold medal; success is shared and is merely a stepping stone towards the next goal. It is rare for a leader to be able to declare victory and to finish the leadership race. Unlike athletics, the leadership race never ends.

It appears that there is very little of practical use that leaders can learn from sports people. If you ask anyone who has attended one of these speeches what they remember from it several months later, you will normally get a vague response. Often the speech will be warmly received, but what is actually remembered is normally an anecdote or a choice phrase or stunning fact. In the spirit of the dog that didn't bark, notice what is missing: any insight or practical help on how to be a better leader is marked mainly by its absence.

Why this myth matters

Elliot Carver, the mad media mogul in the James Bond film *Tomorrow Never Dies*, makes a short speech recounting what he learned when he started out in the media: 'The key to a great story is not who, or what, or when, but why.'[1] This is a huge lesson for leaders: by far the most interesting question is why. When the unexpected happens or someone says something odd, always remember to ask why it happened or why they said that.

The question we should ask about sporting heroes making keynote speeches is not 'What can we learn from them?' We should ask '*Why* are they so much in demand, especially as they appear to be poor leadership role models?'

There are powerful reasons for having an interesting, and preferably famous, keynote speaker address your annual leadership conference.

Most conferences are boring. Sports heroes bring a touch of glamour to the conference, and help attendees enjoy the event and engage with it. It is better to have engaged delegates than bored ones.

You can learn from anyone. Sports heroes may not be leaders, but leaders can still learn from them if they want to. To learn, you have to listen critically. The lessons you draw may not be the ones the speaker intends you to draw, but that is beside the point; your challenge is to use every opportunity to learn. By opening another window on reality, sports people offer you an alternative perspective. What you choose to learn is up to you.

Sporting heroes provide powerful insight. The insight is not about leadership; it is about yourself and the nature of success. Sports people are highly driven and make huge sacrifices to succeed. They provide a call to arms for those who want to succeed. They also make the choice clear: success is hard work, and if you want a balanced life then there are other ways of living.

Sports heroes, or other celebrities, are a very good way of keeping the boss happy. If the boss is able to meet the celebrity, then they will be able to dine out for weeks on the story: with each re-telling they will become ever more intimate friends with the celebrity. If you want a happy boss, hire a celebrity speaker they want to meet.

Lessons for leaders

Success is hard work

This lesson carries across from sports to leadership. Sports people can normally tell tales of the sacrifices they have had to make and the setbacks they have faced on the way to success. The same is true of leadership. We may all want to win, but between wanting and doing there is a huge gap to be bridged. The challenge that sports people implicitly ask is: 'Are you prepared to make the sacrifices required to lead and succeed?' A legitimate answer is to seek a fulfilling life which is not about chasing someone else's definition of success. Make your decision a deliberate decision, not an accidental default.

You can learn from anyone and any situation

It is easy to treat sports heroes as pure entertainment. If that is what you want, that is what you get. But leaders can learn from any situation, even from watching a James Bond movie. The chance to learn is always there, especially if we know what we are looking for.

Listen critically

Most of us are poor at listening, even when we learn to shut up: we may hear but we do not understand. If we want to understand, we have to master the art of critical listening. An easy way of doing this is to think about what you expect to hear before a presentation starts. This will enable you to accept or reject ideas more critically than if you simply listen with an open mind.

CRITICAL LISTENING: THE ART OF LOOKING SMART

Five partners shared one room. This meant they all knew what was happening with the firm all the time. Four of them were very bright. And then there was Mark, who sputtered like a 10-watt lightbulb. But all the staff loved him and rated him as the smartest partner, much to the irritation of the other four.

One day a partner saw Mark scribbling notes furiously to himself. When asked what he was doing he explained:

My team is coming to present to me. This is their test to see if I am any good. So I am making some notes to prepare. I always note three things in advance of a presentation:

- My point of view on the topic: this means I am not filled with their brilliance, but can challenge them where I need to.

- What I expect them to cover: this lets me spot the invisible. I can see if they have missed anything.

- At least one topic where I can give them some coaching and support: this means they value my input rather than seeing it as a challenge.

The other partner looked shell shocked. He realized why Mark always looked so smart. Listening openly is fine for social discourse, which is a journey of discovery. But critical listening means listening with prejudice and with an agenda.

A good way of thinking critically is to follow Mark's advice: make notes on your viewpoint and what you expect to be covered before you hear someone speak and before you read a document (even this book). It will make you a more demanding and more insightful thinker and reader.

Conclusion

Sports people are not leadership role models. But the myth does not get a full five unicorns because sports people can be inspirational, and in practice you can learn from anyone and any situation: even from sports people. What you choose to learn and what they attempt to teach may be completely different. Four unicorns.

Endnote

1 IMDB, Quotes for Elliot Carver [online] http://www.imdb.com/character/ch0000305/quotes.

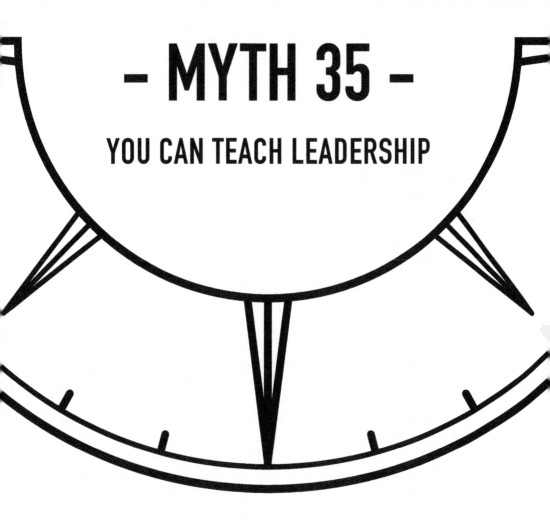

– MYTH 35 –

YOU CAN TEACH LEADERSHIP

Leadership cannot be taught, but you can learn it.

The nature of the myth

If we can all learn to lead, then it should be possible to teach people how to lead. There are endless leadership courses and books which claim to be able to teach you how to lead. The fact that people offer these courses and people buy them indicates that people believe leadership can be taught. So at first glance, teaching leadership appears to be reality, not myth.

But we should pause before writing off the myth.

It is clear that you cannot read a book on leadership and become a leader by page 278. Equally, the two-day leadership course will not turn you instantly into a leader. If you can be taught leadership, it is neither easy nor instant.

As an exercise, I ask groups how they have learned to lead. I let them choose two main ways of learning from six sources. You might try the exercise as well. Choose which two of the following have been most important for you in learning about leadership:

- books;
- courses;
- peers (inside and outside work);
- role models (inside and outside work);
- bosses (good and bad lessons);
- personal experience.

Virtually no one chooses books or courses. That could be bad news for an author who runs courses on leadership. Everyone chooses some combination of personal and observed experience. This makes perfect sense. We see someone do something well, and we try to copy it. We see another person implode spectacularly and we make a note not to repeat that particular mistake. We see what works in practice and in our context. We create our own unique formula for success, based on how we work and where we work.

The problem with discovering leadership this way is that it is a random walk: bump into good bosses and experiences and you accelerate your career. Poor bosses and experiences lead you straight into a dead end. You have to convert your random walk of experience into a structured journey of discovery. This is where books and courses can help: they help you make sense of the nonsense you encounter and to structure your journey of success.

Why this myth matters

This myth matters for two reasons, because it shows:

- how organizations should develop leaders;
- why most leadership training is doomed to fail.

How organizations should develop leaders

The best leadership organizations build their leadership programmes around how people actually learn: from experience. That means they will structure your leadership journey for you. The Royal Marine Commandos put aspiring officers through a gruelling 18-month training programme; the best firms put new graduates through a series of experiences as well as training to develop them.

Inevitably, the best firms also select rigorously, but they are all selecting on different criteria. What it takes to succeed in the Royal Marines, versus the Civil Service, versus investment banking or the creative arts are completely different: attitudes to risk, courage, compliance and creativity are different in each. Although they select on different criteria, they all recognize that managing the leadership journey involves developing and testing people with a range of relevant experiences.

Why most leadership training is doomed to fail

Look back at the list of sources of learning about leadership: very few people claim to have learned about leadership from training courses. The symptom of this is the frequency with which people find themselves unable to attend a training course (unless it is in a nice location away from the office) and the frequency with which training is one of the first items to be cut in the annual budget squeeze. There are three reasons why leadership training is not valued:

- Going on any form of leadership training is often perceived as a sign of weakness. Going on a course to learn a technical skill such as IT, or finance is not weak. Going on a course to learn about motivating people implies that you are no good at motivating people.

- Leadership courses are generic solutions to specific challenges. The skills you need and how you deploy them depend on your context. Working out how to adapt universal lessons to your needs is hard in theory and even harder in practice.

- There is a time lag between learning and doing. Managers rightly want learning which helps them now; they need to try new ideas while they are still fresh in the mind. The half life of any learning is very short, unless it is constantly tested and put into practice.

None of these challenges are about the quality of the course. Some courses are excellent, others less so. These are all structural challenges which are inherent to the nature of all formal courses. The best programmes attempt to address these challenges, but it is as thankless as pushing water uphill.

Lessons for leaders

Leadership cannot be taught, but you can learn it. This is because your path to leadership is a journey of discovery. You have to discover what works for you in your context: there is no universal formula for success. And as your context will keep on changing, you must keep on learning throughout your career. The people who stop learning are the ones who get marooned in their career.

Ultimately, the only person who can navigate the leadership journey is you. You have to make sure that you get the right experiences, projects, assignments and bosses to build your career.

Your challenge is to make sure that your journey is not a random walk, and that you do not get lost in all the noise and nonsense you encounter day to day. That is where books and courses come in: they can help you step back and see more clearly where you need to go and what you need to do. Hopefully this book is your map: it shows you what your options are, where some of the pitfalls are and lets you decide where you want to go on your leadership journey.

Conclusion

In its narrow sense, this myth deserves five unicorns. You cannot read a textbook and become a leader. But you can learn to lead, and firms can structure experiences and support to help you learn. Given you cannot be taught leadership but you can learn it, this deserves three slightly confused unicorns.

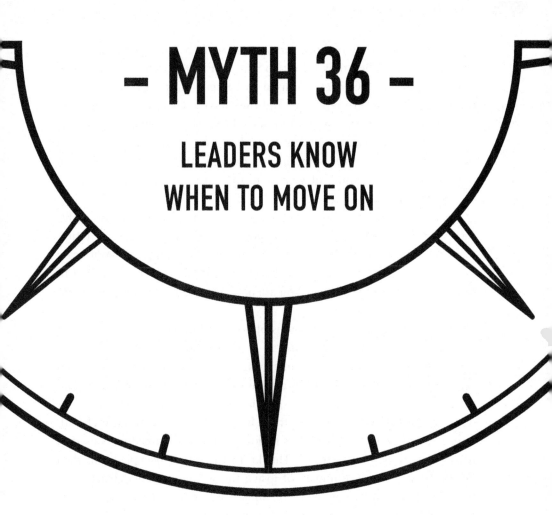

– MYTH 36 –

LEADERS KNOW
WHEN TO MOVE ON

*Leaders live in a gilded cage where few people dare to challenge
them, and many people choose to flatter them.*

The nature of the myth

Most firms pay attention to succession planning. Firms need a pipeline of
talent at all levels to provide the leaders of the future, and to provide cover
for the present. A deep reservoir of talent is insurance against losing key
executives unexpectedly.

Leaders pay lip service to the idea of succession planning. They know it
is good for the firm; they are less enamoured of the idea that they should
make themselves redundant. What is good for the firm is not always so good
for the individual.

If you really want to both annoy and scare a CEO, ask what they are going to do when they retire. To many CEOs, retirement is a sort of living death. As CEO, they are used to being a master of the universe; the world revolves around them and they have a clear sense of purpose and relevance. They may work hard, but the work gives structure to their lives, and the firm creates a society for them. When they retire, they lose everything: they lose the structure of the day, the society of the firm, the purpose and meaning of work and they are no longer the centre of the world.

Logically, leaders may see the need for succession planning. Emotionally, they want to avoid it for as long as possible. To avoid the fate of retirement death they often seek a halfway house where they can pontificate on committees, commissions and charity boards. This is often referred to dismissively as 'going reactive': you are no longer pushing your agenda, but reacting to those of others.

Leaders are right to be suspicious of downshifting. Evidence shows that retirement is bad for your health. A May 2013 report published by the London-based Institute of Economic Affairs found that retirement increased the chances of suffering from depression by 40 per cent, while it increased the probability of having at least one diagnosed physical ailment by about 60 per cent.[1] There is a familiar pattern. In the first year of retirement, health improves as the stress of the job is removed; new-found freedom is used to fulfil life dreams such as travel. This keeps the retiree occupied. But then health deteriorates. The impact of losing the social and daily structure of work hits home. Watching television aimlessly from day to day is not great for health. Depression and a serious ailment normally strike within six years of retirement.[2]

Finally, leaders want to stay in post because they start to believe they really are indispensable to the fate of the firm. Leaders live in a gilded cage where few people dare to challenge them, and many people choose to flatter them. If things go well, that proves to the leader that they are doing a great job. When things go wrong, it is even stronger proof that the boss is indispensable: setbacks are clear evidence that the rest of the team are not up to their current jobs, let alone the top job.

Quietly, many leaders are happy with poor succession. If the firm struggles after the CEO departs, that is proof positive (at least to the departed CEO) that they really were the key to success, and that no one else could possibly emulate them. In reality, a failure of the new CEO is the failure of the old CEO in not securing the succession properly.

Why this myth matters

It is very hard to get rid of a CEO, especially in countries where the governance allows for the concentration of powers in the hands of the CEO. When the CEO is also the president and chair of the board, you have a real problem. There is no one to challenge the CEO, especially as the CEO is able to fill the board with friends and allies. These friends are often other CEOs or chairs who all appoint each other to each other's boards. They create a CEO self-preservation society which is good for them, not for the firm.

Even with proper governance in place, most boards are deeply risk averse. Dumping a CEO and finding a new one is the riskiest thing a board can do, and it causes a lot of work. Non-executives have limited appetite for work or risk. This means that they will only move when there is a real crisis and when the CEO is obviously failing: that is too late.

Lessons for leaders

Here are five things you can do to deal with the problem of moving on. All good actors and actresses know how to time their entrances and their exits. Leaders need to do the same.

Visit a graveyard

It is full of executives who thought they were indispensable. Earlier ages were more robust about death than we are. Memento mori were paintings or artefacts which sent out a simple message: 'Remember you must die'. They were popular all the way from the Middle Ages to the Victorian era. They are reminders of how precious and fleeting life is: we have to make the most of every moment.

Prepare for your next move

Leadership is a journey, even when you are the CEO. Work out how you will either sustain or replace what you value about what you do currently: the social network, the structure to the day, the sense of meaning and purpose. These things are far more valuable than your next long-term bonus payment. If you are a CEO you probably have enough money to pay the rent. But money cannot buy you the things that become increasingly important: networks, structure and meaning. These things cannot be developed overnight. You need to start building them at least a few years ahead.

Pay attention to governance

Most CEOs regard the non-executive board as a nuisance: they are a necessary evil which has to be managed. But the governance structure is there for good reason. It is a vital check and balance for the firm and its shareholders. It should be the source of constructive challenge for the CEO. A weak board makes for an easy life for the CEO; a strong board can help deliver strong performance. The CEO should prefer performance to an easy life.

Set yourself term limits

Death concentrates the mind, so does retirement or the prospect of moving on to another role. If you know you have a 'sell by' date stamped on your forehead, then that forces you to think about how you will make a difference in the time available. It creates a sense of urgency and purpose, and does not allow you to drift on endlessly. The US presidency was informally subject to the two-term rule from the time of George Washington, and this was formally acknowledged in the 22nd amendment to the constitution after FDR's long stint as president. The contrast with other nations where dictators and demagogues cling on to power for life shows the wisdom of clear term limits.

Plan your succession

When Isaac Newton was being acclaimed for his achievements, he modestly replied: 'If I have seen further, it is by standing on the shoulders of giants.'[3] He knew that his success was built on the work of all the scientists who preceded him. This is your opportunity to be the giant on whose shoulders the next leader can stand, and perhaps achieve even greater things. The success of your successor is also your success. Help them on the path to greatness.

Conclusion

This myth is both pervasive and dangerous. It is pervasive because leaders do not know when to move on: they normally have to be nudged or kicked. And it is dangerous because leaders who stay too long damage the firm and ultimately themselves by not knowing what they will do next. Five unicorns.

Endnotes

1   Gabriel H Sahlgren (2013) IEA discussion paper no 46: Work Longer, Live Healthier, Institute of Economic Affairs [online] https://iea.org.uk/wp-content/uploads/2016/07/Work%20Longer,%20Live_Healthier.pdf.

2   DFI (2013) Can retirement kill you? [online] http://defenceforumindia.com/forum/threads/can-retirement-kill-you.57285/.

3   Wikiquote, Sir Isaac Newton [online] https://en.wikiquote.org/wiki/Isaac_Newton.

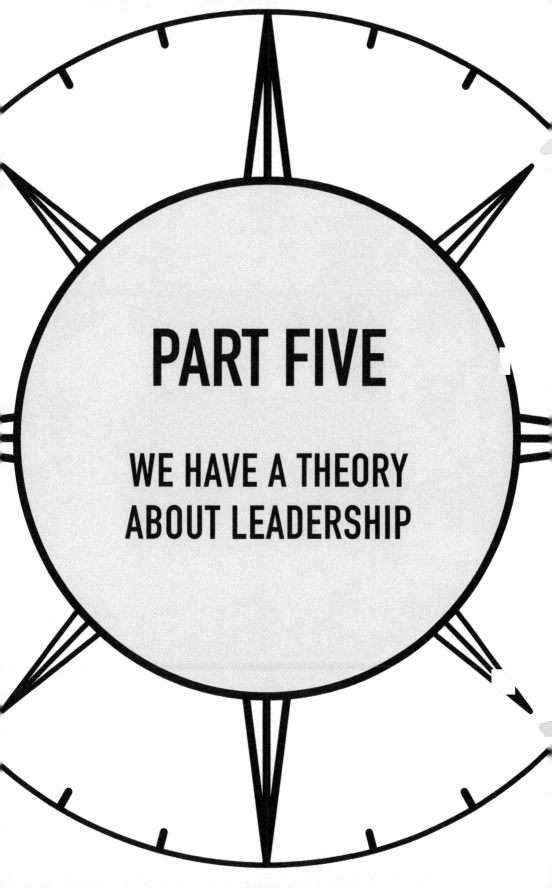

PART FIVE

WE HAVE A THEORY ABOUT LEADERSHIP

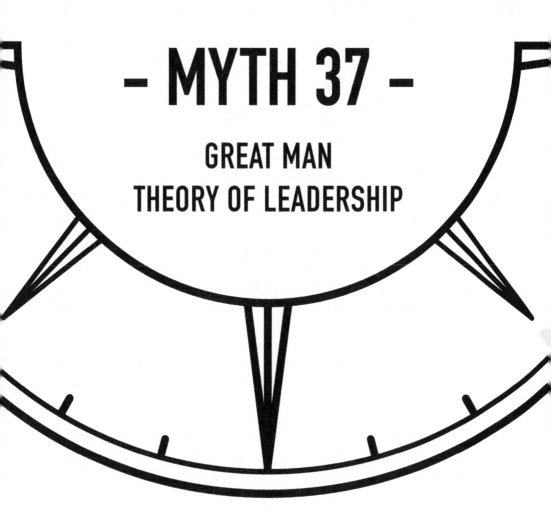

– MYTH 37 –

GREAT MAN
THEORY OF LEADERSHIP

*The world changes so fast that most firms fail
to survive much longer than one generation.*

Nature of the myth

This theory has its origins in the 19th-century belief that 'the history of the
world is but the biography of great men'.[1] This made for gripping history:
it was the history of heroes achieving great things and changing the course
of mankind. It was the sort of history which could inspire generations of
schoolchildren.

The Great Man theory of history was supported by philosophy. Thomas
Hobbes' solution to the problem of life being 'solitary, poor, nasty, brutish,

and short' was that society needed a Leviathan[2]: this is a powerful leader who can create an ordered society. This was echoed later by Nietzsche, who called for an Übermensch[3] (overman – great leader) who would risk all to save humanity. It was a philosophy admired by Adolf Hitler.

There was just one small problem with this approach to history: it was wrong. The counter argument, put by Herbert Spencer, was that great men do not make society; society makes the man: 'Before the Great Man can remake his society, his society must make him.'[4] This put the primacy of economics, society and technology at the heart of history. Karl Marx made an early attempt to explain history through the force of economics and society. Since then, the practice of history has become more professional and the deep forces of economics and society have become better, if imperfectly, understood.

The Great Man theory of history lives on as the Great Man theory of leadership. The idea is that the leader changes the destiny of a business through sheer will of leadership. As evidence for the Great Man theory of leadership we have the billionaire entrepreneurs of today: we owe Microsoft, Google, Apple, Facebook and other breakthrough firms to the driving force of their founders. And most of the great firms of today, from Ford to Sony to Toyota, were founded by great visionaries who conjured their businesses out of the thin air of imagination and courage.

The counter argument is that businesses are shaped by their times. The evidence for this is the survival rate of the top firms. Research from the World Economic Forum shows that firms do not shape their destiny successfully for very long.[5] The life expectancy of a Fortune 500-sized firm is 40 to 50 years. In just 15 years from 1999, over 50 per cent of the firms in the Fortune 500 disappeared from the list. These firms did not change the world: the world changed them.

This still leaves the entrepreneurs who are the celebrity poster pin ups of the business media. They appear to have changed the world. But did they?

Microsoft got its big break when Bill Gates was asked to provide the operating system for IBM's newfangled PC back in 1980.[6] IBM certainly did not see that the money was in the software, not the hardware. But what would have happened if IBM had managed to reach agreement with Digital Research, who were their first target partner? Gates would still have been a brilliant writer of code, but few would have ever heard of him. Instead we would be telling the story of how Digital Research became the owners of desktop operating systems.

Similarly, many people tried to develop a successful search engine. Someone, somewhere, had to find the winning formula: step forward

Larry Page and Sergey Brin. It would be wrong to suggest that they are no different from lottery winners. Unlike lottery winners, these great entrepreneurs have to put in huge amounts of hours, have real talent and take serious risks.

So are the great entrepreneurs people who shape the world, or are they simply products of the time they live in?

If in doubt, turn to Shakespeare. He normally has the answers, and he finds a way of expressing them well. Hamlet says: 'There's a divinity that shapes our ends, Rough-hew them how we will...'[7] This suggests that destiny, in the form of economics, society and technology, shapes the nature of businesses which rise or fall. Leaders are in the business of 'rough-hewing' those ends to make sure their business is the one that makes the most of destiny.

Why this myth matters

The theory matters greatly, because it poses a fundamental question: how much can leaders really change the course of events?

If you believe that leaders do re-shape the future fundamentally, then it can make sense to pay them vast sums of money. If you believe that leaders drift with the tide of history and that half of the Fortune 500 firms will disappear from the list every 15 years, then there is not much point in paying top dollar for your leader.

The Great Man theory also lives on in gender stereotyping. At a girls' school, I asked pupils to imagine an airline pilot, a surgeon and a chief executive. When asked the gender of the people they had imagined, all of them had imagined males in those roles. None of them saw themselves going into those sorts of roles.

Lessons for leaders

Shape the future

The Great Man theory of leadership is useful insofar as it is a call to action. It challenges leaders to shape events rather than be shaped by them. You may not change the destiny of the world, but you can change the destiny of your team. Leaders believe they can control, or at least influence, events; victims believe they are controlled by events.

Build your team

The Great Man theory is dangerous because it leads to the belief in the all-powerful, all-wise leader who knows it all and does it all. The modern world is so complicated and inter-connected, and it is changing so fast, that no leader can know it all and change it all. Leadership is a team sport. That means that forming the team is a key task for any leader.

Stay paranoid

Andy Grove, the founder of Intel, wrote a book called *Only the Paranoid Survive*.[8] It is one of those great books you never need to read, because the message is in the title. It is also the antidote to the Great Man theory. The world changes so fast that most firms fail to survive much longer than one generation. You have to stay paranoid: understand the forces that can shape or destroy your firm and then learn and adapt fast. If you cannot change the world, you have to change yourself and adapt to the world.

Leadership is not just about men

In the 19th century, only men were seen as leaders; poverty, famine and disease were rampant; small boys had to climb inside chimneys to clean them; the average working year was 3,000 hours long.[9] Fortunately, we have made progress since then.

Conclusion

The Great Man theory of leadership is largely discredited and is dangerous to the practice of leadership: you do not need to be great or male to lead, and nations and firms are in trouble when they look for a hero to save them. That should give us five unicorns trampling all over the history books. But only four appear, because there remains a kernel of truth in the myth. Some people do have the 'will to power' and can change the future. They may be the exception that proves the rule, but they are often vital exceptions. Four unicorns.

Endnotes

1 Thomas Carlyle (1840) The hero as divinity, in *On Heroes, Hero-Worship and the Heroic in History*, various editions.

2 Thomas Hobbes (1651) *Leviathan*, Oxford University Press.

3 Nietzsche, F (1885) *Also sprach Zarathustra*, various editions.

4 Herbert Spencer (1896) *The Study of Sociology*, Appleton, p 31.

5 Mark Goodburn (2015) What is the life expectancy of your company? *World Economic Forum* [online] https://www.weforum.org/agenda/2015/01/what-is-the-life-expectancy-of-your-company.

6 This story is told in many places, including here: http://thisdayintechhistory.com/11/06/ibm-signs-a-deal-with-the-devil/.

7 William Shakespeare, *Hamlet*, Act V, Scene II.

8 Andrew Grove (1998) *Only the Paranoid Survive*, Profile Books.

9 Michael Huberman and Chris Minns (2007) The times they are not changin': days and hours of work in Old and New Worlds, 1870–2000, *Explorations in Economic History*, **44** (4), pp 538–67.

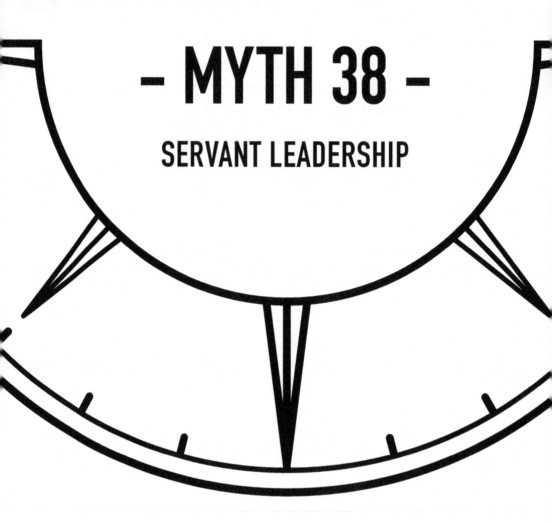

– MYTH 38 –

SERVANT LEADERSHIP

*This management fad was as fashionable as watching your dad (or CEO)
attempting to throw a few shapes on the dance floor.*

The nature of the myth

Traditional leadership involves a leader accumulating and exercising power
over people and other resources. The idea of servant leadership runs in the
opposite direction. The servant leader is not the ruler, but the server. The
servant leader serves in two ways:

- serve the mission;
- serve the organization.

The idea of servant leadership has deep roots:

- *Servus servorum Dei* is the Latin title for the Pope: Servant of the Servants of God.
- 'Ich Dien' is the slightly implausible German motto for the Prince of Wales and means 'I serve'.
- 'Serve to Lead' is the motto of Sandhurst, the officer training centre for the British Army

This myth became fashionable in business circles early in this millennium. It became a staple of business talks, and CEOs often liked to present themselves as a servant leader by inverting the organization pyramid. The traditional organization pyramid looks something like Figure 38.1: there is one person at the top who leads many people at the bottom through various layers of management. That is conventional and simple to understand.

Figure 38.1 Traditional organization pyramid

The servant leader presented the pyramid upside down. The idea was to show that the most important people in the firm are the front-line workers who make things, move things, sell things or deal with customers. The job of management and leadership was simply to support the front-line staff. To make the point even more clearly, sometimes the pyramid would have customers at the top. A simplified version of the upside-down pyramid is shown in Figure 38.2.

Figure 38.2 Upside-down organization pyramid

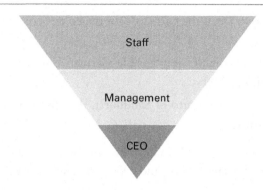

Why this myth matters

The servant leadership involves two linked, but separate myths:

- the leader serves the organization;
- the leader serves the mission.

We will treat each individually.

The leader serves the organization

The upside-down pyramid is trying to convey two important messages: front-line staff are key to success and the mission matters. These ideas are becoming more important as the workforce changes. Staff are becoming more professional and better educated, and they expect to be treated better. Treating them like they are slaves toiling away at the bottom of the pyramid is not motivational. Turning the pyramid upside down was about attempting to change mindsets at all levels:

- show staff that they matter and treat them with respect;
- show managers that their job is to support, not just control;
- show top management that they need to serve the mission, not themselves;
- show everyone that they need to focus more on the customer.

It turned out that this management fad was as fashionable as watching your dad (or CEO) attempting to throw a few shapes on the dance floor. It was not inspirational: it was cringe making. The reason it went wrong is because what the CEO said was different from what the audience heard.

The CEO may or may not have believed his own speech about being less important than the people on the front line. But what the staff heard and saw was this:

- The upside-down pyramid looked like a spinning top out of control: that was an apt metaphor for many firms.

- The entire spinning top seemed to depend on the balance of one person at the bottom of the spinning top: the CEO. That looked more like hubris than humility.

- If the CEO really was so unimportant, then why did he make so much money, and why did he retain so much power in terms of decision making, budgets, resource allocation and rewards and recognition?

The leader serves the mission

Mission-led organizations include some of those that are the most transformational and long-lasting. That is longevity compared to most businesses: only 27 of the original 100 firms in the FTSE 100, which was formed in 1984, are still in the index.[1] The others have all been taken over or overtaken. The oldest business in the world is a hot spring hotel in Japan, called Nishiyama Onsen Keiunkan, which has existed since the year 705.[2] But the Catholic Church is getting on for 2,000 years old: that is longevity. And some of the most transformational organizations have a strong sense of mission: they are not in it just for the money. Leading not-for-profit organizations such as Oxfam or Medecins Sans Frontières make a huge difference. Mission-led firms, like Google in its early days, can be disruptive and transformational. Elite units of the armed forces achieve extraordinary things under extraordinary circumstances: uniformly, they have a strong sense of mission. All these mission-led organizations also have a very strong sense of values.

Clearly, if mission is so important, it makes sense to have a leader who serves the mission. Leaders with a sense of mission can be both visionary and inspiring. They can be a huge force for good or for evil. Not all missions are good missions, as the dictators of the 20th century showed.

Sustaining the sense of mission in both the organization and the leader is hard, especially in today's world. If the average tenure with an employer is five years or less (see Myth 9), then employees will be focused on their own mission of building a career.

Demanding passion and loyalty and then downsizing shows inconsistency between words and actions: staff will believe your actions, not your words. Over time, many mission-driven leaders also go through a transformation:

they start by serving the mission and slowly the mission comes to serve them. The mission becomes a vehicle for promoting themselves and building their profile and prestige. They remain passionate about the mission, but only because it serves them so well. This is a subtle change which their staff notice, and it leads to hubris and eventually to nemesis. My lawyers have advised me not to name the case examples of this.

Lessons for leaders

Always deliver on what you say

That means being very careful about what you say. The latest management fad (like upside-down pyramids) may look and sound great, but check whether it reflects a reality you are willing to create, and whether it is a credible message for your organization.

Avoid fads

They impress no one.

Treat front-line staff well

That is the core message of servant leadership, and it is valid. But there are other ways of respecting and supporting staff besides showing them upside-down pyramids.

Mission is powerful, but...

Ensure consistency between what you say and what you do. Commitment is a two-way process. If you demand commitment from your staff, you have to show that you are committed to them. You can have a deal where they serve the mission for a few years, gain great experience and then move on: if that is the contract, be explicit about it.

Be honest with yourself

Make sure you really are serving the mission and that the mission is not just there to serve you. How much would you be prepared to sacrifice for the mission personally or professionally? Would you give up pay, bonus and promotion for the mission, or is the mission a vehicle for optimizing your pay, bonus and promotion?

Conclusion

The greatest fads and myths are mountains of nonsense built on a kernel of truth. Servant leadership is a classic. While the true servant leaders are notable, honourable and successful, they are the exceptions that prove the rule. This was a fad which deserves to fade into history. It is not as lethal and damaging as some fads, so qualifies for just four unicorns instead of five.

Endnotes

1 Harriman Stock Market Almanac (2015) FTSE 100 Index original share constituents [online] http://stockmarketalmanac.co.uk/2015/02/ftse-100-index-original-share-constituents/.

2 Guinness World Records, Oldest hotel [online] http://www.guinnessworldrecords.com/world-records/oldest-hotel/.

- MYTH 39 -

THE HUMBLE LEADER

Most of us think we are above average, which is statistically
impossible but emotionally inevitable.

The nature of the myth

It is no longer enough for leaders to be visionary, charismatic, inspirational, decisive and motivational. You have to be humble as well. That is a big ask. Superman is perhaps the role model of the humble leader; he had everything, but was humble with it. Clearly, it is time for leaders to emulate Superman: start wearing your underwear outside your trousers.

The idea of the humble leader is a reaction to the Great Man theory of leadership. Casual observation of your own office and of real life shows that most leaders are not charismatic and inspirational great men and women. They are more likely to fit the stereotype of ordinary people achieving extraordinary things. The question is whether ordinary really means humble, and what humble really means.

There is no set and agreed definition of what a humble leader is. Different people project different qualities onto the humble leader, to suit their needs and opinions. Within this diversity, there appear to be three distinct humility themes:

1 humble about self;

2 humble with others;

3 humble in terms of ambition.

Why this myth matters

If the Great Man theory of leadership is largely discredited, then there needs to be an alternative. Humility appears a good candidate because it is pretty much the opposite of being a Great Man. As with all leadership theories, you can find a few leaders who fit your theory. From there it is a small, but spectacularly wrong, leap to claim that you have found the secret of leadership. All that you have proved is that some form of humility works for some leaders in some contexts. Unfortunately, such a nuanced message does not sell books or make for a great conference speech; you have to be bold and offer The Answer, preferably in three easy steps.

No leadership theory stands up to any form of scientific test for long, because every theory can be quickly falsified. There is no universal formula for leadership like $E = mc^2$. But every leadership theory has some value; it opens a new window on reality and invites us to think again about what really works and does not work. In that spirit, it is worth searching the humble leadership theory to see what we can learn.

Lessons for leaders

Humble about self

Research on 69,000 managers' 360-degree feedback shows that leaders either over estimate or underestimate their capabilities: no surprise there.[1] But the leaders who underestimate their capabilities are seen to be better leaders by their teams. Teams engage better with a humble leader than an overbearing one. Teams also rate humble leaders as being more effective. This is a subjective rating: teams rate highly leaders they like.

In practice, this sort of humility is hard to come by. Most of us have a superiority complex. Here are some examples:

- Eighty-seven per cent of Stanford MBA students rated themselves as above average.[2]

- Of 1 million students sitting SAT exams, 85 per cent thought they were above average in ability to get on with others; 25 per cent thought they were in the top 1 per cent.[3]

- Ninety-three per cent of drivers think they have above-average driving skills; even among the modest Swedes, 69 per cent think they are above average.[4]

Now test yourself: do you think you are below or above average in terms of honesty, reliability, hard work, decency and driving ability? Most of us think we are above average, which is statistically impossible but emotionally inevitable.

This aspect of humility can be taken to mean that leaders have to admit to their failings, weaknesses, doubts and shortcomings in public. This is taken to be authentic leadership (see Myth 42) which humanizes leaders and makes them more approachable. This takes humility too far. Leaders are dealers in hope: you have to craft a positive vision of the future for your team. If instead you are always mumbling about your fears, doubts and weaknesses you will not convince your team that you can lead them to a sunny future. They will doubt that you can lead them anywhere.

The benefit of being humble about your own abilities is that it encourages you to learn and grow. It also encourages you to respect the views and talents of other people. It makes you more inclusive on decision making, and more willing to delegate. These are all useful traits for a leader to have.

Humble with others

Humble leaders are better at empowering their teams. Even in China, which is traditionally seen as a very hierarchical society, more humble CEOs create better management engagement and empowerment than those who are less humble.[5]

As ever with these studies, engagement and effectiveness tend to get mixed up. Humility clearly leads to more engaged teams, up to a point. All things being equal, a more engaged team will perform better than a less engaged team. But all things are never equal. There is a downside to humility, and that is lack of ambition.

Humble in terms of ambition

This is the dark side of humility. Humble leaders are less likely to challenge the system, to force change or to build a compelling vision. If you under-appreciate your own talents, and defer to the skills and capabilities of others, you are unlikely to be the revolutionary leader who takes people where they would not have got by themselves. In other words, you are not leading. The humble leader may not be a leader at all, but could be an exceptionally good manager.

Conclusion

As with all myths, it is fantasy built on a sliver of reality. There are undoubtedly real cases of humble leaders succeeding. But the overwhelming evidence points in the opposite direction. If you want to lead, you have to have ambition for your mission; most of us suffer from a superiority complex which is not consistent with humility. Four unicorns for this myth; one is missing in deference to the sliver of reality behind the myth.

Endnotes

1 Jack Zenger and Joseph Folkman (2015) We like leaders who underrate themselves, *Harvard Business Review* (November) [online] https://hbr. org/2015/11/we-like-leaders-who-underrate-themselves.

2 E W Zuckerman and J Jost (2001) What makes you think you're so popular? Self-evaluation maintenance and the subjective side of the 'Friendship Paradox', *Social Psychology Quarterly*, **64** (3) pp 207–23.

3 Mark Alicke, David Dunning and Joachim Krueger (2005) *The Self in Social Judgement*, Psychology Press, pp 85–106.

4 Ola Svenson (1981) Are we all less risky and more skillful than our fellow drivers? *Acta Psychologica*, **47** (2), pp 143–48.

5 Amy Y Ou, Anne S Tsui, Angelo J Kinicki, David A Waldman, Zhixing Xiao and Lynda Jiwen Song (2014) Humble chief executive officers' connections to top management team integration and middle managers' responses, *Administrative Science Quarterly*, **59** (1), pp 34–72.

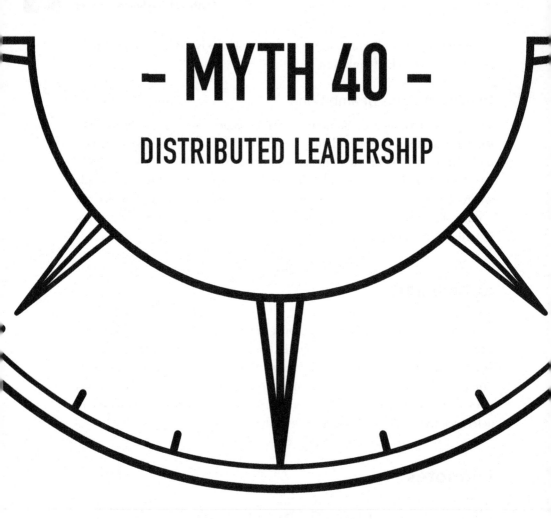

– MYTH 40 –

DISTRIBUTED LEADERSHIP

Delegation is a matter of trust.

The nature of the myth

Distributed leadership is a new reinvention of a very old idea which addresses an eternal problem: how do you lead across a system which is complex and dispersed? In its current format, the idea started in education and has moved out from there.[1] The challenge has existed for millennia. The Roman Empire was large, complex and highly dispersed. They lacked e-mail and phones, which meant that Rome could not keep up with all the minor variations in salt tax receipts in far-off Britain. It also meant that if your man in Judea happened to crucify the wrong person, well… woops. They had no choice: the Romans had to distribute leadership to run their far-flung Empire.

At the heart of the idea is sharing leadership among a group, rather than relying on one person. It is a way of engaging the whole team effectively and optimizing performance. It is an idea of its time in that it kicks back against the traditional idea of the leader being the Great Man or Great Woman. It is also highly relevant in a global context where there is tension between maintaining central control and distributing power to teams around the world. Making global teams work shows just how challenging the idea of distributed leadership is in practice.[2]

The exact nature of the theory depends on who you talk to. Its practical implementation is vague: since the concept is fashionable in schools, any school leader who delegates anything says they have distributed leadership.

Why this myth matters

The myth touches on two vital aspects of leadership: control and delegation. Distributing leadership requires delegation, but the more you delegate the more you face the challenge of control. Put the other way around, if you have a smart way of ensuring control, then you can be more confident of delegating. Understanding the control and delegation trade-off gives more insight into the nature of distributed leadership.

Levers of control

Historically there are four ways in which organizations exert control:

- **Standards and skills.** The medieval guilds were a triumph of standardization. It meant that no matter where you were, you knew what you were buying when you bought a loaf of bread: the weight and ingredients were consistent and predictable. This tradition lives on in the modern crafts of accounting, teaching, dentistry, plumbing and medicine, where independent bodies verify that individuals are qualified to practice.

- **Values.** The East India Company was one of the first truly global firms.[3] It made its fortune by becoming the world's largest drug runner, exporting opium from India to China. It could trust its officials around the world for one reason: they all had the same British public school education, which was largely geared to producing people who could run an empire. They all had the same values and outlook. This is a tradition which still holds true in many global firms. Some show complete home nation bias: all key posts are held by nationals of the home nation. Others build a single set of values: you can be of any race, faith or gender but you have to adhere to the idea of the 'one firm firm'. Diversity of values is not tolerated.

- **Information.** The great conglomerates of the past managed wildly diverse business portfolios, where they had no obvious expertise. What they did very well was to use information to monitor management, and then provide strong incentives for them to perform well. The explosion of data available to leaders today means that it is possible to have more information faster than ever before. Information and trust are usually inversely proportional: high levels of reporting reflect low levels of trust. Very high levels of information allow the leader to micro-manage. They should also allow the leader to delegate more: you can be confident that the data will show you when you need to step back in.

- **Processes.** Process control is obvious on an auto production line. If this is matched with excellent real-time data, it allows front-line operators to take control to the extent that any one of them can halt the entire production line if required. Process control also applies to management. Walter Lingle is an unsung hero of globalization. He globalized Procter & Gamble and its brand management system with a simple insight: if all the successful processes and procedures of Cincinnati HQ could be replicated down to specifying the length and format of the monthly brand report, then you could let each country manage its own brands successfully. Control was vested in the system, backed up by a few international executives who ensured the systems were being applied correctly. In the days before the internet, it was highly practical and successful.[4]

In practice, firms and leaders use a mixture of all control methods.

Delegation

Leaders often find it hard to delegate. Some overt and real reasons for not delegating are shown in Table 40.1.

Ultimately, delegation is a matter of trust. When you delegate a task, you create a dependency: you depend on someone else to deliver for you. Most leaders prefer to be in control than to be dependent. This is where you have to be able to rely on effective control systems to be confident that you can delegate.

Table 40.1 Stated versus real reasons for not delegating

Stated reason for not delegating	Real reason for not delegating
This is too important	I don't trust my team on this one
It is quicker for me to do it	I don't trust my team on this either
Only I have the skills for this one	I don't trust my team to have the talent for this
I am accountable for this	Trust my team? You must be joking
My team is too busy	I will never trust my team

Lessons for leaders

If you are not going to be the lone hero leader, you need to distribute your leadership responsibilities across your team. At its most basic, this is a grand way of saying that you need to delegate.

Building the trust to delegate is partly about building personal trust in each member of your team. You will know what they can and cannot do. But it is also about building the control mechanisms which can give you the confidence to delegate more. If you have the right information and processes, and the team have the right standards, skills and values, it should be easy to delegate to them. If you find it hard to delegate, you can do two things:

- look in the mirror and see if you have a high need for control;
- look at how you can improve the control levers: values, skills and standards, information and process.

Conclusion

The need for distributed leadership has been around for thousands of years. It is not really a theory of leadership: it is a reality of leadership which many leaders struggle with. Zero unicorns.

Endnotes

1 Richard Bolden (2011) Distributed leadership in organizations: a review of theory and research, *International Journal of Management Reviews*, **13** (3), pp 251–69.

2 Jo Owen (2016) *Global Teams*, Pearson/FT.

3 George P Landow (nd) The British East India Company: the company that owned a nation, The Victorian Web [online] http://www.victorianweb.org/history/empire/india/eic.html.

4 Jo Owen (2016) *Global Teams*, Pearson/FT.

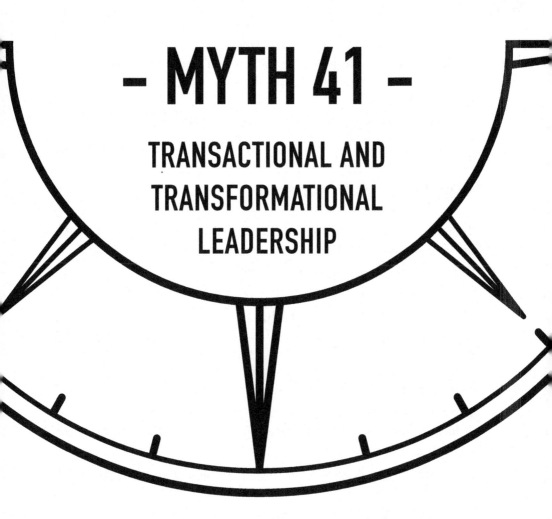

– MYTH 41 –

TRANSACTIONAL AND TRANSFORMATIONAL LEADERSHIP

Your job is to master leadership, not to master leadership theory.

The nature of the myth

These are two linked myths, so you get two myths for the price of one. Bargain time. To add to the bargain, this myth will also refer to five other myths and theories of leadership. There is a reason for this: transactional and transformational leadership theories reflect a much wider debate about the nature of leadership.

These myths have their origins in the 1970s. Important people at big conferences would argue over the merits of the two approaches to leadership. The debate followed the true dialectic tradition of Marx and Hegel,[1] in which a thesis (transformational leadership) generated an antithesis (transactional leadership) which led to a synthesis: you need a bit of both. Whether the leaders of the capitalist world saw themselves following a Marxist tradition is questionable.

Although the leadership debate has moved on, the original debate illustrates some basic challenges and truths about the nature of leadership.

Why this myth matters

Transactional and transformational leadership showed two fundamentally different approaches. It matters which approach you take. Here is the basic debate: decide which way you would vote.

Transformational leadership

- **Tasks.** Focus on building trust with your team. Engage them and bring them to a higher level of motivation, morality and purpose. Create a strong sense of identity and mission.
- **Nature of the leader.** You will be charismatic and inspirational, with a high ability to motivate, influence and persuade. You will challenge the status quo and seek change.
- **Guiding beliefs.** People want to perform well and you can trust them. Your team will find purpose in reaching for a demanding vision and will be prepared to put the vision and the group before themselves.

Transactional leadership

- **Tasks.** Build an organization machine which works. Establish clear goals, rewards and sanctions. Appeal to the self-interest of each team member.
- **Nature of the leader.** You will be organized, analytical, objective and fair and maintain the status quo.
- **Guiding beliefs.** Teams are self-interested and utilitarian: they seek to maximize pleasure and minimize pain.

This myth reflects an endless debate in leadership, which comes up in different forms. Here are three ways the debate is echoed in three other classic theories of management:

- **Maslow's hierarchy of needs.** Maslow argued that we are all needs junkies.[2] Once we have satisfied our base needs for food, safety and water we simply progress to higher-order needs until we seek immortality by endowing a university. One way or another, we always want more. Transactional leadership assumes teams are at the lower end of Maslow's hierarchy; transformational leadership assumes that teams have their base needs satisfied and are now looking for meaning in their work.

- **Theory X and Theory Y.**[3] These take two different views of employees. Theory X is pessimistic and assumes that people only work out of self-interest and are motivated by clear rewards and sanctions. Theory Y is more optimistic: people are self-motivated to do well, they seek to improve themselves and they find meaning in work. How you manage, control and reward people changes depending on whether you believe in theory X or theory Y. Theory X is consistent with transactional leadership; theory Y is consistent with transformational leadership.

- **Task-focused versus people (or relationship)-focused leadership.** This trade-off lies behind many evaluation systems. Do you focus on goal, results, tasks and structures or do you focus on communication, relationships, team well-being and effectiveness? The answer, of course, is that you need to do both. But most leaders have a strong bias to one side of the equation or the other.

If you have not yet voted for transactional or transformational leadership, here is one more theory which may allow you to vote for both forms of leadership.

- **Contingency theory**[4] does what it says on the tin: it argues that you need different sorts of leadership in different sorts of context. Inevitably, there are endless variations on the theme, but the basic message is simple: you need to adapt to circumstances. For instance:

Transactional leadership works well in an immediate crisis where the focus is on survival: fires and other catastrophes are not the time for inspiring visions for the future. It also works well where people have relatively low engagement with their work and simply want to know what they need to do. This finds expression in the modern trend to management by algorithm: drivers, warehouse pickers and the like are organized by a computer which tells them what to do and how to do it. The algorithm is highly efficient and learns fast: if your boss is an algorithm, then your boss is a tyrant who constantly demands more and more from you.

Transformational leadership works well with professionals who push back against micro-management, but want to find meaning and purpose in their work. But as a theory it demands too much of leaders. Few leaders can be inspirational and charismatic; lifting your team to a higher moral purpose is nice, but is neither necessary nor very doable.

Lessons for leaders

Avoid too much theory

If you start to swim in the ocean of leadership theory, it is easy to drown. Your job is to master leadership, not to master leadership theory.

Leaders have to be transformational

This is essential if they are to make a difference. But you do not have to be charismatic to make a difference.

Transactional leadership is closer to management

It is about building a machine which you can rely on to deliver. Leaders need the machine (transactional management) but they also need to engage the team (transformational leadership). The Marxist dialect between transactional and transformational leadership has reached its synthesis: you need bits of both theories to lead.

Conclusion

Myth and reality weave their way through both theories. Leaders need to be transformational and transactional; they have to manage people and tasks; they have to motivate and control. It is not either or: leaders have to do it all. Since both theories are true it should be zero unicorns but since the debate was framed as a choice it should be five unicorns. That leads to an unsatisfactory compromise: three unicorns.

Endnotes

1 Marx argued that his form of dialectical materialism contradicted Hegel's dialectics. Never get in the middle of an argument between two philosophers.

2 A H Maslow (1943) A theory of human motivation, *Psychological Review*, 50 (4), pp 370–96.

3 Douglas McGregor (1960) *The Human Side of Enterprise*, McGraw-Hill.

4 F E Fiedler (1967) *A Theory of Leadership Effectiveness*, McGraw-Hill.

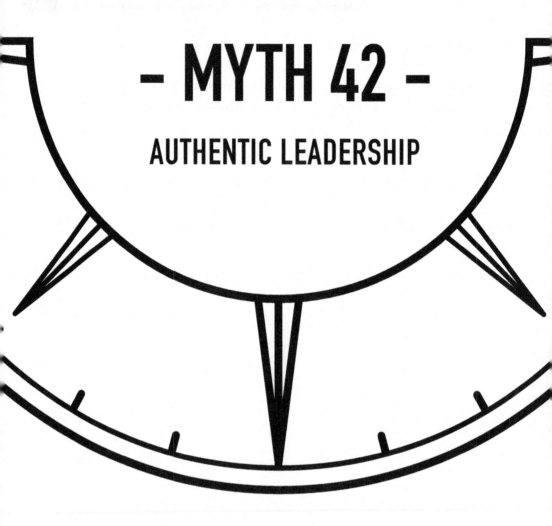

– MYTH 42 –

AUTHENTIC LEADERSHIP

You cannot succeed by trying to become someone else,
and you cannot succeed just by being yourself.

The nature of the myth

Authentic leadership is a slippery myth because there is no agreed version of what it is. It means different things to different people.

Two traits appear consistently in discussions about authentic leadership:

- a leader has to be true to who they are;
- authentic leaders are open about their thoughts and beliefs.

From these twin pillars, people add whatever else they want onto the idea of an authentic leader: the authentic leader solicits feedback, is fair minded, has a strong ethical foundation. In other words, 'authentic' is a code word for 'ideal'. The broader the definition becomes, the less useful it is.

Why this myth matters

For the sake of this myth, we will focus on the two traits identified above.

A leader has to be true to who they are

At one level, this is a truism which challenges much of the leadership literature. You can find many books out there which claim to reveal the leadership secrets of everyone from Genghis Khan to Steve Jobs. But there is a flaw with all these books: you cannot succeed by trying to be someone else. If you try to become some combination of Nelson Mandela and Admiral Lord Nelson, you will just land up confused.

But equally, if you just try to be yourself you will fail. If you hang around like a teenager in full hormonal angst waiting for the world to recognize your true genius, you will have a very long wait.

So now we have a paradox: you cannot succeed by trying to become someone else, and you cannot succeed just by being yourself (authentic). At this point, it appears we may as well give up. But there is a solution to be discovered.

Authentic leaders are open about their thoughts and beliefs

This belief appears to be non-controversial. If you are to be trusted, you have to be honest. That means being honest about what you think. But as you think of your personal, as well as professional life, there are plenty of times when being honest can cause problems. Discretion can be better than honesty.

The tension between honesty and discretion was highlighted by one CEO who was reflecting on his leadership journey:

> When I was young I used to get angry and frustrated, and I showed it. It always got me into trouble. I still get angry and frustrated, but I have learned to wear

the mask of leadership. My team picks up their mood from me. If I want them to be professional and positive, that is the mask I have to wear at all times. My mask has made all the difference.

Should you always be open and honest about your thoughts and beliefs?

Lessons for leaders

A leader has to be true to who they are

The resolution of the leadership paradox is simple: leaders have to become the best of who they are.

You cannot pretend to become someone you are not. Nor do you need to become someone else. Fortunately, leadership is a team sport. You can and should build your team so that it has a balance of skills, styles and strengths. Find team members who can fill in for areas which are not your strengths. If you hate book keeping, learn to love book keepers: they can save you from the hell of book keeping.

But it is not enough just to be who you are. Every leader has one or two signature strengths. Understand what your strengths are and build on those; find roles and firms where your strengths are in demand because that is where you will flourish. If you are to become the best of who you are, you have to commit to a lifetime of learning and development. No leader is ever the finished article; there are always new challenges to meet and new skills to learn.

Authentic leaders are open about their thoughts and beliefs

If your thoughts are always positive and constructive, you are fortunate and you have the foundations of being a very good leader. Most of the time, most of us can stay positive and constructive. But most of the time does not count. We do not want to have a heart which works 'most of the time'. The moment of truth is when things are going awry: how do you react then?

This is where being open and honest is dangerous. You need to be open and honest about the situation because people want to know what is going on and where they stand. But if you are feeling angry, frustrated and vengeful then being open and honest about that is destructive. It will cause your team to implode in a mixture of fear and finger pointing. It is at these times you need to wear your mask of leadership: project the style which you want your team to follow.

You need to be careful even with your thoughts. From time to time you may think that someone has been idle, careless, dishonest or plain foolish. If you are open with these thoughts to that individual, and to others, you have a recipe for conflict. And it may even be that your initial judgement is wrong; there are often plenty of innocent explanations for mishaps. Instead of being authentic, it pays to be discreet. Keep your views to yourself; buy some time to allow you to find out what really happened.

Summary

1 Dial up your strengths and dial down your weaknesses. Leadership is a team sport (although some people would argue that is a myth as well; see Myth 43), so find people who have strengths where you are not so strong.

2 Be ready to wear the mask of leadership to set an example for your team to follow.

Conclusion

This myth is true, but potentially very misleading. You have to be authentic, because you cannot be someone else. But that is not enough. You must become the best of who you are. So this myth leads you astray by letting you just be who you are. This means that even though the myth is true (zero unicorns) its potential to mislead earns it two unicorns.

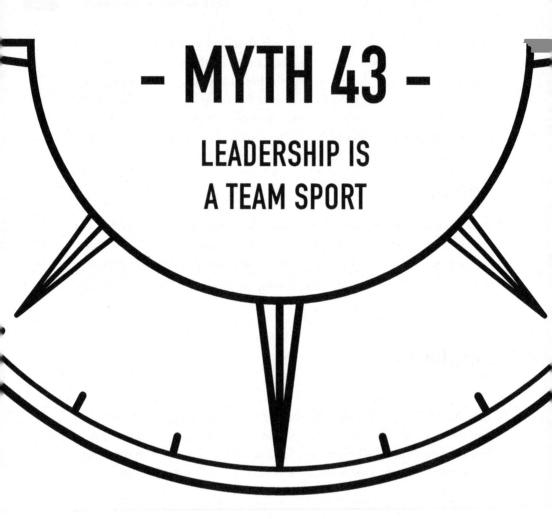

– MYTH 43 –

LEADERSHIP IS
A TEAM SPORT

*You face a trade-off between creating a team
and creating a group of individuals.*

The nature of the myth

This is a dangerous myth, because it is at the heart of *Myths of Leadership*.

The myth arises because the nature of leadership has changed. Leadership is no longer about the great man and lone hero leading the multitude to a sunny future. Business is too complicated and changes too fast for any one person to master. And 'the multitude' are no longer poorly educated masses who have few choices in life. They are more likely to be highly educated professionals who expect to be involved in shaping their future. In this new context, leadership has to be a team sport rather than an individual one.

But the essence of this book, and of all good leaders, is to be ready to challenge everything. Assumptions are useful mental short cuts most of the time. They can also be dangerous if they are not fully understood. In that spirit, it makes sense to challenge the idea that leadership is a team sport.

Why this myth matters

There is a world of difference between the concepts of the lone hero leader and leadership as a team sport. It makes sense to know which sort of leadership is most effective.

In theory, team leadership makes sense. It enables the full creativity and power of the team to be unleashed; it enables different talents and styles to flourish; it reduces the risk of depending on one person.

In practice, leadership fails to follow the theory. That is the problem with reality: it never lives up to the theory. To see the difference between theory and practice, observe a board meeting or meeting of the executive committee. In theory, this is where the leadership team comes together to lead and manage the business. In practice, the leadership team fails to act as a team. The meeting is more like a series of table tennis matches between the chair and each person sitting around the table. Each business unit or function will serve up a few proposals; the chair will bat back a few questions and challenges. At the end of the match between the chair and the first business unit, it will be the turn of the next business unit to have a match with the chair. Everyone else shuts up and watches, trying to pick up any tips on how to play the chair; to observe what mood she is in and what sort of tactics she is deploying.

In practice, the leadership team is often acting as a group of individuals and not as a team. There are rational, political and emotional reasons for this:

- **Rational.** Responsibility can be shared, but accountability cannot. Clear accountability means that each business unit and function has to answer for its own performance. That leads to the series of table tennis matches with the chair.

- **Political.** There is a rule of survival at board level: keep your nose out of other people's business. While it might be tempting to offer your views on the failings of your colleagues, this simply invites nuclear-scale retaliation. To survive, you keep firmly on your own territory.

- **Emotional.** Bosses like to boss. Board meetings are the moment when they can hold court. It is relatively easy to deal with board members one at a time. The moment you invite an open discussion in which everyone contributes, it becomes much harder to control the outcome. The chair is simply one voice out of many in an open discussion; in a one-to-one discussion the boss is the boss who is dispensing wisdom, justice and decisions.

The idea of team leadership is slippery. Teams can be highly interdependent, such as with synchronized swimming or the NFL. In the NFL, each player has to perform well, but is completely dependent on the rest of the team for being effective. In contrast, in team golf events, the performance of each golfer does not depend on the performance of the rest of the team: one player can have a good day even if the team loses.

Lessons for leaders

This myth has one general and one specific lesson for leaders.

The general lesson is to be ready to challenge every assumption, even your own most basic ones. Even if you find that your assumption was correct all along, you will understand why it was correct and how you can use it effectively.

The specific lesson is about how you build your leadership team. You face a trade-off between creating a team and creating a group of individuals. This comes down to balancing accountability versus responsibility.

To drive performance, you need clear accountability: you need to know who to hold to account for what. This forces the team to become a group of individuals, rather than a team. It is consistent with the traditional command and control style of leadership.

But there will be some areas where you need collective responsibility, and you need to act as a single team rather than a group of individuals. Typically, there are five areas where you need the team to act as a team, not as a group of individuals:

1 **Strategy.** You need the insight of the team to arrive at the best strategy, and you also need the commitment of the team to make it happen. Any strategy will lead to 'winners' and 'losers' within the team, and some parts of the firm will get more resources than others. Having a good strategy process requires having a team with the right values of putting team before self.

2 **Values**. The team sets the tone for the rest of the firm, so it is important that the team shows a consistent set of values. One of the core values should be teamwork. If the leadership team does not act as a team, then you cannot expect much collaboration across the organization at lower levels.

3 **Budgets**. Resource allocation is a core duty of leadership. The temptation for senior executives is to act like union representatives, seeking the best deal for their members rather than looking after the interests of the firm as a whole. This is where values matter: do people believe they should be playing for the firm or for themselves?

4 **People**. People are the most valuable resource of most firms, and especially in service businesses. The whole leadership team needs to be aligned on finding, keeping and developing the right talent for the future.

5 **Major initiatives**. Most firms have one or two major initiatives which are meant to drive the business forward. The most powerful initiatives require the involvement of every aspect of the business. For instance, putting customers first is not just for sales: even finance and IT have vital roles to play.

Conclusion

This is the sort of myth which should be true in theory (no unicorns) but is often false in reality (five unicorns). Reality has a pesky habit of not living up to theory. In this case however, most leaders at least attempt to make leadership a team sport. One unicorn.

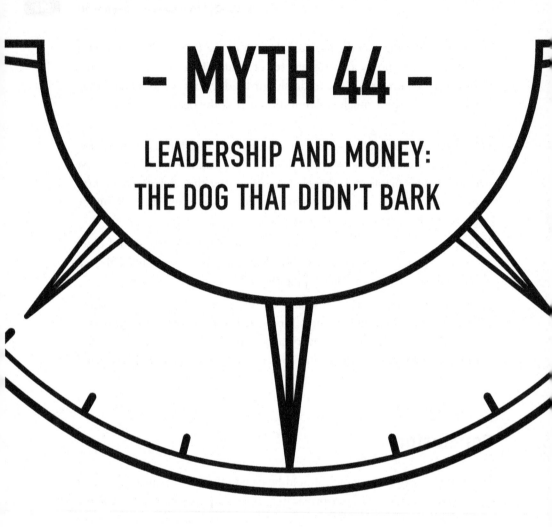

- MYTH 44 -

LEADERSHIP AND MONEY: THE DOG THAT DIDN'T BARK

Great wealth is not a sign of great leadership.

The nature of the myth

Sherlock Holmes drew the attention of the police officer to 'the curious incident of the dog in the night-time'. The officer protested that the dog did nothing in the night-time. 'That was the curious incident,' replied Holmes.[1]

Occasionally, what we do not hear or see is as important as what we can hear and see. But, as Holmes' story shows, it is very hard to notice what is not there. So what is missing from theories of leadership?

The glaring omission is money. No one talks about money. At grand dinner parties, money, along with sex, death and religion, is normally avoided as being too controversial. There is certainly much that could be written about sex and leadership, but we will focus on money. Is money too grubby for leadership experts?

Money matters for leadership for two reasons:

1 if you want to lead, normally you need money;

2 many leaders earn great wealth. This raises a basic question which remains unanswered: what motivates people to lead?

We will explore each of these money puzzles in turn.

Why this myth matters

The need for money

Sometimes, leaders lead and need no money. William Rodriguez is reputed to have been the last person out of the World Trade Centre on 9/11. The reason he was last out was that he had gone back in to lead people out to safety. He was truly leading, if the definition of leadership is 'taking people where they would not have got by themselves'. His leadership required bravery, not money.

But for the most part, leaders discover that you cannot change the world without money. Even leaders who eschew wealth or attack capitalism need funding to succeed:

- Mahatma Gandhi famously lived in poverty. His close friend and poet Sarojini Naidu complained to him: 'Do you know how much it costs us to keep you in poverty? A fortune.'[2] This meant he was dependent on wealthy backers such as Ghanshyam Das Birla to keep his campaign going.[3]

- Karl Marx depended on rich capitalist Friedrich Engels[4] to keep him afloat while he wrote Das Kapital, paving the way for the communist revolution. He needed capitalists to destroy capitalism.

- Most of the great explorers who go through huge hardship on their adventures spend little of their lives actually exploring. More prosaically, they spend most of their lives raising money from investors, speeches and books. Living in extreme hardship can be extremely expensive.

Money is the rocket fuel of ambition. A great idea without any funding is a pipe dream. To turn ideas into reality, leaders need money. This is true whether you are leading a nation or a service team. In practice, money is one of the three pillars of successful leadership:

1 Idea: you need an idea about how you will make a difference.

2 People: you need a great team to turn dreams into reality.

3 Money is the fuel for your idea and your people.

The importance of money is reflected in who becomes CEO. Of the top 100 publicly quoted firms in the UK, half the CEOs have a financial background and a quarter are qualified chartered accountants.[5] A quarter of Fortune 500 firm CEOs were appointed from a CFO role.[6] The finance function is taking control. And money does not matter for leadership?

Leaders and wealth

Not all leaders are driven by money. It would be hard to accuse the Pope of being a money grubber. José Mujica, who was president of Uruguay from 2010 to 2015, famously donated 90 per cent of his salary to charity; he drives a 1987 VW Beetle and lives in a very humble house.[7] These tend to be the exceptions which prove the rule.

Most leaders show great attachment to money: more money than anyone can reasonably need. Total average compensation for each CEO of America's top 350 firms reached US $16.4 million in 2014. That is more than you need for all the champagne you can drink in one lifetime. It is also 300 times more than the average worker earns. In 1965, average CEO compensation was just 20 times that of the average worker.[8] It is not clear how many of these CEOs are actually leading, and how many are simply managing a legacy they inherited.

Historically, money and power have walked hand in hand. Louis XIV of France is reputed to have told Parliament, 'L'état, c'est moi'[9]: I am the state. He echoed the belief of rulers down the ages: the wealth of the state belonged to the king. The same applies to the entrepreneurs of today: 'the firm is me'.

The question this wealth raises is whether money is required to motivate people to become leaders. There is no reason for this to be the case. People normally want to lead to make a difference, whether it is in a community group or elsewhere. Making a difference and making money are different concepts. Great wealth is not a sign of great leadership, nor should it be required to motivate people to lead.

Lessons for leaders

Money matters

If you want to change the world, money is the fuel you need for your idea and for your team.

Become money literate

This does not mean that you have to become an accountant. It means you have to know how to raise money, allocate resources and budget well.

Know your own motivation

Self-worth is not measured by net worth. Wealth simply proves you are wealthy. When bank robber 'Slick Willie' Sutton was asked why he robbed banks he replied: 'Because that is where the money is.'[10] If you want money, go where the money is; if you want power, go where the power is; if you want fame, go where the fame is. If you want to be a leader, make a difference. Know what you want.

Money does not prove that you are a good leader

If you want to be seen as a leader, the measure of your success is how far you have taken people where they would not have got by themselves, and how you are remembered as a role model.

Conclusion

Money matters in leadership. It matters because it is hard to make a difference without money, and it matters because leaders (or at least CEOs) now earn unprecedented amounts of money, which helps to fuel popular discontent with elites. This is an unspoken and highly dangerous myth; five unicorns.

Endnotes

1 If you want to find out why the dog did not bark, read the short story 'Silver Blaze' by Sir Arthur Conan Doyle in *The Memoirs of Sherlock Holmes* (1892).

2 Aviott (2013) Keeping an old man in poverty [online] https://aviott.org/2013/12/20/keeping-an-old-man-in-poverty.

3 Salman Rushdie (2007) Mahatma Gandhi, *Time* [online] http://content.time. com/time/world/article/0,8599,1653029,00.html.

4 Engels' wealth was largely inherited: he was the eldest son of a wealthy textile manufacturer.

5 Richard Crump (2015) Quarter of FTSE 100 bosses are qualified accountants, *Financial Director* [online] https://www.financialdirector.co.uk/financial-director/ news/2409128/quarter-of-ftse-100-bosses-are-qualified-accountants.

6 Jason Karaian (2014) Rise of the number crunchers: how CFOs took over the boardroom, *Quartz* [online] http://qz.com/179301/how-cfos-took-over-the-boardroom/.

7 Vladimir Hernandez (2012) Jose Mujica: the world's poorest president, *BBC* [online] http://www.bbc.co.uk/news/magazine-20243493.

8 Lawrence Mishel and Alyssa Davis (2015) Top CEOs make 300 times more than typical workers, *Economic Policy Institute* [online] http://www.epi. org/publication/top-ceos-make-300-times-more-than-workers-pay-growth-surpasses-market-gains-and-the-rest-of-the-0-1-percent/.

9 Address to the Parliament of Paris, attributed by Weatard-Antoine G, *Histoire de Paris* (1834), vol 6, p 298, probably apocryphal.

10 Wikipedia, Willie Sutton [online] https://en.wikipedia.org/wiki/Willie_Sutton.

– MYTH 45 –

LEADERS ARE LIKE TEA BAGS

If we want to learn, we can learn from anything: even from tea bags.

The tea bag theory of leadership is that leaders are like tea bags: you only know how good they are when they land up in hot water.[1]

Put more directly, leaders are defined by a few moments of truth which are often crises. It is only in a crisis that you find out just how good a leader is.

Why this myth matters

This myth matters because many leaders like to portray themselves as successful people, and often airbrush setbacks out of their memory. This gives a false impression of your leadership journey. The vast majority of leaders face setbacks and crises at some point. People who have never failed have brittle confidence; they look good and sound good but at the first sound of gunfire they crumple. To paraphrase Nietzsche: 'That which does not break you, makes you stronger.'[2] Crises sort the follower sheep from the leader goats: followers step back, leaders step up.

Crises are not obstacles on the path to leadership. They are the high road to leadership. Embrace them, don't avoid them.

Lessons for leaders

If crises can make or break you, it is worth knowing how to make the most of them. The steps below provide a cheat sheet for you, but the best way to learn about handling crises is to go through a few of them. Ideally, you start by observing how others handle or mishandle a crisis; preferably your first few crises will be smaller ones which let you learn and grow. Learning to handle crises is like learning any other aspect of leadership: it is mainly a matter of pattern recognition. Once you have seen the movie a few times, you know what will happen next and you can adjust accordingly. But learning pattern recognition from experience can be painful, so here is a quick guide to how you should act when you land up in hot water.

1 Recognize the problem early. Problems rarely go away by themselves; they usually get worse. The earlier you act, the better.

2 Take control: step up, offer solutions. Take responsibility for success, regardless of who was responsible for causing the crisis. Leave the blame game for another time: another lifetime.

3 Focus on what you can do, and do it fast. Look forwards, not backwards; drive to action, not analysis; focus on the possible, not the impossible.

4 Find support. Don't be a lone hero, because lone heroes normally become dead heroes. A problem shared is a problem halved.

5 Over-communicate. Control the gossip mill and make sure that the positive and constructive messages you want to be heard are heard.

6 Stay positive. People will remember how you were much more than what you did. If you project confidence and purpose you are more likely to succeed than if you project fear and confusion.

Finally, remember that crises are very valuable learning opportunities. No matter whether you had a good or bad crisis, you will have done some things well and you could improve other things. Learn from the good and bad. Grow your crisis capability.

The alternative tea bag theory of leadership

The second tea bag theory of leadership is that all a leader needs for success is a large supply of tea bags. This theory is evidenced by Helen's story below.

HELEN'S STORY

Helen was appointed to lead a plant hire business nationally. Plant hire is Bob the Builder territory; it is mainly a boy's club full of diggers and cranes. Helen was not a boy. She still isn't. This caused consternation among the boys, who doubted that a girl could ever really become Bob the Builder.

However, Helen had a secret weapon: tea bags. She visited each depot around the country and sat down for tea with the boys. She asked them what they would change. Mostly it was simple things. In one town, the boys were not happy that the national flag was old and dirty: they felt embarrassed raising the flag each morning. Next morning, she made sure they had a brand-new flag. At another depot, the boys were not happy that they had nowhere to store their personal kit. Within a week, there were personal lockers in the depot for each team member.

By the time Helen had finished her tour, she had become a legend. Even the crustiest of the boys admitted she might be quite good... even if they doubted whether she could really handle a digger properly.

From then on, whenever she visited depots, she made sure she had a good supply of tea bags because talking is good, but listening is even better.

Why this myth matters

This tea bag theory is the opposite of the first one. The first tea bag theory focuses on defining moments of truth; this second theory focuses on the small things that make a big difference.

Myth 10 showed that there is a big motivation gap between leaders and followers. This tea bag theory illustrates one of the ways in which leaders can pass the crucial motivation question: 'My boss cares for me and my career (agree/disagree)'. Showing that you care takes time, and possibly tea. There is no simple four-step, tick-box guide which you can check off to motivate your team. It is a never-ending process made up of endless small and not-so-small events. A quick thank you, a short chat by the water cooler, or a cup of tea at the depot: all these are chances to show that you care. Find what works for you.

Lessons for leaders

Leadership is full of fancy, and occasionally wacky, theories. The reality is that we can learn to lead anywhere and from anyone and anything. The key is to open our minds and open our eyes. If we want to learn, we can learn from anything: even from tea bags.

Conclusion

Just because something appears to be wacky, that does not mean it is untrue. The idea that the earth was round was a totally wacky idea in the Middle Ages. In a more modest way, leaders may be able to learn from tea bags. This is a unicorn-free zone because the myths are true.

Endnotes

1 I am slightly indebted to Dame Julia Cleverdon for recounting this theory to me. I am hugely indebted to her for all her support to me over the years.

2 Friedrich Nietzsche (1889/1895; 1977) *Twilight of the Idols and the Anti-Christ*, trans R J Hollingdale, Penguin. The original quotation was: 'From life's school of war: what does not kill me makes me stronger.'

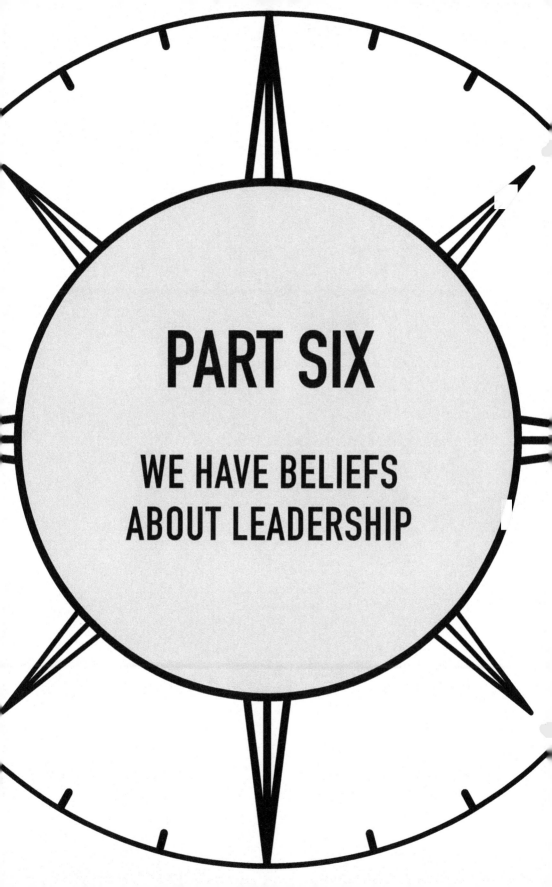

PART SIX

WE HAVE BELIEFS
ABOUT LEADERSHIP

– MYTH 46 –

IT'S LONELY AT THE TOP

Power creates distance.

The nature of the myth

At first glance, this myth is… a myth.

Look at the diary of most leaders and it will be jam-packed with meetings all day, and the average working day of a leader is often long. The real problem for leaders appears to be that they are not lonely enough; they do not have enough quiet time where they can think and review.

The literature on leadership is split between the hyper-active doers who trumpet their ability to work 100 hours a week, and the hyper-deep thinkers who trumpet how much time they spend thinking. Warren Buffet, the legendary investor, is reputed to spend 80 per cent of his time reading or thinking.[1] But Buffet is an outlier in more or less every way. As a fund manager, he needs to spend time thinking, reading and analysing: that is his job. Among leaders, the doers heavily outnumber the thinkers. Leaders like to be seen as dynamic and active, and so that is how they act and how they manage their diaries.

But look again, and you find that this myth may not be a myth at all. It accurately reflects the experience of most leaders. How can leaders be lonely when they are meeting people all day?

Here is how loneliness comes about. As a middle manager, you are used to having your ideas challenged: bosses will tell you what they think about your performance; your failings will be noted. But when you reach the top everything changes:

1 Everyone laughs at your jokes, which they ignored before.

2 Your half-baked idea is no longer trashed; instead you find someone has gone away and worked it into a proposal.

3 You find all sorts of things happening in the firm because that is what you wanted, even when you have not expressed a view on the topic.

4 Everyone comes to you with an idea, and they all want a slice of your time, your support and your budget.

5 Every project you start is deemed to succeed, even when it has failed.

Why this myth matters

At the heart of the problem is power: power creates distance. It is distance which creates a sense of loneliness for the leader. Ultimately, the leader starts to doubt if there is anyone they can trust. The lack of trust takes two forms.

Can I trust anyone to tell me the truth?

The more reflective leaders realize that they are being told what they want to hear. They know that when they were on the way up, they learned loyalty: don't give the boss bad medicine and they supported the boss at all times. But loyalty comes at the price of honesty, and this is why so many leaders value the art of 'MBWA': management by walking around. They want to hear and see for themselves what is really happening in the market, or in operations and elsewhere. They trust their own eyes more than they trust the reports that land on their desk. They take to heart the message from John Le Carré: 'A desk is a dangerous place from which to view the world.'[2] That is as true of leaders as it is of spies.

Can I trust anyone with vital decisions?

Some leaders take the reactions of their team at face value. They start to believe that they are genuinely witty and that the team now depends on their unique brilliance and insight. This is how power corrupts. The leader starts to believe that they are indispensable. They take all the key decisions themselves, and when things go wrong blame their team for poor implementation. This is standard operating practice for dictators around the world. Moving from being a leader to a dictator means everyone suffers except for the dictator and a few lucky cronies.

When you find there is no one you can trust, you start to feel very lonely.

Lessons for leaders

The more powerful you are as a leader, the more everyone wants a piece of you: they want your time, support and resources. This means that they will flatter you, support you and praise you. You will find fewer and fewer people who challenge you or criticize you to your face.

Stay objective

You need to discover the truth, however awkward it may be. Talk to customers, suppliers, competitors and staff; bypass the formal channels of communication. Inside the firm, recognize flattery for what it is: flattery. Focus on what is being said, not how it is being said. Given that leaders receive little challenge or feedback, you have to be your own fiercest critic. Constantly challenge and test yourself and your assumptions.

Listen more, talk less

A famous slogan in the Second World War warned people about the danger of spies: 'Idle talk costs lives'. Leaders soon learn that idle talk is very expensive: your throwaway remark will be taken as approval or disapproval for an idea, and action will be taken as a result. It is no use later saying, 'What I really meant was...' The damage will have been done. The best leaders have two ears and one mouth, and they use them in that proportion: they listen at least twice as much as they talk. Observe leaders in meetings and the most effective ones will say little, but they will ask smart questions at the right moment. If you ask the right question, you can rely on the team to provide the answer.

Trust your team

Asking questions is a good way of delegating; providing answers is a good way of assuming responsibility personally. As a leader, you do not have to prove your heroism by doing everything yourself. You will be judged by what your team achieves, not by who does it. Even if you do not trust your team to tell you the whole truth all the time, you have to trust them to make decisions and to take action. If you try to be the hero, you will be overwhelmed.

Find someone to keep you honest

Julius Caesar, on his triumphal march, had an Auriga (slave) constantly repeating 'memento homo': remember you are human. As a leader, you will not have a slave, but you need someone to challenge, criticize and support you personally. You have to trust them to tell you the truth if you are to stay on top of your game, or raise your game. Without challenge, you will make poor decisions. Without challenge, you will only find out the truth about your performance when your chairman very elegantly slips the knife between your shoulder blades. Your truth teller could be a coach or spouse; it could be a staff person nearing retirement who has nothing to fear, nothing to gain and nothing to lose from telling you the truth. Find someone you can trust with the truth.

Conclusion

At a literal level, it is obvious that leaders are never lonely, so this should rate five unicorns. But the myth turns out to be true at a psychological level: the leader has few people they can turn to and trust completely. To make the point that power is lonely and dangerous, this rates zero unicorns.

Endnotes

1 Thinking or doing? A good example of the trade-off is here: http://www.inc.com/empact/why-successful-people-spend-10-hours-a-week-just-thinking.html.

2 John Le Carré (1977; 2002) *The Honourable Schoolboy*, Scribner Book Company.

– MYTH 47 –

THE BUCK STOPS HERE

Sharing the credit is a good way of claiming the credit.

The nature of the myth

President Truman kept a sign on his desk saying 'The Buck Stops Here'. It is a sign which has been copied many times and used on many desks elsewhere, at least in the era when leaders still had a desk to call their own.

The sign strikes at the heart of two leadership ideas which are frequently confused: accountability and responsibility. The essential difference between the two is that only one person can be accountable, but many people can share responsibility. From the leader's point of view, that means you can never delegate your accountability, but you must delegate as much responsibility as you can. When you delegate responsibility, you ask someone else to do the task: that is the essence of both leadership and management. You remain accountable for the outcome of that task, however well or poorly it was done.

Why this myth matters

The myth matters because it is frequently misunderstood or misused. Two examples will make the point.

The accountability trap

All leaders, and managers, sign up to the idea that they are accountable, until the moment they are held to account. Human nature is to want to be accountable for the good stuff, but not for the bad.

Even CEOs fall into the accountability trap. Reading an annual report when times are good is to discover that the firm is led by people who have improved the fortunes of the firm through their dedication and brilliance. When results are not so good, we get to discover the role of outrageous fortune in sabotaging the work of the CEO: government has, or has not, intervened; the market has been soft so those pesky customers have not been buying enough at the right price; the weather conspired against us; sneaky competition did things which were clearly unfair. But whatever happened, it was not the fault of the CEO, who still deserves an outsized bonus.

The responsibility trap

It is a small step from believing that the buck stops here to believing in the hero leader who knows it all and does it all. It is a step which many leaders and their teams are happy to take.

A leader who believes the buck stops here is often unwilling to delegate. They may delegate the routine rubbish, and they may delegate the blame when things go wrong. That is a parody of delegation. But they are often most unwilling to delegate the most challenging tasks. The leader turns to the only person they trust on such challenging tasks: themselves. The greater the challenge, the greater the need for the whole team to rise to the challenge.

Many teams are happy with letting the buck stop with the leader. This gives them the chance to delegate responsibility for the toughest decisions and challenges upwards. By delegating decisions upwards, the team can no longer be held responsible if the decision is the wrong one. Delegating upwards is a safe and lazy way of being a team member. Leaders need to push back: trust the team and challenge the team to take responsibility.

Lessons for leaders

Be accountable for good times and bad times

The best leaders take an unexpected approach to accountability in good times and bad.

In good times, the best leaders do not hog all the glory. They are generous in sharing the praise. This has several positive effects. First, it builds huge goodwill among the people who share the glory: most people feel under-recognized, so a little recognition goes a long way. Second, it reinforces the role of the leader: only the person who was at the heart of the success knows who to praise. In effect, sharing the credit is a good way of claiming the credit.

In bad times, the most effective leaders take accountability to heart. They take the blame. This has a transformative effect. It means that the team can move on from finger pointing and passing the buck. Instead of playing politics and analysing the past, they can look to the future and work out how to solve the problem. It also creates an atmosphere which is positive, productive and trusting. As a leader, you do not want to be making excuses: you want results. Accepting the blame means you move past the excuses stage and onto action and results.

You are accountable for your own feelings

This is perhaps the hardest accountability lesson of all. Imagine you have had a long, hard and frustrating day; you have been running hard to stand still while everything seems to conspire against you. And then someone comes along and decides to wind you up. They know exactly which buttons to press to get a reaction. At this point, you have every right to feel angry, annoyed and upset. But there is no law that says you must feel angry, annoyed and upset: that is your decision.

Knowing that you are accountable for your own feelings is daunting and liberating. Once you know you can choose how you feel, you are no longer at the mercy of external events dictating your mood. It is also a vital leadership technique. You will not be remembered for beating this year's budget by 6.4 per cent: you will be remembered for how you are. In particular, you will be remembered for how you behave at moments of truth, crisis and uncertainty. You can only project a positive and professional face to the world if that is how you feel inside. However you choose to feel, choose well.

You cannot share accountability, but you must share responsibility

This is where President Truman's sign rings true: the buck does stop with the leader. You can delegate everything except your accountability. Ultimately, you are accountable for the outcome. If you delegated responsibility to someone who did not deliver, you are still accountable for that: you chose to delegate, and you have to live with the result of that decision.

In contrast to accountability, effective leaders have to delegate responsibility. You cannot do it all yourself, however brilliant and heroic you may be. If you find it hard to delegate, that is a sign that you do not trust your team. That means there is either something wrong with you or with your team. A key task of any leader is to build the right team. You will know you have the right team when you are confident in delegating the most challenging roles to them.

Conclusion

This myth is a reality, which should mean no unicorns. But the nature of 'the buck stops here' is easily misunderstood. It does not mean micro-managing: it means sharing responsibility, sharing success and being accountable for yourself, your career and your feelings. In recognition of the potential for misunderstanding, this earns two unicorns.

- MYTH 48 -

IT'S TOUGH AT THE TOP

If you want to discover real stress, do not go to
the top of the firm: go to the middle.

The nature of the myth

How many leaders say it is easy at the top? Probably as many as the number of work–life balance gurus who advise more work. And if it is so tough at the top, why does everyone want to get there?

If we believe that it is easy at the top, then it destroys a large part of the leadership myth. There would be no need to pay leaders large sums of money for doing something easy and enjoyable. The idea of the leader as a hero would bite the dust.

Leaders are happy to live with the idea that it is tough at the top, even if the evidence points in the opposite direction. There are three main elements to the myth:

1 it is stressful at the top;

2 it is hard work at the top;

3 unique skills are needed at the top.

As ever, this makes the assumption that the person at the top is actually leading. Many people at the top fail the leadership test of taking people where they would not have got by themselves.

It is time to put each part of this myth to the test.

Why this myth matters

'It's tough at the top' is at the heart of leadership mythology. Here is what the evidence shows about each part of the myth.

It is stressful at the top

If you want to discover real stress, do not go to the top of the firm: go to the middle. This is the paranoia zone where stress is at its greatest. The two great drivers of stress are control and ambiguity. People often raise their performance when under pressure, as long as they know what they have to do and they are in control of events. If there is the same pressure to perform but you face ambiguous or contradictory goals, stress levels soar: it is not clear where you should invest your time and effort. If you then also lose control over the outcome, stress levels hit the red zone. Losing control is routine if you depend on colleagues or suppliers to deliver part of your outcome, or to give you permission, or to supply information or resources. Suddenly, you are dependent.

Now look at how ambiguity and control change at different levels of the firm. When you start out, you typically have low control but low ambiguity. It is very clear what you have to do. It may be dull and it may be hard work, but at least it is clear what you need to do to succeed. At the top of the firm, the equation is reversed. You have very high control as the CEO: you are the master of your own destiny. You also have very high ambiguity: there are myriad ways of achieving your goals. Your high level of control effectively converts ambiguity into freedom to act as you wish. Stress should be low.

Leaders in the middle do not get the best of both worlds. They get the worst of ambiguity and control. Leaders in the middle face competing priorities from across the firm. They also have to compete to ensure their own priorities get the support and resources they need. The middle is where ambiguity is high and control is low: it is the real stress zone of the firm.

Leadership is hard work

At one level, leadership is hard work. But at the top, leaders can choose to make it as hard as they want. Ronald Reagan was one of the more successful US presidents: he saw the demise of the Soviet Union and end of the Cold War, he introduced Reaganomics to the world, and negotiated a breakthrough treaty to eliminate an entire class of nuclear weapons. That is not bad for someone who was regarded as lazy: he was reputed to be in his pyjamas watching TV with a TV dinner by 8pm every evening.

Business leaders may want to boast about their achievements, but few will match those of Reagan, however hard they work. They could learn from Reagan's approach to leadership:

1 He knew what he wanted to achieve and focused clearly on that.

2 He knew what he was good at, and focused his energies on that; for all his faults, he was seen as the great communicator. He used that talent to pull the nation and Congress behind him.

3 He was excellent at delegating. At the time the business buzzword was MBWA: management by walking around. He practised an alternative version of MBWA: management by walking away. He trusted his team to do the heavy lifting for him.

You need unique skills at the top

This is true, but irrelevant. You need unique skills in any role. The real question is whether leadership skills are in abundant or limited supply. There appears to be no shortage of talent seeking the top jobs.

Lessons for leaders

One of my professors at university decided to give me some unsolicited career advice: 'Don't join a firm as a junior. Always join as a partner.' The professor correctly understood that life is far better at the top of the firm than at the bottom or the middle. It was, of course, completely useless advice: how do you join at the top, unless you set up your own business?

Leaders at the top can follow Reagan's example if they want to be more effective and work less:

1 focus on the big issues where you will make a difference;

2 focus on doing what you do best;

3 delegate everything else.

Following in Reagan's footsteps, one of the best bosses I ever had was also one of the idlest. He did three things very well:

1 He built trust with senior clients who would open their wallets for him.

2 He negotiated smart budgets. He worked on the basis that it is better to work hard for one month a year negotiating a good budget than to work hard for 11 months being macho trying to chase a 'challenging' budget.

3 He delegated everything else, which meant that teams loved him. His delegation showed that he trusted them, and they responded by performing for him.

These are options which are more easily available at the top of the firm than in the middle. The middle is where it is hardest work. In practice, leaders at the top prefer the hard work, as it reinforces their sense of purpose and importance. But that does not make you a good leader.

Conclusion

It is hard to have sympathy with leaders who complain that it is tough at the top. Everyone has a tough life, and leaders live a gilded life compared to most. Leaders choose to lead and they are fortunate compared with most people. Leaders should enjoy what they do, not complain about it. Five unicorns.

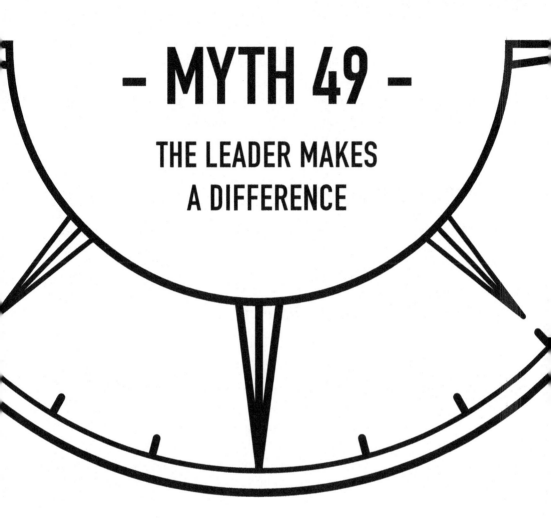

- MYTH 49 -

THE LEADER MAKES
A DIFFERENCE

Activity is not the same as achievement.

The nature of the myth

This myth is potentially a tautology. If leaders take people where they would not have got by themselves, then if you are not making a difference you are not leading. Instead, we will relax the definition of leadership and define the leader as the boss. So does the boss make a difference?

Subjectively, it is obvious that all bosses make some sort of difference, for better or for worse. A good boss will energize the team and a bad boss will demotivate them. But the leadership test of 'making a difference' is tougher than the effect you have on your team. The test is whether you have changed the future for the team and taken them where they would not have got by themselves.

Against this tougher benchmark, many leaders would argue that they are making a difference. Every firm will point to the initiatives they are taking to build market share, open new markets, cut costs, attract and retain customers, simplify their operations and strengthen their talent pool. Firms are a coruscating whirl of activity and change. This activity and change is what leaders are leading, so the evidence points to them making a difference.

Why this myth matters

This myth is central to leadership. If leaders are not making a difference, they may as well pack their bags and go home. But this myth contains two bear traps for leaders.

The myth of the stable baseline

This myth is a killer in business. All your work on improving the business often has little positive effect, for two reasons:

1 **Corporate entropy.** Everything inexorably slides towards chaos. Experienced staff leave and are replaced by more junior staff; customer requirements change; regulations change but never get lighter; the tax man always wants another cut; suppliers let you down and random acts cause crises even before the competition attempts to wreck your day. In this world, simply maintaining the current level of performance is hard work.

2 **Competition,** which is the curse of capitalism. The benefits of every initiative you take are likely to be competed away to the ultimate benefit of your customers, who are the only winners in the corporate race called betterfastercheaper. If you cut costs by 10 per cent, then the chances are your competitors will cut them as fast. Unless you are in an oligopoly, the cost cuts will not show up in your bottom line, but in prices to your customers. Your leadership team may be brilliant, creative and diligent, but the chances are that the leadership teams of your competitors are equally brilliant, creative and diligent. It is hard to outrun them.

Competition and entropy mean that many leaders find themselves following the advice of the Red Queen in Lewis Carroll's *Through the Looking Glass*: 'If you want to get somewhere else, you must run at least twice as fast as that!' As we shall see, that is the second bear trap for leaders.

Activity is not the same as achievement

The standard response to the problem of the declining baseline is to work harder and do more. How many managers complain that there are not enough initiatives in the firm? We know that in most firms, people are working hard and introducing lots of new initiatives. But few of them actually change the future. We noted in Myth 37 that half the firms in the Fortune 500 disappear within a generation. These were not firms led by idiots; they were firms led by people like you or me.

In practice, most firms are prisoners of their past. They suffer inertia, which makes it hard to change direction when they need to. In most firms the best predictor of next year's budget is this year's budget; the best predictor of next year's strategy is this year's strategy. Of course, the budget and strategy will move over time and each minor change will be the result of major discussion. But the despite all the activity of the leadership, the destiny of the firm rarely changes.

That is not an indictment of leadership; it is a reflection of just how hard it is to reach the stable baseline. If leaders really want to make a difference, they have to do more than run faster. They need to change the rules of engagement: buy a bicycle instead of running.

Lessons for leaders

If you are to make a difference as a leader, you have to beat the challenge of the declining baseline. This is a tough challenge which few leaders can achieve consistently.

Leaders operate at three levels:

Maintaining performance

This deals with the day-to-day noise of organizational life. It is hard work because of corporate entropy: you have to stop the slow slide towards chaos. Every day brings new challenges. The battle against the declining baseline never stops. This supervisory work is necessary but not enough.

Improving performance

This is where leaders launch endless initiatives which ultimately get competed away to the benefit of competition. This is classic managerial work: find ways of improving what already exists. It is hard work but essentially safe work. You are dealing with existing systems and ways of working.

Changing performance

This is not about improving performance or seeking excellence. It is about daring to rethink what you do and how you do it. Create new rules of the game. Stop running faster and faster and either change direction or buy that bicycle. This may sound exciting and inspirational, but the reality is different. It is highly risky because you have to challenge how things are done today. That makes it hard work, because you will encounter widespread political resistance to anything that makes deep change, rather than simply improving on existing ways. It is the fast track to success, or failure.

If you aspire to lead, you have to make a difference. But making a difference in a way that changes the future is exceptionally hard. You have to beat the challenges of competition, corporate entity and the declining baseline. If you can do all that, you know you are a leader.

Conclusion

Leaders are often confused about what makes a difference and whether they are making a difference. 'Making a difference' is much claimed but little achieved, which takes it firmly out of the realms of reality and into the realms of fantasy. Leaders claim to make a difference more than they do. Three unicorns.

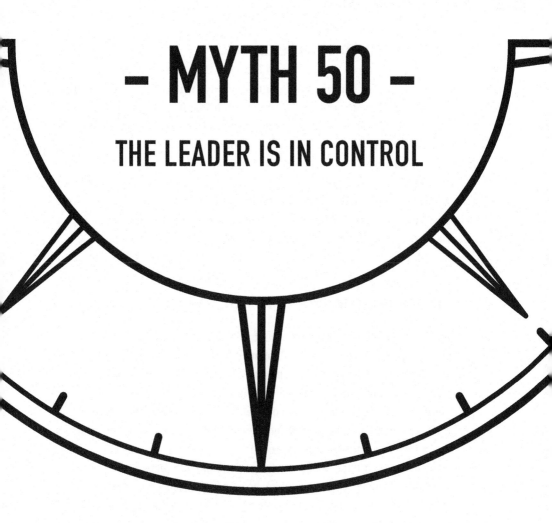

– MYTH 50 –

THE LEADER IS IN CONTROL

We only discover the true value of plumbing when it goes wrong.

The nature of the myth

No leader will ever say that they are not in control: if you are not in control you are not leading.

But just because you have a big position, it does not follow that you are in real control. Even prime ministers have fallen into this trap. British PM John Major was attacked, in public and by his own side, for 'being in office, but not in power'.[1] The point was that the prime minister seemed to lack an agenda of his own and he was drifting with the tide: others were shaping the agenda for him.

Are you in office or are you in power?

Why this myth matters

In practice, no leader can be in full control of any large organization. Unlike a deity, most leaders are not omnipresent, omniscient and omnipotent. The leaders who think they have these powers are well worth not working for. It is impossible to know in real time what is happening everywhere, let alone to do anything about it.

So the challenge for leaders is to know what they can and should control directly, and what can be left to the organizational machine. Organizations generate huge amounts of noise: meetings, reports, e-mails and reviews can absorb all of the leader's time without actually achieving anything.

MAXIMIZING THE SIGNAL TO NOISE RATIO

Darwin's *Voyage of the Beagle*[2] recounts his epic trip around the world which formed the basis for his development of his revolutionary ideas of evolution. You might think it would be a tale of unending scientific inquest, with setbacks and breakthroughs along the way. It was not like that. Instead, it was a tale of a Victorian gentleman slowly making his way round the world, visiting acquaintances and having a relatively leisured time. But it was a five-year journey with a purpose.

It took Darwin another 20 years to publish *Origin of Species*.[3]

Looked at from today's perspective, he was hopelessly unproductive. Five years to go around the world while a productive executive can do a transatlantic trip overnight, clear out e-mails, have a series of meetings and still have quality time with the children via video conference. And all Darwin did was to produce one book in 25 years.

Never mistake activity for achievement. Effective leaders maximize their signal to noise ratio. Noises are the daily distractions of business life; your signal is where you are going to make a difference.

Lessons for leaders

Leaders have to control the noise, but they also have to maximize the signal. This is always a tough juggling act.

Maximizing the signal means having a clear vision and clear agenda; managing the noise depends on having a great team and strong organizational machine.

Have a clear vision

You maximize the signal when you have a very clear agenda. You need a clear idea, or vision, of how things will be different or better as a result of your leadership. What will happen that would not have happened without you?

Have a clear agenda

Your vision will tell you what you want to see achieved, and you have to support that with a clear idea of how that will happen. This normally comes in the form of a simple set of priorities or a campaign which everyone can understand. This may be as simple as:

- we will put our customers first;
- we will simplify our operations;
- we will be first to market;
- we will achieve six sigma quality.

At first blush, these appear to be no more than slogans. And if all you do is make the motivational speech about customers, it will remain a slogan. You then have to push the idea through to its logical conclusion. If customers come first, then that might mean making our products easy to use, making the helpline helpful, being generous on refunds, listening to what customers actually want, and much more.

Unlike Charles Darwin, who had the luxury of focusing on his scientific mission, leaders have to deal with the noise of business. There are endless battles to be fought every day. If they are not fought, chaos quickly ensues. This is where leaders can get stuck in the weeds, and they find they are no longer leading but simply surviving.

Manage the noise: build your team and organizational machine

To deal with the noise, the leader needs to put things in place: a great team and a strong organizational machine. Your team is your most vital asset: they can deliver the signal and manage the noise for you. But your team needs a machine that works. The plumbing of the firm is vital: decision-making systems, financial controls, reporting processes, operating systems,

IT and people development systems all need to work. Plumbing may not be glamorous but it is essential: we only discover the true value of plumbing when it goes wrong.

The strong team and machine means that you do not need to be omnipresent and omnipotent. Your team and machine will look after the noise for you, allowing you to focus on maximizing the signal. You only need to get involved in the noise on an exception basis. You will never achieve 100 per cent control: that is impossible and unnecessary. But focusing on the signal will allow you to control what you have to. It will let you make a difference and take people where they would not have got by themselves.

Conclusion

Leaders cannot control everything but must control the right things: they have to maximize their signal to noise ratio. What makes this myth lethal is that many people get stuck in the weeds. They think that if they are very busy dealing with the day-to-day noise then they are in control and they are leading. They may exercise control, but they are going nowhere and not leading. So this gets four unicorns: control is a dangerous myth and much misunderstood. The reason it is not five unicorns is that leaders must control something: their destiny.

Endnotes

1 Norman Lamont in his resignation speech on 9 June 1993.

2 First published in 1839 as *Journals and Remarks*.

3 Charles Darwin (1859) *On the Origin of Species by Means of Natural Selection, or the Preservation of Favoured Races in the Struggle for Life*, John Murray.

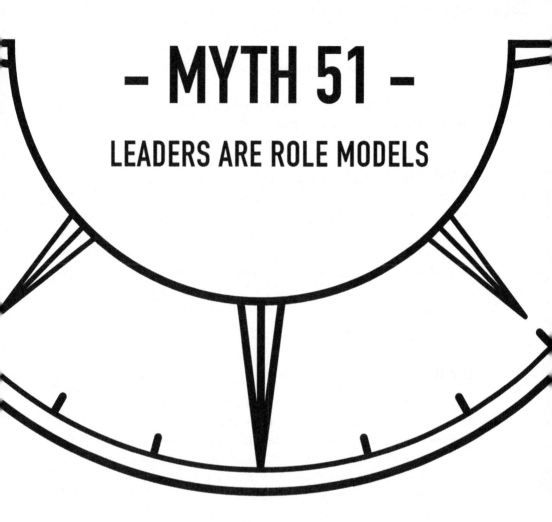

– MYTH 51 –

LEADERS ARE ROLE MODELS

Leaders tend to underestimate the influence they have.

The nature of the myth

Try this simple exercise. Think of some of the bosses you have worked for. Remember what they achieved. Now try to remember what they were like. What do you remember the most?

The chances are that you remembered little, if anything, about what they really achieved or what difference they made. But you will probably remember vividly what they were like: the sort of clothes they wore, what they looked like, how they talked, what sort of character they were.

Now think about how you will be remembered: will you be remembered for what you achieve or for what you are like? And how do you want to be remembered?

In practice, all leaders are remembered mainly as role models. Some role models are good and others are bad.

Why this myth matters

The idea of a role model is usually a positive one. A role model is someone we would like to emulate, and a leader should be held up as an aspirational role model. Why would we want to work for someone we despise or dislike? But leaders can be positive or negative role models: either way, they set the tone for their team.

Leaders tend to underestimate the influence they have in terms of substance, style and learning.

Substance

In terms of substance, leaders have to use words carefully. What you say will be used and misused to justify actions far away from you. One senior leader was shocked to find that the office was being redesigned on the basis that that was what he wanted. The leader had no view and had not expressed an opinion, but it had proven an expedient way for a manager to force through the redesign. If managers want something done, the easy way to push it is to claim that is what the boss wants: no one argues with the boss.

Style

At least with matters of substance, you can see what is happening and you can deal with it. Matters of style are much harder to deal with, and the consequences can be much more damaging. If you find that you have a team which is Machiavellian, low on trust, competitive and individualistic you can blame the team, or you can look in the mirror. Teams pick up their behaviours from their leader, for better or for worse. This means you have to pay constant attention not just to what you do, but to how you do it.

Learning

We saw in Myth 35 that emerging leaders learn heavily from their boss, both good and bad lessons. You are constantly under the microscope, with your team peering at your every action. This is where you are a highly influential role model.

Lessons for leaders

Effective leadership is not something that just happens. You cannot just turn up in the morning and start leading. To lead well requires conscious effort. It is obvious that you need to make conscious effort and conscious decisions around matters of substance. But since you will be remembered more for how you are than for what you do, you also have to make conscious decisions about how you behave. Your decisions will influence how your team reacts and performs.

Manage your mood

If you come into the office feeling gloomy, your gloom will soon spread like a major depression across the office. Your team will try to avoid seeing you, knowing that any discussion will be less than productive, and their avoidance will probably just annoy you even more. Leaders have to learn the basic truth that we can choose how we feel. We are accountable for our feelings. If we want to feel gloomy and suspicious, that is our choice. If we want to be positive and professional, that is also our choice. As humans, we have good days and bad days. On good days, it is easy to project the right mood. The real test comes on bad days. That is when leaders have to make a conscious choice about how they want to present themselves to the team. Choose well.

Manage your style

You are who you are and there is no point in trying to become someone else. The challenge for the leader is to become the best of who you are. If you are deeply analytical and not great with people, then that is how you are. Recognize this and, in your deeply analytical way, work out what you need to do to bring people along with you: use your strength to address your weakness.

As a role model, make conscious decisions about how you want to be seen. You will not get any direct feedback on this, but you will get clear indirect feedback in the way that your team behaves: they will be following or reacting to your lead. They will remember you for how you are. How do you want to be remembered?

Encourage learning

Since everyone is watching you and learning from you, make this process explicit, not implicit. This does not require you to ask people for feedback, because no one gives honest feedback to their boss face to face. But you can instil the basic discipline of debriefs. The Red Arrows, the UK air display team, do this after every show and every practice because they chase perfection and mistakes can be fatal. In the debrief, the hierarchy is suspended: the focus is purely on the performance and how it can be improved. Asking WWW (what went well) and EBI (even better if...) is a positive and non-threatening way of extracting the learning (see Myth 31).

This learning will help your team improve fast, and it will also help you.

Conclusion

All leaders are also role models, for better or worse. That should rate zero unicorns. But this myth is easily misinterpreted as indicating that leaders are only positive role models, when many are less than positive. For this reason, the myth scores two unicorns.

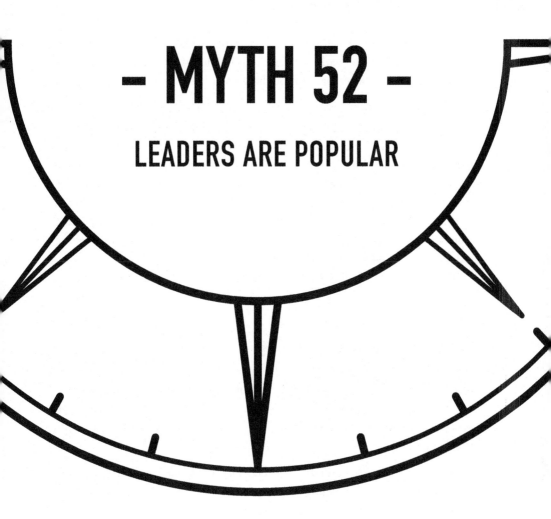

– MYTH 52 –

LEADERS ARE POPULAR

The true currency of leadership is respect and trust.

The nature of the myth

Even leaders are human, mostly. And it is human nature to want to be liked. Leaders like to be liked. This is a universal truth, which is reflected in the use of flattery down the ages:

- 'A person who seeks and desires rank must be obsequious and use flattery as powerful men and rulers require. Otherwise it will be impossible for him to attain any rank' (Ibn Khaldun, 1377).[1]

- Machiavelli (1513) wrote an entire chapter of advice in *The Prince* entitled 'How flatterers should be avoided', noting that, 'In general men are ungrateful, fickle, false, cowardly, covetous, dissimulating, hungry for profit and quick to evade danger.'[2] Not much has changed in 500 years. He did not say whether he thought women were better or worse than men in these respects.

The popularity myth is also part of the hero leader myth. The successful leader is portrayed like Julius Caesar returning to Rome on a triumphal march in front of adoring and cheering citizens, with less adoring conquered slaves in chains at the back of the procession. Annual reports and company newsletters reinforce the popularity myth. The great leader is always portrayed doing worthy things just like royalty: opening a plant, inspecting some new machinery, delivering a great speech, handing out awards, making a donation to charity or meeting celebrities.

The idea of a popular leader seems to be both natural and harmless. But is it?

Why this myth matters

Machiavelli went to the root of the problem when he asked whether it is better for a leader to be loved or feared. He concluded that love is weak because it is temporary; people will like you as long as you are doing favours for them:

> As long as you succeed and do them good, they are devoted to you entirely; they will offer you their blood, property, life and children… but only when danger is far distant; when danger approaches they turn against you.

He recommended that the Prince execute a few people to tame the population. Be cruel to be kind: once the population see that you are serious about law and order, they will not fool around. It was the equivalent of a business reorganizing and firing a few people.

Popularity is also a recipe for weakness in a business setting. Good ways to gain popularity include:

- not giving people bad news;
- not stretching people and demanding that they achieve more;
- accepting second best and not complaining;
- always adjusting your diary to suit the needs of others;
- keeping a bowl of candy on your desk for passers-by (and yourself).

The popularity problem is acute for leaders in democracies. Elections are essentially auctions where different sorts of promises are made to different parts of the electorate. The side which bids the most to the most people wins, but then suffers winner's curse: they have to make good on impossible promises. If politicians are honest, they will not make promises and they will not get elected. If they want to get elected, they make promises they cannot keep and then no one trusts them. Part of the fault is with the politicians; part of the problem is with us in voting for the impossible.

Lessons for leaders

Machiavelli assumed that a leader cannot be both loved and feared, so he chose fear as the true currency of leadership. There are still a few bosses who operate like that. They are the psychopaths who believe that a team player is someone who does what they are told.

But love and fear is a false choice. There is a stronger currency of leadership than fear or love. The true currency of leadership is respect and trust. Take the list of popular actions above and see what a respected leader would do instead:

- **Not giving people bad news.** Be open about the situation. Have an honest, positive and constructive conversation about options for the way forward. This is a difficult conversation, but if you handle it well it builds trust and respect. The alternative of trying to suppress bad news until everything blows up, or until the annual review, is a good way of losing both trust and respect.

- **Not stretching people.** Effective team leaders will stretch their team and be demanding, but they will also support the team in getting there and be flexible about how they do it. Stretching the team helps each team member grow and develop.

- **Accepting second best.** Effective leaders have high standards and high expectations. Most professionals have pride in what they do and want to do a good job. You gain more respect from having high standards than from giving everyone an easy life.

- **Adjusting your diary to suit others.** This is both weak and leads to massive loss of time. If you do not value your time, your team will not value your time either. Be clear about your needs and interests. Optimize the use of time for yourself and your team.

- **Keeping a bowl of candy on your desk is simple bribery**. As a leader, you have a far more powerful weapon at your disposal: recognition. Giving specific and positive feedback is powerful: everyone likes to be flattered. Public recognition from your boss is flattery on steroids.

Achieving this sort of respect requires strong-form honesty. Weak-form honesty is politician's honesty: they assume they are honest until they have been convicted in court of lying. But in day-to-day life, leaders are not presumed innocent until they are proved guilty. Strong-form honesty does not permit shading the truth or omitting vital information. It follows the legal requirement to 'tell the truth, the whole truth and nothing but the truth'. The challenge for the leader is to tell the truth in a way which is positive and constructive.

Respect lasts longer than popularity, and will serve you well in hard times as well as good. It is the way to high performance, not adequate performance. You do not need to be feared or loved: you need to be respected.

Conclusion

This myth is widespread and it is lethal to the effectiveness of leaders. That merits five unicorns. But some leaders can be both popular and effective, even if they are exceptional. In recognition of the exceptions, this scores just four unicorns.

Endnotes

1 Ibn Khaldun (1377) *The Muqaddimah* (307), various editions.

2 Niccolò Machiavelli (1532) *The Prince*, chapter XVII.

– MYTH 53 –

LEADERS DESERVE EXCEPTIONAL REWARDS

Senior executives show that they are very good at rent seeking, but fail to prove any link between the rents they extract and the performance they deliver.

The nature of the myth

Nearly 250 years ago, Adam Smith saw the dangers of public firms as opposed to private firms. Owners look after their money carefully; managers of other people's firms are not so careful:

> The directors of such companies... being the managers rather of other people's money than of their own, it cannot well be expected that they should watch over it with the same anxious vigilance with which the partners in a private

co-partnership frequently watch over their own. Negligence and profusion, therefore, must always prevail, more or less, in the management of the affairs of such a company.[1]

In the last 50 years, this 'negligence and profusion' has been to the benefit of senior executives of large firms. Whether these senior executives are actually leading or succeeding is another debate. For our purposes here, we will define the CEO as the leader of the firm.

Pay of the median S&P 500 CEO is now 300 times that of the median employee.[2] In 1965, the CEO earned just 20 times the compensation of the median employee. There has been an explosion of pay at the top. Average CEO compensation at top firms now runs at $16.4 million annually.

Various reasons for high pay are put forward:

1 **It's tough at the top.** We have already seen (Myth 48) that it is tougher in the middle than at the top.

2 **CEOs have little job security.** Median CEO tenure at S&P 500 firms is now 6.6 years, up one year since 2005. Job security is rising and is better than that of staff who have median job tenure of 4.2 years. Only 16 per cent of CEOs who move on are dismissed.[3]

3 **If we don't pay top dollar we will lose top talent.** There is no evidence of top CEOs moving from one firm to another for a salary increase.

4 **The CEO makes all the difference.** Pay certainly seems to make a difference, in the wrong direction. Research shows that of 1,500 large firms, higher executive compensation led to worse performance over three years.[4] Despite performance-linked pay, there is no evidence that pay drives better performance.

5 **It is the market rate.** But the market fails on top pay: every board thinks they want an above-average CEO so they pay above average, which means the average rises remorselessly. Adam Smith, the high priest of capitalism, foresaw this (above). The problem will get far worse before it gets better.

Why this myth matters

Perhaps we should not worry about high CEO pay. We do not complain about the huge sums earned by football stars, film stars and entrepreneurs.

In the UK, average pay of footballers in the top division has risen even faster than that of CEOs. In 2000, they were earning an average of £10,000 per week;[5] by 2015 it had risen to £44,000 per week.[6] This includes many journeyman players; top players earn nearer to £10 million a year.

The public find it easier to accept high pay for film and sports stars because the contract between us and the star is very transparent. We volunteer to pay the star and we watch him or her perform; we see what they do and we can stop paying when we no longer like what they do. A different sort of transparency works for entrepreneurs. We can all see that they started and built something themselves and they deserve the rewards for that.

There is no such transparency for CEO pay. We see that they earn a lot, but it is not clear what they deliver in return, nor have we given clear consent to their pay, unlike film and sports stars.

So what is the problem with high CEO pay?

- Breakdown in trust and respect for the leaders within the business. When the CEO demands that staff show passion and loyalty, and then downsizes and fires 20 per cent of the staff while pocketing millions more in compensation, a serious trust problem arises. It looks like the CEO is acting in pure self-interest.

- Excess pay leads to social conflict. Popular movements are on the rise in the democratic world, to the consternation of the elite. But this is not surprising. In the 25 years from 1989 to 2014, real median US household income rose from $53,327 to $53,718, or less than 1 per cent. At the same time, business leaders were enriching themselves to an unprecedented degree.

- Public loss of trust in business and its leadership. The Ipsos MORI veracity index[7] shows that business leaders are one of the least trusted professions that exist: only 35 per cent of the population trust leaders to tell the truth. If leaders are seen to be greedy liars, then a popular backlash against the elite is not far behind.

- CEOs start to believe that they are special. If you are paid very highly and treated very well, that is evidence that you must be special. This creates a circular logic: 'I am special so I deserve top rewards, which shows I am special.'

Lessons for leaders

There are three possible lessons for leaders:

- The cynical lesson is simple: become a top executive and stick your snout in the swill while the swill is still there. If you don't take it, others will.

- Know what you really want in life, and how much money you need to achieve that: do you really need to earn $16 million a year, and what would you do with it anyway? Self-worth is more than net worth.

- If you want to lead people where they would not have got by themselves, it helps if they trust and respect you. Excess pay erodes trust.

Boards or shareholders need to get a grip, otherwise government will get a grip, and it is unlikely to be a warm embrace.

Conclusion

Senior executives show that they are very good at rent seeking, but fail to prove any link between the rents they extract and the performance they deliver. So this myth is true; it is also toxic because of the way it breeds mistrust and populism. Five unicorns.

Endnotes

1 Adam Smith (1776) *Wealth of Nations*, W Strahan and T Cadell.

2 Lawrence Mishel and Alyssa Davis (2015) Top CEOs make 300 times more than typical workers, *Economic Policy Institute* [online] http://www.epi. org/publication/top-ceos-make-300-times-more-than-workers-pay-growth-surpasses-market-gains-and-the-rest-of-the-0-1-percent.

3 Matteo Tonello (2015) New statistics and cases of CEO succession in the S&P 500, *Harvard Law School* [online] https://corpgov.law.harvard.edu/2015/04/23/ new-statistics-and-cases-of-ceo-succession-in-the-sp-500.

4 Michael Cooper, Huseyin Gulen and P Raghavendra Rau (2010) Performance for pay? The relation between CEO incentive compensation and future stock price performance, *SSRN* [online] https://papers.ssrn.com/sol3/papers. cfm?abstract_id=1572085.

5 Nick Harris (2011) From £20 to £33,868 per week: a quick history of English football's top-flight wages, *Sporting Intelligence* [online] http://www.sportingintelligence.com/2011/01/20/from-20-to-33868-per-week-a-quick-history-of-english-footballs-top-flight-wages-200101/.

6 Nick Harris (2016) Mind the gap…, *Mail Online* [online] http://www.dailymail.co.uk/sport/football/article-3456453/Mind-gap-Premier-League-wages-soar-average-salaries-2014-15-season-1-7million-rest-creep-along.html.

7 Ipsos MORI veracity index 2016 [online] https://www.ipsos-mori.com/researchpublications/researcharchive/3685/Politicians-are-still-trusted-less-than-estate-agents-journalists-and-bankers.aspx#gallery[m]/1.

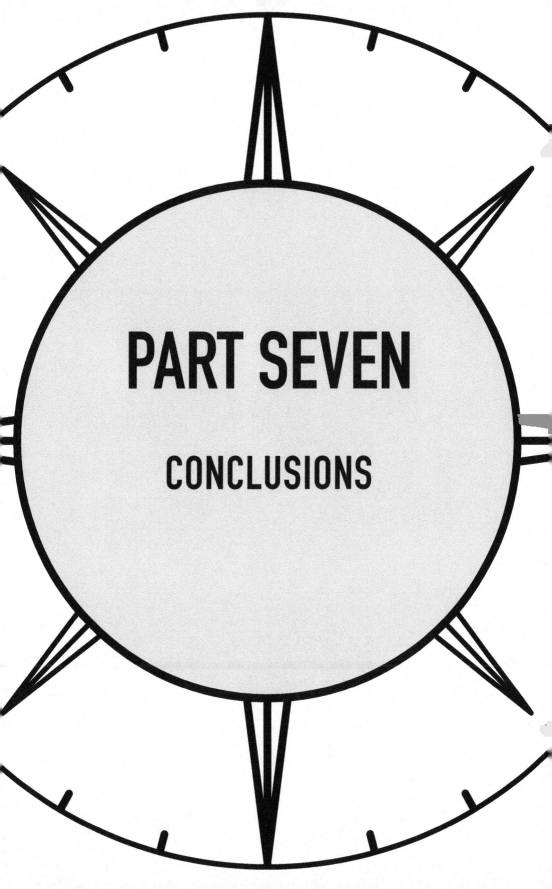

PART SEVEN

CONCLUSIONS

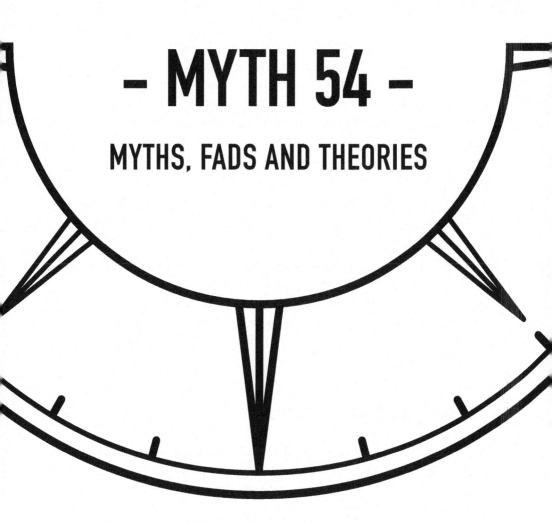

– MYTH 54 –

MYTHS, FADS AND THEORIES

Copying symptoms without understanding causes is bound to fail.

The nature of the myth

Leadership is a land of myths, fads and theories. They come in two main flavours:

- Insights into what leaders are like: what are the qualities you need to succeed?

- Insights into what leaders should do: how can you really make a difference?

These myths may be peddled in an *HBR* article, or by consultants selling their wares, or in an inspiring conference speech, but they all have a simple promise: follow me and you will be better. These myths may be as robust as the latest breakthrough in medical science, or they may be as credible as the quack doctors of the Wild West selling potions to cure everything from drooping morale to drooping profits and drooping libido.

It is easy to mock many of the myths, but that is to miss the point. Two characteristics of these myths stand out:

- They vary widely: there is not a single unifying theory of leadership. No one can agree what leaders are like, what leaders should do or even what leadership is.

- There is an insatiable demand for the myths of leadership. It is easy to mock the peddlers of myths, but they only exist because we seek them out, pay them and encourage them. Consultants are the easy butt of jokes, but they make very good money and have grown in number very fast for 30 years. So who is the fool: the fool or the person who pays for the folly?

Why this myth matters

A book called *Myths of Leadership* should probably mock all the myths and fads of leadership. The peddlers of the myths may deserve mockery, but that does not mean we should mock the leaders who pay for the myths and use them.

In practice, there is good reason for the myths to exist and for leaders to use them: both the myths and the fads have value. That is not necessarily the expected conclusion from a book with this title.

The wide variety of leadership theories is very good news for leaders. If there was a single formula for leadership, leaders would soon be following the fate of Korean baseball fans,[1] camel racing jockeys,[2] dairy hands[3] and Japanese waitresses[4]: we could all be replaced by robots. The fact that there are so many leadership theories shows that leadership remains more of an art than a science. You do not have to slavishly follow a set of leadership rules. You can find your own way to lead; there are countless ways to succeed or to fail. This makes the leadership journey endlessly challenging and rewarding. Make the most of it.

Leadership gives rise to an endless conveyor belt of new theories and new fads, all of which promise to help leaders succeed. These fads flow through business with great regularity. In the last 30 years, a few of the major fads that have swept through business include:

- re-engineering;
- strategic intent and core competence;
- portfolio analysis and management;
- shareholder value management;
- blue ocean strategy.

These fads should carry a public health warning. I should know: I helped the academic creators of several of these myths deploy them into the market place. Taking strategic intent and core competence as an example, here is why it needs a warning:

- The theory is an idea which was retrofitted onto the experience of successful firms. The exemplar firms never actually implemented strategic intent and core competence consciously, and it is not clear that the ideas were the drivers of their success.
- Practice and theory are different. In practice, the theory became a call to action. It was a way of stretching the firm and getting executives to think about business not as usual.
- The theory and practice degrade rapidly over time. Once the idea spreads, it becomes simplified so that junior consultants can implement it. This was the fate of re-engineering which was reduced to juniors mapping processes at great expense. Nowadays 'strategic intent' simply means a goal we want to achieve and a 'core competence' is a grand way of saying we think we are good at something.

These fads spread like wildfire once they reach a tipping point. An esoteric fad is risky to implement: if it does not work, then the sponsoring executive has wasted time, money and opportunity. But once a fad becomes fashionable, the risk equation goes into reverse. If you have not implemented re-engineering, then the question is why not? The business universe will be full of dramatic success stories, which may or may not be accurate. You cannot afford to be left behind.

The surprise finding from these fads is that they can all help. This became apparent when working in education. More or less any initiative can help: philosophy for children,[5] building a skateboard park in a remote village school in India,[6] and putting table tennis tables in an inner-city school in London[7] are all deeply implausible interventions. However, they are all associated with some outstanding successes which have been widely written up. When other schools mindlessly copy the intervention, the fad fails. The same happens when fads are mindlessly copied across businesses. The copying school or firm does not understand why the fad appears to have worked. If you do not understand why it works, you will not understand how to make it work. Copying symptoms without understanding causes is bound to fail: it is like using spot remover to cure measles.

The reason the fads work has little to do with the fads themselves. Instead a fad helps because it:

1 mobilizes management to raise its game;

2 provides a platform for implementing a wider change programme;

3 gives permission to leadership to take action: the intervention is normally heavily customized to the needs of each situation;

4 offers insight and challenges management to think differently about what they do and how they do it.

Lessons for leaders

There is a surprising lesson for leaders from these fads and theories: they can all help.

All leadership theories offer some insight. None of them offer a universal truth.

All fads can help, if you use them well. Use them as a call to action and tailor the implementation to your needs and situation. Where possible, understand why the fad works; copy the causes, not the symptoms of success.

Conclusion

Leadership myths serve the same purpose as ancient myths: to explain the inexplicable, to give comfort and insight, to guide behaviour and occasionally to entertain. This means that behind even the wildest fantasy, there is often a nugget of truth or an insight to be gained, provided that the myth is not taken at face value. And all myths and fads can be used as calls to action. For this reason, you can choose to award this myth as many or as few unicorns as you like.

Endnotes

1 A struggling Korean baseball team tried to solve the problem of its lack of support by installing robot fans in the stalls: https://www.youtube.com/watch?v=PHTK63fgl4M.

2 Camel racing is enjoying a resurgence in the UAE, with robots riding the camels rather than children, which was once the case but has been outlawed: https://www.youtube.com/watch?v=pDBGdEZa9eM.

3 Tom Heyden (2015) The cows that queue up to milk themselves, *BBC* [online] http://www.bbc.co.uk/news/magazine-32610257.

4 Japanese waitresses: https://www.youtube.com/watch?v=8pYY3LQFAVU.

5 Education Endowment Foundation (nd) Philosophy for children [online] https://educationendowmentfoundation.org.uk/our-work/projects/philosophy-for-children.

6 Pratik Chorge (nd) No school, no skateboarding: India's first rural skate park, *Hindustan Times* [online] http://www.hindustantimes.com/static/groundglass/no-school-no-skateboarding.

7 Morpeth School in south London had a strong table tennis programme for years, and in 2011 was selected as the training centre for the UK and Japanese teams for the 2012 London Olympics: http://www.bbc.co.uk/news/uk-england-london-12848896.

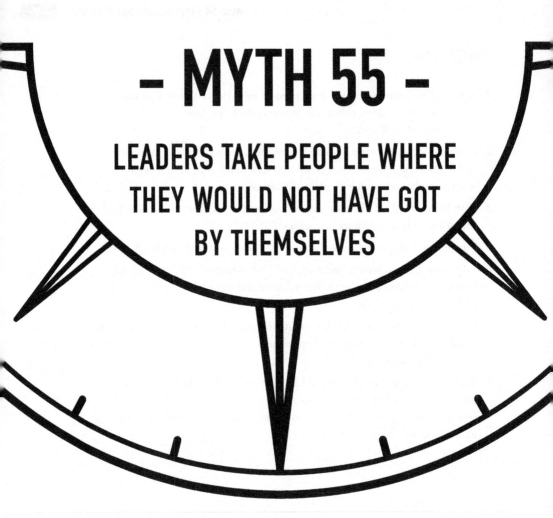

– MYTH 55 –

LEADERS TAKE PEOPLE WHERE THEY WOULD NOT HAVE GOT BY THEMSELVES

*If you do not know where you are going, then you are
unlikely to go where you need to.*

The nature of the myth

This is the myth that is at the heart of this book, and is a definition of leadership used by Henry Kissinger. Any book about the myths of leadership cannot avoid creating more myths of leadership. It is only fair that these myths should be exposed and challenged.

To challenge the myth, you need criteria for what a good definition of leadership achieves. Here is a suggestion, noting on the way that even these criteria may be myths in their own right. You decide.

A good definition of leadership will:

1 Differentiate what a leader does from what other managers and staff do; does the definition only work with people you regard as leaders?

2 Be actionable and practical: it should give guidance to what leaders should and should not do and how they should act.

3 Be universal: it should apply to all leaders in all situations.

Why this myth matters

If you do not know where you are going, then you are unlikely to go where you need to. So it matters to know what leadership is. Many books on leadership do not even attempt to define leadership, which means that they can say whatever they want. The books which do attempt a definition all have different definitions.

Three top writers on leadership have attempted definitions of leadership. Here they are:

Peter Drucker: 'The only definition of a leader is someone who has followers.'[1] This definition fails on two counts:

- Stars of film, stage and music, and top writers and thinkers like Drucker have followers: that does not make them leaders.

- Every boss has a team which follows them: just because you are the boss it does not mean you are leading your followers.

John Kotter: 'Leaders set a direction, align people, motivate and inspire.'[2] This reads well, but does not work. Look closely at each characteristic of Kotter's leader:

- Leaders may align and motivate people, but don't managers do that as well?

- Not all leaders are inspirational, even if they are highly effective. You have probably worked for an effective leader without being inspired all the time.

- That leaders set a direction is closer to the truth, but if the direction is simply a continuation of the past direction, is that leading or following?

Warren Bennis: 'Managers are people who do things right and leaders are people who do the right thing.'[3] This is a nice aphorism, but the language is better than the thinking. There are plenty of leaders who do catastrophically wrong things. They lead people into the desert, not into the Promised Land. Even leaders who succeed do plenty of things which are wrong: Churchill, Stalin and Mao Tse-tung were all leaders who did plenty of things wrong, not right. The hallmark of most leaders is that they have repeatedly done things wrong, they have failed and they have had the resilience to come back.

Lessons for leaders

The idea that leaders take people where they would not have got by themselves spawns an epic saga of other myths, which you can choose to challenge or accept. But if the core idea is correct, then these myths may be reality. For that reason, we will treat them as lessons of leadership, not myths of leadership.

Here are the top 10 consequences of believing that leaders take people where they would not have got by themselves:

1   You can lead at any level. Anyone can learn to lead, and everyone can learn to lead better, even if few of us will become leadership superstars.

2   The person at the top is not necessarily leading: never confuse position with performance.

3   Don't confuse activity with achievement. You may be working very hard, but that does not mean you pass the leadership test. Leaders need to maximize their signal to noise ratio. The signal is how they make a difference; the noise is the day-to-day survival of organizational life, which can consume all your time.

4   Leaders need a clear idea of how things will be different as a result of their leadership. You can call this a mission, vision or strategy if you want to sound important.

5   Leaders require more than formal power to succeed. They need to be able to influence and persuade people they do not control. This becomes more important as firms de-layer and outsource: no one controls all the resources they need to succeed.

6   Leaders do not need to be charismatic and inspirational, but they do need some signature strengths and skills and they need a clear idea of how they will make a difference.

7 No leader has all the skills required to succeed; no one gets ticks in all the boxes. Since you can only excel at what you enjoy, find the context which you will enjoy and where your strengths flourish.

8 Leaders need to build a strong team to deliver for them and to compensate for any weaknesses they may have.

9 Leaders need to build a strong operational machine with effective managers: the leader may lead the revolution, but the leader needs managers to manage the world before, during and after the revolution.

10 Leaders have to keep learning and growing because the context in which they work keeps on changing: what works in one role does not automatically work in the next role.

Ultimately, leadership is like life: it is a voyage of discovery. It may be challenging, but it is rarely dull. It is as good as we want to make it. So whatever your journey is, enjoy it.

Conclusion

As the author of the book I will claim that this myth is true, so it rates zero unicorns. But we live in a post-truth world where the truth is what you want to believe. That means you get to decide whether this is myth or reality and how many unicorns it merits.

Endnotes

1 Peter Drucker (1996) Your leadership is unique: Good news: there is no one 'leadership personality', *Greek Orthodox Metropolis of Boston* [online] http://boston.goarch.org/assets/files/your%20leadership%20is%20unique.pdf.

2 J P Kotter (2001) What leaders really do, *Harvard Business Review*, 79 (11), pp 85–96.

3 Warren Bennis and Burt Nanus (1985) *Leaders: The strategies for taking charge*, Harper and Row, p 21.

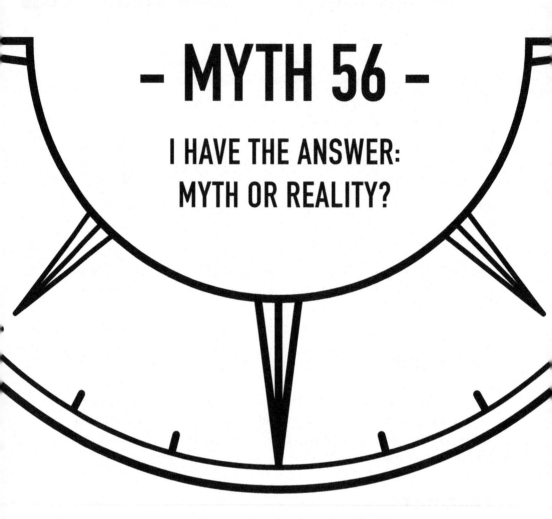

– MYTH 56 –

I HAVE THE ANSWER: MYTH OR REALITY?

Leaders need to build their own success formula.

The nature of the myth

This book is about myths, which presents the kind of big temptation that few teenagers can resist. The best way to show that you are smart is to show that everyone else is really dumb. Attacking myths implies that no one else knows what they are talking about. But there is no point in attacking myths if you have no alternative to offer. If you do not know what reality looks like, how can you tell myths from truth?

Throughout this book I have attempted to respect most myths. The tales of Greek mythology were not attempting to tell the truth; they were telling stories from which listeners could learn if they wanted to. The same holds with myths of leadership: we can learn something from all the myths if we choose to. If we choose to learn nothing, that says something about the myth and something about us.

In challenging the myths, I have suggested alternatives where possible. The alternatives may be the truth, or they may be reality. This is the point at which to pull together all these alternatives: you decide whether they belong to the land of myths or the land of reality.

Why this myth matters

Leaders need to build their own success formula. It helps if you know what the choices are. This lays out some of your choices.

Lessons for leaders

Here are seven major themes which this book has laid out as an alternative to the myths of leadership:

1 **A leader is someone who takes people where they would not have got by themselves**. Leadership is about what you do, not about your position. You can lead at the bottom of the organization, and you may not be leading even if you are at the top.

2 **Anyone can learn to lead and everyone can learn to lead better**. Leadership is like a playing a sport or a musical instrument: a little practice will make you far better than most people and you can always improve, even if only a few people can become superstars. You do not need to be born a leader.

3 **Leadership is contextual**. There is no universal formula for leadership: there is only what works for you in your context. This means you have to keep on learning and growing because your context keeps on changing. Leadership is a journey, not a destination.

4 **No leader gets ticks in all the boxes**. There is no such thing as a perfect leader, and you do not need to be a charismatic superhuman to lead. You do need some signature strengths which you can build on and use in a

context where you can succeed. Learn to be the best of who you are, rather than attempting to copy some leadership idol.

5 **Leadership is a team sport.** Leaders succeed with other people. They have to build a balanced team which compensates for their weaknesses, has a balance of styles and allows each leader to focus on the one or two things where they can make the most difference. Everything else has to be delegated to the team. Leadership is not about being the lone hero or the Great Man.

6 **Leaders need a vision, but you do not need to be a visionary.** A vision is just a story about how you are going to make a difference. It is a story in three parts: this is where we are, this is where we are going and this is how we will get there. To make it motivational, customize your story to each team member with part four: 'and here is your vital role in helping the team get there.'

7 **Leadership is becoming more challenging.** The core skills required of a leader are growing. In the 19th century, leaders needed IQ: bosses had the brains and workers had the hands. An educated workforce in the 20th century could do more but demanded more: leaders needed EQ (emotional quotient) to deal with people. In the 21st century, leaders need to make things happen through people they do not control: they need PQ (political quotient) skills of influencing, building networks of trust and support, aligning agendas and fighting the right battles.

Conclusion

You decide whether these are myths or reality, and how many unicorns to award. But beware the sting in the tail. If they are myths, then what is reality? And perhaps that is the ultimate lesson of leadership: you have to make your own reality.

INDEX

Note: page numbers in *italic* indicate figures or tables.

9/11 215

accountability 126, 229–32
  for feelings 231–32
  passing the buck 230, 231
  vs responsibility 229–30, 232
  upwards delegation 230–31
adaptability 139
Alexander the Great 8, 119–20
alumni networks 143
Amazon 120
'analysis paralysis' 62
Apple 182
Attlee, Clement 17
authentic leadership 194, 206–09
  'being yourself' 207, 208
  openness 207–09

balanced scorecard 66
Barnes & Noble 120
Barone, Guglielmo and Mocetti, Sauro 80
Bayesian analysis 61
BBC 120
Bennis, Warren 9, 267
Birla, Ghanshyam Das 215
blue ocean strategy 263
Bonaparte, Napoleon 133
Boston Consulting Group (BCG) 120
Boston Matrix *see* growth/share matrix
Brin, Sergey 104, 161, 183
British Airways 120
Buffett, Warren 225–26
Bush, George H 80
Bush, George W 80

Caesar, Julius 228, 250
Carroll, Lewis 238
Carver, Elliot 165–66
Catholic Church 189
CBS 120
change, resistance to 240
charisma 87–90, 268
  vs crisis management 90
  vs decision-making 89

vs effectiveness 88
heroes, need for 87–88
vs honesty 90
vs manipulativeness 88
vs motivation 89
teachability of 88
vs vision 89
Churchill, Winston 8, 85, 122, 133, 137, 268
Clinton, Bill 80
collaboration 127
comfort zones 140, 149
communication 51
  and control 54
  email 56
  employee engagement 51
  face-to-face 56
  in writing 57
  jargon 54
  listening 55
  'making words count' 55–56
  and persuasion 54
  phone calls 56
  presentations 57
  technology, influence of 54, 56
  and understanding 54–55
  video conferencing 56
contingency theory 202
control 54, 241–44
  agenda, role of 243
  delegation 244
  in distributed leadership 197–98
  establishing, in the first 90 days 158
  signal to noise ratio 242, 268
  vision, role of 243
core competence 263
courage 95–98, 126
  and decision-making 96
  and difficult conversations 96
  pattern recognition 97, 98
  and risk-taking 96–97
  'stepping up' 96
credibility 93–94
crisis, moments of 90, 219–21

charisma, importance of 90
learning, importance of 220–21
pattern recognition 220
transactional leadership 203
critical listening 166, 167–68
cultural factors 32–36, 35
cultural intelligence, building 34
Western bias 33

Darwin, Charles 242, 243
Das Kapital 215
debriefs 248
decision-making 59–62, 96
delegation 62
logic, role of 61
politics, role of 62
'selling' the decision 62
upwards delegation 60
Deezer 120
defining leadership 7–11, 24–27
academic definitions 9
achievements 10
Bennis definition 267–68
context 27, 33
core skills and mindsets 27, 124–27, 269
Drucker definition 267
'goodness' 8
hubris 26
Kissinger definition 10, 266–69
Kotter definition 267
learning, importance of 27
managers' interpretations 8
'success formulas', personal 9, 25, 271
delegation
and control 244
in distributed leadership 198, 199
and trust 198, 199, 236
upwards delegation 60, 230–31
Deming, W Edwards 31
depression 174
destiny 183
difference, making a 237–40, 268
activity vs achievement 239, 268
change, resistance to 240
competition 238
entropy 238
difficult conversations 96
Digital Research 182
disruptive entrepreneurs 120, 120–21
distributed leadership 196–200
control methods 197–98
delegation 198, 199
and globalization 197
vs the Great Man theory 197
Drucker, Peter 9, 267
Dyson 120

Eagly, Alice 108
East India Company 197
École Nationale d'Administration 143–44
emerging leader 46
employee engagement 48–52
and communication 51
compliance vs engagement 49
defining 50
and expectation setting 50
goals, setting 50–51
and positivity 51
sources of 49
and vision 50
Engels, Friedrich 215
entrepreneurial leader 46
EQ (Emotional Quotient) 105–06, 272
expectation setting 50
experience, role of 150–54
learning, importance of 152–53
seniority vs leadership 152
vs youth 150–51

Facebook 150, 161, 182
Fire Service 97
first 90 days 155–59
acceptance and understanding 156–57
control, establishing 158
first impressions 158
reorganization 156
vision, new 156
first impressions 158
first mover advantage 29, 30
fishbones 61
fitness, physical 137–38
sleep, role of 137–38
five competitive forces 120
Ford, Henry 119
Ford Motor Company 120, 147, 182
Fox 120

Gallup 50
Gandhi, Mohandas (Mahatma Gandhi) 215
Gates, Bill 104, 161, 182
gender differences 107–12
balance, importance of 109, 111
gender stereotypes 108, 109
leadership development 109–10
leadership stereotypes 108
and respect 111
General Motors 120
Genghis Khan 88, 207
George II 95
globalization 197, 198
goal-setting 50–51, 63–67
cheating the system 66
competition and teamwork 66

context 65
difficulty of 64
sacrifices, making 65–66
'selling' the goal 64–65
Goldman Sachs 143
'goodness' 8
Google 120, 150, 161, 182, 189
Great Man theory 68, 181–85, 210, 272
destiny, making the most of 183
vs distributed leadership 197
gender stereotypes 183
history of 181–82
vs humility 192, 193
paranoia 184
team, your 184
Grosvenor Group 17
Grove, Andy 184
growth/share matrix 120

habit 125
Hegel, Georg 201
Henry V 87
Henry VI 151
hierarchy of needs 202
Hitler, Adolf 88, 182
Hobbes, Thomas 181
honesty 90, 91–94, 228
and credibility 93–94
and intimacy 93
vs popularity 251, 252
and risk-taking 94
and selfishness 94
and servant leadership 190
and trust 92
Hoover 120
hubris 26, 69
humility 192–95
ambition, in terms of 195
and empowering your team 102, 194
vs the Great Man theory 192, 193
others, with 194–95
self, about 193–94
humour 139–40

IBM 182
Ibn Khaldun 249
influencing skills 148–49
information and reporting 72–75
data vs people 75
information vs intelligence 73–74
materiality of data 74
trust vs control 73, 198
Institute of Economic Affairs 174
Intel 184
intelligence 103–06

EQ (Emotional Quotient) 105–06, 272
IQ (Intelligence Quotient) 105, 272
learning, importance of 105
MBA, having an 104
PQ (Political Quotient) 106, 272
Scientific Management 104
total quality management (TQM) 104
Ipsos MORI 255
IQ (Intelligence Quotient) 105, 272

jargon 54
Joan of Arc 87
Jobs, Steve 207
Jordan, Michael 139

Kennedy, John F 83
King, Martin Luther 8, 83, 86
Kissinger, Henry 10, 21, 266
Kotter, John 9, 267

Le Carré, John 227
leaders vs founders 28–31
first mover advantage 29, 30
learning, importance of 31
start-ups 29–30
survivor bias 29
leaders vs managers 20–23, 160–63
challenge of management 22
'discovery' of leaders 161–62
expectations mismatch 22–23
Kissinger definition 21
management skills, value of 162
promotion, inappropriate 162
pyramid principle 160–61
resilience 162, 163
risk-taking 163
'title inflation' 21
undervaluing leadership 21
leadership courses 169, 171
leadership journey, managing your 43–47, 172
emerging leaders 46
entrepreneurial leaders 46
learning, importance of 42
openness 47
'signature strengths' 41
typical leadership journey 44, 45
learning to lead 79–82, 169–72, 268
physical traits of leaders 80–81
social background of leaders 80
learning, importance of 152–53, 247, 248, 269
debriefs 248
Even Better If... (EBI) 153, 248
and your leadership journey 27, 42, 127

learning from a crisis 105, 220–21
  and scaling up 31
  What Went Well? (WWW) 153, 248
legacies, managing 17, 19
  legacy teams 69–70
Lingle, Walter 198
listening 55, 227–28
loneliness 225–28
  listening 227–28
  management by walking around
      (MBWA) 226, 235
  objectivity 227
Louis XIV 216
luck 131–35
  pay and rewards 132
  persistence 133
  perspective 134
  practice 134
  trust 132–33

Machiavelli, Niccolo 249, 250
Major, John 241
management by algorithm 203
management by walking around (MBWA)
      226, 235
Mandela, Nelson 8, 207
manipulativeness 88
  in psychopathy 115, 116
Marx, Karl 182, 201, 215
Maslow, Abraham 202
McKinsey 143
Medecins Sans Frontières 189
Met Life 70
micro-management 198, 204
Microsoft 161, 182
mind maps 61
money, need for 215–16
Mother Theresa (Anjezë Gonxhe Bojaxhiu) 8
motivation
  ability to motivate 89, 221–22
  and charisma 89
  empowerment of the team 100
  motivational speakers 165
  wealth as a motivator 216, 217
Mujica, José 216
Mussolini, Benito 88

Naidu, Sarojini 215
Nelson, Horatio (Admiral Lord Nelson) 207
nemawashi 62
networks, building 142–45
  alumni networks 143
  personal network, your 144–45
  profile building 145
  vs talent 144
Newton, Isaac 120, 176

Nietzsche, Friedrich 182, 220
Nishiyama Onsen Keiunkan 189

Obama, Barack 80
objectivity 227
Only the Paranoid Survive 184
openness 47, 207–09
Origin of Species 242
Orwell, George 51
Oxfam 189

Page, Larry 150, 183
Palmer, Arnold 134
paranoia 184
pattern recognition 61, 97, 98, 105, 220
pay and rewards 253–57
  average CEO salary 254
  luck, role of 132
  reasons for high pay 254
  trust, effect on 255, 256
  wealth as a motivator 216, 217
people-focused leadership 203
perfection 12–15
  context 13, 14
  limelight, role of 13–14
  'signature strengths' 14
  'success formulas', personal 15
  weaknesses, working with 14–15
persistence 133
personal network, your 144–45
Pol Pot 88
popularity 249–52
  and honesty 251, 252
  and respect 251–52
  and weakness 250
Porter, Michael 120
portfolio analysis and management 263
positivity 126–27
  and resilience 139
  and your team 51
power and influence 146–49, 268
  functional silos 147
  influencing skills 148–49
PQ (Political Quotient) 106, 272
Prahalad, C K and Hamel, Gary 121
presentations 57
Prince, The 249
process control 198
Procter & Gamble 198
profile building 145
psychopathy 113–17, 251
  characteristics of a psychopath 114
  labels, applying 116
  manipulation 115, 116
  prevalence of 113–14

Quality Movement 33

Reagan, Ronald 80, 235, 236
reason 118–23, 148
    vs belief 120
    data, role of 119
    disruptive entrepreneurs 120, 120–21
    excuses 122
    ruthlessness 121, 122
    Scientific Management 119
Red Arrows 248
re-engineering 263
relationship-focused leadership 203
resilience 126, 138–40
    adaptability 139
    in career management 162
    comfort zones 140
    and failure 163
    humour 139–40
    perspective 139
    vs popularity 251–52
    positivity 139
    stress 139
respect 111, 251–52
retirement 174
risk-taking 96–97, 168
    'burning platform' story 94
Rodriguez, William 215
role model, being a 245–48
    debriefs 248
    mood 247
    style 247–48
    words, use of 246
Roosevelt, Franklin D 137, 176
Royal Marine Commandos 97–98, 139–40
ruthlessness 121, 122, 127
Ryanair 120

Scientific Management 104, 119
selfishness 94
servant leadership 186–91
    fads 190
    honesty 190
    organization pyramid 187, 188
    serving the mission 189–90
    serving the organization 188–89
Shakespeare, William 57, 87, 183
shareholder value management 263
'signature strengths' 14, 41
skills and mindset, of leaders 27, 124–27
    accountability 126
    collaboration 127
    courage 126
    habit, role of 125
    high aspirations 125–26

learning 127
    positivity 126–27
    resilience 126
    ruthlessness 127
Sky 120
sleep, role of 137–38
Smith, Adam 253–54
Socrates 53
Sony 120, 182
Spencer, Herbert 182
sporting heroes, lessons from 164–68
    context 171
    critical listening 166, 167–68
    experience 170–71
    goals 165
    hard work 166
    leadership courses 169, 171
    motivation 165
    nature of success 166
Spotify 120
Stalin, Joseph 8, 268
'stepping up' 17, 96
stereotypes
    gender stereotypes 108, 109, 183
    leadership stereotypes 108
strategic intent 263
stress 139, 234–35
'success formulas', personal 9, 15, 25, 271
succession planning 173–77
    board, role of 175, 176
    poor succession 174
    retirement and depression 174
    term limits 176
Sun Tzu 148
survivor bias 29
Sutton, Willie 216
SWOT analysis 61

task-focused leadership 203
Taylor, Frederick 104, 119
Teach First 24
team leadership 210–13
    accountability 211
    collective responsibility, areas of 212–13
    emotions 212
    politics, role of 211
team, your 68–71, 99–102, 269
    accountability 100, 101
    churn 70
    competition and teamwork 66
    humility 102, 194
    legacy teams 69–70
    loyalty vs competence 70
    motivating 100
    parent–child relationship 99–100, 101

trust vs control 102, 228
    values vs skills 70
Thatcher, Margaret 17
theory X and theory Y 203
Through the Looking Glass 238
Tidal 120
Timpson 71
titles and ranks 16–19
    founders 30
    legacies, managing 17, 19
    'stepping up' 17
    'title inflation' 21
total quality management (TQM) 104
Toyota 120, 182
transactional leadership 201–05
    in a crisis 203
    vs management 204
    nature of 202
transformational leadership 201–05
    charisma, role of 204
    and micro-management 204
    nature of 202
Truman, Harry 229, 232
Trump, Donald 80
trust
    vs control 73, 102, 198, 228
    and delegation 198, *199*, 236
    and high pay 255, 256
    and honesty 92, 207–08
    and influence 148
    and luck 132–33
    and reporting 198

and respect 251
and sycophants 226–27
in transformational leadership 202
Tse-tung, Mao 8, 88, 268
Tyson, Mike 139

Uber 120
Universal 120

values 197–98
    setting 213
    vs skills 70
video conferencing 56
vision, having a 83–86
    call to action 85–86
    establishing a new 156
    grand vs small visions 83–84
    idea 84–85
    and motivation 50, 89
    promise of hope 85
    'What's In it For Me?' 86
Voyage of the Beagle 242

Wall Street 114
Warner 120
weakness
    and popularity 250
    working with weaknesses 14–15
Wellesley, Arthur (Duke of Wellington) 133
World Economic Forum 182

Zuckerberg, Mark 104, 150, 151, 161